The Myth of International Order

The Myth
of International Order

Why Weak States Persist and Alternatives to the State Fade Away

ARJUN CHOWDHURY

University of British Columbia

OXFORD
UNIVERSITY PRESS

OXFORD
UNIVERSITY PRESS

Oxford University Press is a department of the University of Oxford. It furthers
the University's objective of excellence in research, scholarship, and education
by publishing worldwide. Oxford is a registered trade mark of Oxford University
Press in the UK and certain other countries.

Published in the United States of America by Oxford University Press
198 Madison Avenue, New York, NY 10016, United States of America.

CIP data is on file at the Library of Congress
ISBN 978–0–19–0–68672–7 (pbk.); 978–0–19–0–68671–0 (hbk.)

1 3 5 7 9 8 6 4 2

Paperback printed by Webcom, Inc., Canada
Hardback printed by Bridgeport National Bindery, Inc., United States of America

Why bother with the false?

       Hegel

CONTENTS

List of Figures ix
List of Tables xi
Acknowledgments xiii

1. Incapable Yet Central 1

2. The Self-Undermining State 11

3. Europe as an Other 37

4. Restaging the State 65

5. Sympathy for the Neoliberal 95

6. Origins of Anarchy 133

7. Suffering Spectators of Development 161

8. Full Circle 191

9. A World of Weak States 217

Bibliography 229
Index 247

LIST OF FIGURES

3.1   Francisco de Goya, *The Second of May, 1808*   41

3.2   Number of interstate conflicts, 1816–2000   45

4.1   Yves Klein, *Hiroshima*   66

5.1   Social transfers in selected OECD states as percentage of GDP   98

5.2   US Treasury Department posters from the 1940s   110

5.3   Percentage of respondents who "agree" or "strongly agree" that "government should reduce environmental pollution"   118

5.4   Percentage of respondents identifying "economic growth" as "No.1 priority of country"   119

5.5   Ratio of respondents saying "economic growth" is No. 1 priority compared to respondents saying "strong defense forces" is No. 1 priority   120

8.1   Frequency of terms "savages," "minorities," "human rights," 1800–2000   203

LIST OF TABLES

1.1   Failed States Index   3
2.1   Possible Outcomes   16
2.2   War and State-Making   21
2.3   Examples of Institutional Trajectories   28
4.1   War and State-Making after 1945   78
5.1   Tax Burden (% of Income) in the United Kingdom, including Direct and Indirect Taxes   108
7.1   Contrasting Exchange in West, Postcolonial Gamble, Colonial Non-Exchange   171
7.2   Insurgencies in Areas Colonized by Major European Powers, then Decolonized, 1800–2000   177
7.3   Insurgencies in Areas Colonized by Major European Powers, plus Insurgencies in Areas Occupied by Austrian Empire, Japan, Russia, and Indian Wars in North America   177

ACKNOWLEDGMENTS

I took an embarrassingly long time to write this book. Over this period, I depended on the patience of many people at three different institutions. I began this book at the University of Minnesota. Among the many excellent faculty there, I thank especially Lisa Disch, John Freeman, Vinay Gidwani, David Samuels, and Tom Pepper. Andy Dickinson's passion for intellectual debate is much missed. Sharing an office with David Forrest, Matt Hindman, Darrah McCracken, and Anthony Pahnke was a pleasure. I learned a lot from Mark Hoffman, Govind Nayak, Kevin Parsneau, Aaron Rapport, and Gabriel Shapiro. Most of it was irrelevant for this book but much more important.

I was fortunate to spend a horizon-broadening year at the Penn Program on Democracy, Citizenship, and Constitutionalism at the University of Pennsylvania. Sigal Ben-Porath, Tulia Faletti, Anne Norton, and Bob Vitalis were generous interlocutors. At Penn, I taught a class with Rogers Smith, who remains a model of intellectual engagement and generosity.

At the University of British Columbia (UBC), Allan Tupper and Richard Johnston, as Department Heads, created a supportive research environment. Several colleagues—Bruce Baum, Max Cameron, Cesi Cruz, Alan Jacobs, Gyung-ho Jeong, Chris Kam—provided feedback and helpful advice. Campbell Sharman has been a mentor since I got to UBC. Kaveh Sarhangpour, Rebecca Foley, and Elizabeth Good provided excellent research assistance at various times. Finally, our office staff—Dory Urbano, Amy Becir, Josephine Calazan, Becca Monnerat, and Richard Wright—deserves a lot of credit for keeping our department running smoothly.

I would be remiss not to note the excellence of the three research libraries, at Minnesota, Penn, and UBC, at which I worked and where I was never unable to track down the very many books I needed. These libraries, and the librarians who run them, remain the heart of the university.

At Oxford University Press, thanks are due my editor, David McBride. Dave supported the broad scope of the project and lined up two outstanding reviewers. I am grateful to the reviewers for their generous but demanding critiques. For an extremely efficient production process, I thank Katie Weaver, Jeremy Toynbee, Patterson Lamb, and especially Claire Sibley.

My parents—Angshuman and Indrani Chowdhury—have encouraged me throughout despite general bemusement with their son's career choices. My partner, Ashley Dawson, patiently bore the frustrations of watching me draft, redraft, and redraft again. By contrast, our son Max was magisterially indifferent to the whole process. Maybe I will punish him by making him read the book.

Finally, Bud Duvall and Ron Krebs. Not only did they advise me through the dissertation (which started with a paper in Ron's class), but they also shepherded me through writing this book, including inviting me to Minneapolis to "workshop" an early draft. Throughout, they tolerated the many bad ideas that didn't make it into the final version, in the hope that there would be a few worthwhile ideas at the end of it. I hope there are some of those, and I cannot thank them enough for everything they have done for me.

The Myth of International Order

Incapable Yet Central

In February 2011, Libyan citizens rebelled against their Brotherly Leader and Guide of the Revolution Muammar Qaddafi. Within eight months, the rebels had unseated the Brotherly Leader. The collapse of the regime surprised most observers. In 2010, *Foreign Policy Magazine*'s "Failed States Index" (now "Fragile States Index") had ranked Libya 111 among 177 states in the world, meaning that 110 states were seen to be at greater risk of instability and regime change.[1] Less than twelve months after this ranking was published, Libya descended into civil war, and became a "failed state." Five years later, large areas of Libya are controlled by non-state armed groups—militias and Islamist groups—and Libya is a "weak state" unable to monopolize violence within its own borders, much less eliminate these groups.

The reader will shrug and say that the ranking merely indicates that the people who designed the "Failed States Index" should get out of the predictions business. But Libya's relative position points to a significant phenomenon. More states in the world resemble Libya than resemble the United States or Denmark. Take two states not usually compared to Libya: India and Mexico. India is the world's largest democracy and a rising economic power. Yet, a long-running Maoist insurgency is active in nearly a quarter of India's districts; in addition, there is persisting unrest in Kashmir and northeast India. Mexico is also an established democracy and a member of the Organisation for Economic Co-operation and Development (OECD). But in the recent conflict with drug traffickers, parts of Mexico have seen high levels of violence—Juarez was widely publicized as suffering a higher homicide rate than Baghdad—or have come under the control of traffickers. In 2010, the conflict peaked with 15,000 casualties across Mexico (exceeding the 1,000 casualty threshold for a civil war). The year before, a Mexican deputy had declared, "[Mexico is] not yet a failed state,

---

[1] "Failed States," *Foreign Policy* 180: 2010, 74–79.

but if we don't take action soon, we will become one very soon."[2] This was hyperbole; Mexico was hardly at risk of seeing drug traffickers depose the government as occurred in Libya by militias and Islamist groups. But even if neither India nor Mexico face an existential threat to the state, they cannot be said to exercise a monopoly on organized violence; that is, they can be said to be 'weak but stable.' Other states, like the Democratic Republic of Congo or Somalia, face armed rivals who are materially stronger than the central government. Finally, some states appear to be stable, but because they are controlled by a small elite who retain rather than redistribute the spoils of power, can unravel swiftly, as Libya did (and the vastly imposing USSR did a mere two decades ago). The latter two types of states can be categorized as failed states or 'weak states at risk of failure.' In summary, the majority of states are incapable of fulfilling the fundamental tasks of modern states—monopolizing organized violence in a given territory and providing basic services to their citizens.[3] The majority of states in the international system—about two thirds—are weak states (see Table 1.1).[4]

The language of weakness and failure (and the more recent "fragility") suggests an aberration from a norm. This norm would, presumably, be a world composed mostly of strong states that do monopolize violence and provide services. Yet most states in the system are weak, meaning strong states are the exception. Looked at historically, strong states are even more anomalous. Consider that until the 1950s most polities were empires. Nineteenth-century imperial rule was predicated on the idea that non-Europeans did not have states and were incapable of founding them. It was not just that the majority of polities in the nineteenth century were not states, the *idea* that the majority of people in the world could have states of their own was improbable in the nineteenth century. The organizing principles of this system were imperial, racial, and civilizational, not statist. But the tenuousness of states was not restricted to Africans and Asians; it extended right into Europe. Late in the nineteenth century, what are now taken to be enduring polities like Germany and Italy lacked essential aspects of centralization, and European polities like Etruria appeared on and disappeared from the map. When Imperial and then Nazi Germany invaded Russia and the Soviet

[2] David Luhnow and Jose de Cordoba, "The Perilous State of Mexico," *Wall Street Journal*, February 21, 2009.

[3] Mann 1993; Ruggie 1993, 148–152; Fukuyama 2011, 80–81.

[4] Various scholars estimate forty to sixty states being at risk of failure, or about a fifth to a third of states in the system; Collier 2007; Ghani and Lockhart 2009, 21; Rice and Patrick 2008; Rotberg 2004, 23–24; Weinstein et al. 2004;. Another third are weak but stable, that is, while the central government cannot monopolize violence, it is unlikely to collapse. The Failed States Index allows us to evaluate these categories for the last decade. While individual states may move significantly with adverse events—Libya went from 111 in 2010 to 54 in 2013 and Ukraine from 117 in 2013 to 84 in 2015—the majority of states are consistently classified as weak.

Table 1.1 **Failed States Index**

	Weak with risk of failure (FSI Score > 90)	Weak but stable (90 ≥ FSI Score > 60)	States in index	Weak states as % of total
2006	28	78	146	73
2007	32	97	177	73
2008	35	92	177	72
2009	37	94	177	74
2010	37	92	177	73
2011	35	89	177	70
2012	33	92	177	71
2013	35	91	178	71
2014	34	92	178	71
2015	37	88	178	70
2016	38	87	178	70
2017	35	89	178	70

Source: Fund for Peace, 2006–2017

Union, German decision makers represented the East as a vast space bereft of a state. The history of the modern state is one in which states that have been capable of fulfilling their fundamental tasks—monopolizing violence and delivering services—are the anomaly. Contemporary state weakness is the latest manifestation of this persistent incapability.

"Strong" states —centralized states that monopolize violence and provide basic services—have never been the majority of polities in world politics. Yet strong states are taken to be the primary units of world politics. States are the basic units of analysis in the discipline of international relations. Normatively, scholars and policymakers concur that centralized states are necessary for a range of desirable outcomes: peace and security, economic growth, and the protection of human rights. The absence of state capacity is seen to contribute to low economic growth, the incidence of civil wars, and the spread of terrorism. This list suggests a shift in the fundamental tasks states are expected to perform. If we compare these expectations to the "strong" European state that developed in the nineteenth century, we see an expansion in what I will call "expectations of order." Ironically, contemporary "weak" states are expending greater resources than their nineteenth-century European predecessors. Consider that of the twenty weakest states in the "Failed States Index 2012," sixteen, including Haiti and Afghanistan, spent more than 1 percent of GDP on health. In 1900, only three European states spent more than 1 percent of GDP on health, unemployment, welfare, pensions, and housing subsidies *combined*.[5] Yet the former group is seen to be at risk of state failure. To support these states is a policy priority, manifested in "nation-building." The problems of nation-building in Iraq and Afghanistan notwithstanding, a consensus remains that building "state capacity" remains necessary. It is now a policy truism that "a capable and accountable state creates opportunities for poor people, provides better services, and improves development outcomes."[6] The standards of statehood have increased.[7]

The Paradox

On the one hand, modern states that successfully monopolize the use of violence and provide services are empirically anomalous over time and any given time. On the other hand, this ideal-typical polity is presumed to be the basic organizational unit of world politics, and where it falls short, it has to be constructed. The state has been and is incapable of fulfilling its fundamental tasks, yet it remains the central unit of world politics. Two questions follow:

1. Why has the modern state been consistently incapable of fulfilling its fundamental tasks?
2. Why, despite this incapability, does the state, and not some alternative institution, remain the central unit of world politics?

This book answers these questions. The persistent incapability of the state testifies to a gap between popular demand for protection and public goods (for short, the demand for services), and popular willingness to supply the resources necessary to fund those services and support the institution that would deliver them (for short, the supply of the state). This gap has developed because of the violence—interstate war and imperial conquest—necessary for the formation of "strong" states in Europe and North America. Previous theorizations of this violence, particularly interstate war, have shown it to be a process of positive feedback that increased public willingness to supply the state in the face of external threat. It is only in the presence of costly war that the population becomes willing to support

---

[5] Lindert 2004, 12–13. The data on health spending is from the World Bank's World Development Indicators.

[6] World Bank 2012, 7.

[7] I thank an anonymous reviewer for this formulation.

centralized power and pay a high level of taxes to the center. But war is costly, and as its costs rise, combatants should prefer alternatives to violence that compel fewer sacrifices of them. Put differently, and this is what extant accounts of state formation miss, there are conditions under which the violence of state formation is not replicable because the costs are so high that the population may prefer an alternative to the war-fighting state that will save them the costs of fighting.

But if the population becomes unwilling to supply the state, and its comparative advantage—costly war—becomes less relevant, how does the state remain the central unit of world politics, yet always appear incapable of fulfilling its tasks? Surely, it must either "evolve" to fulfill new tasks other than war-fighting, or be superseded by alternatives. Either way, the state cannot persistently be incapable yet central. This is where alternatives to the state play a hitherto unappreciated role. As state-building through war proves too costly and not replicable, political actors and movements articulate alternatives to the state that would prevent rather than prosecute war. Alternatives "compete" with the state for popular support; to do so, they must offer a new service instead of war that requires a lower level of sacrifice. These alternatives may not gain popular support, but they transform "expectations of order" in that they rule out the activity—costly war—that forced the population to supply the state. If the state is to beat out alternatives, it must be reinvented to fulfill these new "expectations of order." It must provide a different service, like development or welfare, but in the absence of costly war, it cannot demand the same level of sacrifice without being challenged by alternatives that purport to provide the desired services at a lower level of sacrifice. State-building thus becomes more difficult over time as a consequence of alternatives, *even if they fade away*. Put another way, alternatives widen the gap between the demand for services and the supply of the state, and the state cannot close this gap without provoking popular discontent and the articulation of more alternatives.

Yet if these different services can be provided at lower cost, surely the state can satisfy the demand for services even at a lower level of popular sacrifice. This is in part an empirical question, but there is a theoretical reason to expect the costs of new services to increase. To have popular appeal, the new services internalize costs that in prior periods of state formation were externalized onto individuals and groups. Development in the postcolonial world, for example, involves commitments to education and health care provision that the colonial state took little or no responsibility for. This process of internalizing costs is necessary to gain popular support, and as a result, "expectations of order" have increased to take in aspects of everyday life that the nineteenth-century state had no presence in. These new services are costly, and their costs rise as a reaction to prior state formation. Yet the emergence of alternatives in the absence of war chips away at popular willingness to pay for these costly services. The state may remain the central unit, but because of the gap between the demand for services and the supply of the state, it remains incapable of fulfilling its fundamental tasks. State-building is more difficult now than it was a century ago, partly because the mechanism that compelled popular sacrifice has become less prevalent, but also because the same process has expanded expectations of order. State weakness is quite simply the result of the standards of statehood increasing to a greater degree than popular willingness to sacrifice for the state.

Put crudely, people over history have been unwilling to disarm and pay taxes at anything near the rate modern "strong" states require to pay for their operations and provide services (about 25 percent to 35 percent of GDP). I will show that this level of centralization and extraction has in any case occurred only recently under the duress of (a few) costly interstate wars. But costly interstate war cannot be repeated indefinitely; at some point the costs rise to a level at which bargains are preferable to fighting. At this point, which we have reached historically, alternatives to the state can arise, and even if they are not institutionalized and fade away, they compete with the state for popular support by promising a higher level of services or a lower level of sacrifice. The state does survive, but it faces challenges when it has to compel popular sacrifice. At the same time, it must satisfy heightened demands for services. Contemporary weak states are not deviations from the normal course of state development. Rather, they are the product of state formation and are the latest manifestation of a persistent gap between the demand for services and the supply of the state.[8] Stanley Hoffman noted that "nation-states—often inchoate, economically absurd, administratively ramshackle, and impotent yet dangerous in international politics—remain the basic units in spite of all the remonstrations and exhortations .... [T]hey go on *faute de mieux* [for want of a better alternative] despite their alleged obsolescence."[9] That was written in 1966. *The Myth of International Order* documents this process of state incapability *and* centrality over the last 200 years.

---

[8] If pushed to provide a number, I would guess this gap is 10–15 percent of GDP outside of Europe and North America. I am updating the estimate of economists Nicholas Kaldor and W. Arthur Lewis who suggested in the 1960s that developing countries needed 20 percent to 25 percent of GDP for state spending but taxed at only 8 percent to 15 percent. Taxation has improved, but it runs in the 10 percent to 20 percent range, while expectations of services like health, education, and infrastructure, not to mention defense and policing, have only increased, so I estimate that the state is expected to provide services worth 25 percent to 30 percent of GDP. The size of this gap means that these states are more reliant on foreign aid and loans for funding, thus making them more vulnerable to economic shocks and more beholden to foreign funders than to their own populations. But the main problem is that efforts to raise taxation and disarm the population will make alternatives preferable. Given the absence of costly war, we cannot expect the population to supply the state at Euro-American levels, and so, as I discuss in the conclusion, it is important to seriously consider alternatives to the state to make up this gap.

[9] Hoffman 1966, 863.

Analytical Approach

To analyze the development of the modern state, I combine an informal rationalist model with a more dynamic historical narrative. The model takes the modern state as an interaction between a central authority and the population. I then subject the model to historical change, to accommodate different demands in different time periods. The historical material combines first-person experiences of change and secondary sources to substantiate the claims of contemporary observers. While this hybrid approach does not yield straightforward hypotheses that can be tested, it does bring together the analytical strengths of positive theory with the insights of historical sociology, political theory, and postcolonialism.

The benefit of a deductive model is that it clarifies the mechanisms behind state formation. However, given the long time period studied below, the parameters of the model, specifically the expectations the participants have, are not static. Using historical material enables us to situate this change in the model itself, by shifting the parameters conditioning the interaction between central authority and population. The role of parameters requires some explication. Consider, for example, a prisoner's dilemma game, with the parameter being the discount rate, or the value the players place on future payoffs.[10] The discount rate is a function of how many times the players expect the game to be played in the future and thus should vary depending on how long the players expect to live— their life spans, in short. In a dangerous world where the players have shorter life spans, the discount rate will be low, and conversely, a less dangerous world should see a higher discount rate. Different discount rates alter the outcome of the game. If the game is played in a period when life spans are short, the players will be more likely to defect, reasoning that even if the other player will punish them, they might have died before future games were played anyway. When life spans are longer, the players expect to live long enough to reap the benefits of cooperation, so they are less likely to defect. Over a long time period over which life spans change in response to shifting historical conditions, the model must be emended as the discount rate changes, and the outcomes of the game will change.

This example can be complicated further. Life spans can increase for reasons exogenous to the game—say, improved medical care. But they can also change endogenously, that is, as a player realizes the other is willing to cooperate, each expects to live longer and becomes more likely to cooperate. The parameter— the discount rate—changes as the players learn that they can be trusted to

[10] Axelrod 1986, 126–129.

cooperate. One way to track this parametric change is to examine first-person accounts and historical trends, such as the incidence of warfare over time. First-person accounts help us identify whether the shifts are endogenous—that is, if observers and actors are learning from past events to infer that the old parameters require revision; for example, observing cooperation and lowering the discount rate in the prisoner's dilemma game above. Such first-person accounts can either be observations of parametric shifts or advocacy for such shifts.[11] The historical trends allow us to ascertain whether the phenomenon the parametric shift should have led to—cooperation in the case of the prisoner's dilemma, for example—actually happened.

Plan of the Book

The rest of the book comprises eight chapters: one theoretical, six empirical, and a conclusion. In Chapter 2, I flesh out my argument with respect to two literatures: that on state formation, and that on the causes of war. Juxtaposing these literatures enables me to generate a new theory of the formation of the modern state. Rather than see it as a stable institution that the population prefers to alternatives and is willing to sacrifice for, I theorize the modern state as a "self-undermining" institution whose conditions of development—namely, interstate war and imperial conquest—reduce the population's willingness to sacrifice and make alternatives to the state possible. I specify the theoretical conditions under which the state is self-undermining.

I then move, in the next six chapters, to my empirical account. Unlike extant analyses of state formation that rely on aggregate statistics or secondary accounts, I examine how observers and participants understood the tasks—war, deterrence, development—that the modern state developed to carry out, and whether it was doing so adequately or an alternative would do a better job. This enables me to tease out the changing expectations of the state, and how they arose in reaction to prior state formation. Chapters 3, 4, and 5 offer a story of state formation in Europe and North America that departs from extant accounts. In these accounts, the modern state had superseded its alternatives, like empires, by the nineteenth century, which was merely a period of state consolidation. In Chapter 3, I challenge this narrative. In the nineteenth century, the European state was developing in an uneasy relation to empire (most European polities *were* empires). The modern state had not superseded other forms of political organization. As the costs of war rose, culminating in World Wars I and II, it became clear that the European state could no longer engage

---

[11] That is, they can either be constative or performative utterances; Austin 1975.

in war and conquest as its primary rationale. In Chapters 4 and 5, I reveal how the war-making/state-making relationship, the basis for the modern state, was undermined by the very process of state formation and replaced with other functions: of war prevention—namely, nuclear deterrence—and economic intervention to supply welfare. Yet, as the threat of war diminished, the population's willingness to supply the state came to be challenged as alternative modes of providing services, especially through market mechanisms, were articulated by political movements in North America and Europe. These movements promised to deliver a high level of services but to require less of the population in terms of taxes, thus widening the gap between the demand for services and popular willingness to supply the state.

In Chapters 6 and 7, I turn to the decolonized world, where the pattern of state formation was quite different. Rather than interstate war and empire, the dominant experience of warfare in the decolonized world has been intrastate or civil war, which has very different effects on the interaction between central authority and population. These different conflict patterns stem from how anti-colonial movements represented the European model of political development as tainted by war and conquest, and hence not worth emulating. Rather than engage in conquest, anti-colonial movements promised to deliver economic development. These promises, of economic development and transcending the practices of the colonial state, have made state-building harder in the postcolonial world than in Europe in two ways. First, the postcolonial state emerged in relation to alternatives, like federations and forms of traditional organization, which reduced popular willingness to sacrifice. Second, the postcolonial state inherited "customary identities" like ethnicity and tribe that developed in the colonial period. These customary identities have enabled previously disaggregated local conflicts to be connected through alliances into long-running insurgencies. The postcolonial state spends more on its population than the colonial state did (and more than nineteenth-century European states did on their own populations), yet is constantly challenged for not achieving its goal of development. Postcolonial states are weak not despite their role in the lives of their population, *but because of it.*

The delinking of state-making from war-making worldwide would imply that states had outlived the function they emerged to fulfill in nineteenth-century Europe. In Chapter 8, I begin with such expectations and of alternatives to the state, after the demise of the Soviet Union, but then show how, as in the past, a new role for the state was articulated: to provide security and ensure human rights, which has culminated in the state-building projects of the past decade. To fulfill these transformed "expectations of order" is difficult. At the same time that the contemporary state is expected to do more than its nineteenth-century predecessor, actions constitutive of nineteenth-century state-building like war, land displacements, and the suppression of vernacular languages and cultures are either foreclosed or provoke long-running challenges. Through these changes—from war-making to welfare/development to ensuring human rights—the modern state has constantly been undermined, even as its centrality is reaffirmed. This is no accident. In its structure, the modern state is self-undermining, and the process of state formation is more likely to produce weak states than strong ones. In Chapter 9, I conclude by summarizing my argument and discussing its implications.

2

The Self-Undermining State

In the introduction, I suggested that the incapability of the modern state to fulfill its fundamental tasks is the norm at any given time and over time. The majority of states in the international system are weak states, states that face difficulties monopolizing violence within their borders and providing services. Similarly, throughout the nineteenth century, non-Western and indigenous peoples were seen as lacking states. But the impermanence and instability of states was a European phenomenon as well. Contemporary epitomes of "strong" states like Germany lacked essential aspects of centralization until quite late in the nineteenth century. And within three generations, even a superpower like the USSR would cease to exist. Weakness, impermanence, and failure characterize the modern state.

But the modern state continues to be the desired organizational form for world politics. And despite manifold discontent with its efficacy, state intervention in everyday life is increasing, not decreasing. The importance of "state capacity" to prevent civil wars and deliver public goods is trumpeted in the academic and policymaking community. The contemporary policy of "nation-building" is a manifestation of this longer-term desideratum. Why, despite the fact of state weakness over time and at any given time, do people desire and try at great cost to build states? Why, despite persistent claims for the incapability of states, have alternatives not superseded the state? These questions have thus far generated two opposed, but unsatisfying, answers.

The first answer, prevalent in economic and international relations theory, is that there was nothing wrong with the state to start with. Talk of the incapability of states, much less alternatives to the state, is the work of disgruntled intellectuals with too much time on their hands. Theoretically, the modern state, defined as a monopoly on the use of force which allows its public to specialize in economic activity, is the optimal way of "organizing violence."[1] The lack of a

---

[1] North, Wallis, and Weingast 2009; Fukuyama 2011; Fukuyama 2014.

monopoly of violence disrupts economic functioning as individuals and groups, unable to rely on the state to protect them, invest in self-defense, which is inefficient as their comparative advantage lies in productive activities.[2] In essence, a market for force and law is inefficient, and centralized institutions are preferable.[3] Neither the fact of the state nor its centrality as unit of world politics has changed significantly over the last two centuries or so. Otherwise different theories of international politics over the last four decades concur that the state remains the starting point for analysis.[4] As the constituent units of world politics remain mostly unchanged, we can construct theories that enable us to make sense of the present and future in terms of past patterns of war and peace.[5]

However, important patterns of world politics—patterns of war, trade, and organization—have indeed changed. Great power war and imperial conquest have diminished to the point of disappearance, implying that whatever the state does now, its primary role is *not* war-fighting.[6] Barring a few outliers like North Korea, states are open to international capital.[7] While empires have vanished, numerous non-state actors play expanded roles;[8] and international institutions, if not forming a global government, perform many of the functions of governance.[9] For the last two decades, scholars from a range of disciplines have suggested that at the very least the centrality of the state has been challenged.[10] At most, the state is said to be in a "transformative crisis."[11] The present, not to mention the future, looks very different from the past, and the latter's lessons—based on the centrality of a particular type of state whose primary role was war-making—seem of limited utility.

Neither argument is entirely satisfying. The first account seems to be contradicted by the flux of world politics, the rarity of "strong" states, and changes in the role of the state over time. The second account seems to be contradicted by the persistent expectation that states are and should be the foundation for world order. Policymakers seem more, not less, invested in the survival of the

[2] Bates 2008.

[3] Olson 1993.

[4] Waltz 1979; Wendt 1999; Wagner 2007; Glaser 2010; Braumoeller 2012. Even as David Lake contests the representation of the international system as anarchic, he concedes that the basic units are states; Lake 2009, 2.

[5] Mearsheimer 2001.

[6] Pinker 2011; Goldstein 2011. Although a minority of states continue as "permanent Spartas" like Israel where the threat of war leads to a consistently high level of popular mobilization and sacrifice.

[7] Hardt and Negri 2004.

[8] Keohane 2001.

[9] Slaughter 2004.

[10] Sassen 2006, 222–271; Ben-Porath and Smith 2013.

[11] Appadurai 2002, 24.

state; as a United Nations (UN) commission examining the relevance of state sovereignty in an era of globalization would conclude: "it is strongly arguable that effective and legitimate states remain the best way to ensure that the benefits of the internationalization of trade, investment, technology and communication will be equitably shared."[12] The irony, of course, is that "effective and legitimate states," for all their purported benefits, remain the historical exception, and the continued emphasis on the state serves to close out alternatives that may, if given a chance, improve outcomes.

If the first account entirely disregards alternatives to the state and exaggerates the centrality and permanence of the state, the second account underestimates the persistence of the state and exaggerates the importance (and novelty, I will show) of alternatives to it. These two accounts force us to choose between two empirically unconvincing visions: stable states and unchanging patterns of world politics, on the one hand, and alternatives that would supersede the state and fundamental shifts in how world politics is conducted and organized, on the other. Can the (incapable) modern state be theorized in relation to alternatives to it? Can a theory explain both state weakness and state centrality?

In the next four sections, I lay out such a theory. First, I provide a rationalist model of the modern state as an exchange between the central authority and population. A rationalist model provides two benefits: it enables us to specify the conditions under which the state is preferred to other institutional forms instead of assuming that it will be preferred, and it lays an analytical foundation from which to study the bargaining that is said to typify state formation.[13] For the state to endure, both parties to the exchange have to prefer it to alternatives: the state must be "self-enforcing." In addition to being self-enforcing, the central authority must supply a level of services that is roughly equal to what the population is willing to sacrifice. Second, I specify the conditions of war and empire under which the population prefers the exchange to alternatives and are willing to supply the state. These conditions are historically rare, and more important, cannot be replicated indefinitely. At some point, the costs of war rise beyond what the population is willing to endure, and at that point, they may prefer alternatives to the war-making state that require less sacrifice. Third, I lay out the conditions under which alternatives emerge, and how the state is transformed to supersede those alternatives. Alternatives to the state emerge by promising new services that internalize costs previously borne by the population, thus the cost of new services increases even though popular willingness to sacrifice does not increase. This leads to a persistent gap between the demand for services and the supply of

---

[12] I.C.I.S.S. 2001, 7.
[13] Tarrow 2013, 56–57.

the state. Fourth, and finally, I contrast my argument to alternative mechanisms for state formation and state persistence. Throughout, I provide examples from the empirical chapters to illustrate the theory.

The Self-Undermining State: An Informal Theory

I begin with a model of the ideal-typical modern state. Such a state must monopolize organized violence and provide a basic level of services. If the state is to have the good effects said to justify it, the central authority must choose to protect the population and provide it services, and the population must choose to disarm and pay taxes to the central authority rather than some other entity.[14] The state must be "self-enforcing," meaning there are no third parties—for example, imperial or hierarchical orders where the metropole provides material support to local authorities—to enforce the exchange between the central authority and the population. Relatedly, the assumption of anarchy in international relations theory implies a self-enforcing state as the basic unit of world politics.

This emphasis on the population, rather than wealthy elites, requires some historical context. The "strong" modern state extracts at 25 to 35 percent of GDP, compared to a maximum of 10 percent in 1900.[15] The latter level is consistent with the preferences of elites, from medieval nobles to nineteenth-century industrialists, who benefit from paying taxes high enough to provide property rights and basic security but low enough to ensure that the state is not so powerful as to expropriate them.[16] These elites are willing to purchase other services on the market without having to subsidize the rest of the population. Elites should be expected to prefer a minimal state, and, to protect against expropriation, may arm in self-defense, when their assets are immobile like land, or try to exit, when their assets are mobile like capital. Indeed, even in the nineteenth century most European states extracted less than 10 percent of GDP and were far less centralized than they are now. The mechanisms behind the rise of extraction— progressive taxation and conscription—are driven by the involvement of the population in costly war. To see the demand for the wide range of services the modern state has come to provide—and support for the extraction necessary to provide it—we have to look to the population rather than elites.[17]

[14] Here I paraphrase Fearon 2011, 1661.

[15] Piketty 2014, 476. In 1902, all levels of the US government extracted 7.8 percent of GDP as compared to 37 percent in 1992; Wallis 2000, 65.

[16] E.g., Ansell and Samuels 2014.

[17] Here I draw on Braumoeller's reformulation of systemic theory. Braumoeller derives the behavior and interaction of polities—he focuses purely on states—from the preferences of their populations; Braumoeller 2012, 40–43, 100–104. As will become clear, I extend his argument about popular

For this reason, I theorize the formation of modern states as an exchange between a central authority and the population rather than the result of elite bargaining. The central authority provides services—protection from external and internal threats, and public goods like infrastructure.[18] In return, the population provides taxes and conscripts, and disarms. For the exchange to occur (i.e., be "self-enforcing") in the absence of a third party, both sides must prefer the exchange to alternative courses of action, or "outside options." From the perspective of the central authority, an outside option would be to renege on the exchange—for example, by expropriating the population or repressing it. From the perspective of the population, an outside option would be to arm for self-defense, ally with external forces against the central authority (both of these would make a monopoly on violence impossible), or move to a different place (exit).[19] Understanding the exchange as one option of several open to both parties that must be repeated over time allows us to theorize the breakdown as well as the formation of polities. Such breakdowns in the exchange have been common over history, leading to the collapse and disappearance of polities; if anything, it is the self-enforcing exchange that has proven anomalous.[20] Schematically, one can represent the possible outcomes in Table 2.1.

Two points should be emphasized. First, as the reader will object, the population does not *choose* to live under tyranny; to say they "cooperate" is absurd. A more precise (and less objectionable) description is that they are unwilling or unable to defect—for example, because they are unable to coordinate a rebellion.[21] Second, and consequently, if they are not defecting, the central authority can repress and extract at will.[22] Thus, a tyrannical regime can be sustained for a long time. But if the population chooses an alternative, by rebelling, for example, and the central authority is unable to defeat the rebellion, the central authority has to reduce its use of force and extraction over the long term. This is why civil

preferences to the *forms* of polities, including states that vary in capacity and non-state institutions, as well as their behavior.

[18] E.g., Wagner 2007, 118–120.

[19] On the exit option in Africa, see Herbst 2000, 88–89.

[20] For two recent analyses on how a self-enforcing exchange (these authors use the terms "open access orders" and "inclusive institutions" instead of "self-enforcing") arises, see North, Wallis, and Weingast 2009; Acemoglu and Robinson 2012. In these accounts, the important barrier to the exchange's being self-enforcing is commitment problems between elites who fear the rise of a neutral central authority who can expropriate them. Implicitly, these scholars assume that if elites could solve their commitment problems, the population would prefer the exchange to alternatives, whether because they can gain from redistribution or enjoy greater economic opportunities. I will contest this assumption.

[21] Kuran 1991; Fearon 2011.

[22] Mann 1993, 60.

Table 2.1 **Possible Outcomes**

	Central authority cooperates	*Central authority defects*
Population cooperates	Exchange endures (stable state)	Tyranny (risk of eventual state failure)
Population defects	No monopoly on violence (polycentric orders)	Civil war (state failure)

wars do not build centralized states; rather, civil war is better understood as the population's choosing an outside option to reduce extraction from the central authority.[23] Consequently, the alternative must itself commit to using force and extracting at a lower level, for fear of facing the same problem. The existence of an alternative has the net effect of making repression and extraction more diffi- cult (and conversely the absence of an alternative allows the central authority to repress and extract easily). Alternatives to a centralized state should have popu- lar appeal because they promise to reduce extraction and repression. But for that very reason, they cannot be expected to extract at the level of a centralized state.

Representing the modern centralized state as one possible outcome in the relationship between the central authority and the population recognizes that each side may, under certain conditions, prefer another course of action or alternative institution. This contrasts with extant analyses which posit that the population should prefer to give up its outside option to a centralized state in order to reduce transaction costs and focus on economic activity.[24] Instead, seeing the centralized state as one possible outcome opens the question of the conditions under which the population prefer it to an alternative institution, or to retaining their outside option. I will explore this question in the next section.

Representing the modern state as one possible outcome in the relationship between the central authority and the population is consistent with the vari- ety of organizational forms in the historical record, from formal empires rul- ing through intermediaries to contemporary weak states with several wielders of organized violence. At the level of everyday practices, state power may be maintained through violating the terms of the exchange—for example, regimes relying on illegal methods like torture and extra-judicial killings—but which raise the likelihood of sudden, and unexpected, state failure. On the side of the population, there may be transgressions of the writ of the state, of which the

[23] As I will lay out in Chapter 7, the role of ethnicity in conflict is less as a cause of conflict and more as a means of forming alliances, what I call, following Stathis Kalyvas, a technology of rebellion.

[24] Olson 1993; Bates 2008.

most consequential are rebellions and insurgencies.[25] Put this way, and corresponding with the empirical prevalence of weak states and state failure over history detailed in Chapter 1, both parties seem to have very little incentive to establish the exchange and abide by it. The central authority gains from tyranny (indeed analyses of state failure highlight the pernicious decisions of leaders to renege on the exchange).[26] The population gains from, at the very least, remaining armed so that its members can defend themselves against tyranny or pay fewer taxes. The internal logic of the exchange seems to militate against its being self-enforcing.

We can put this even more simply. The contemporary "strong" state is in a position to repress and extract at a historically unprecedented level (between 25 and 35 percent of GDP in Europe and North America compared to 10 percent or less of GDP in 1900, and 10 to 20 percent of GDP in contemporary "weak" states). To reduce the level of extraction and/or provide some level of self-defense against repression, the population gains from the existence of an alternative to the state, as an outside option. At the very least, an outside option serves as a bargaining chip to reduce the level of extraction. Yet the centralized state, by definition, must eliminate alternatives capable of wielding violence and exercising authority that supersedes domestic law, and the population must be willing to disarm and pay taxes. What are the conditions under which the population accepts the risk of repression by foregoing outside options and submits to a high level of extraction? What are the conditions under which the exchange is self-enforcing?

Costly but Winnable

Charles Tilly theorized the condition under which the exchange would be self-enforcing: in the face of large-scale interstate war.[27] As the scale of conflict increases, self-defense for smaller populations, in village militias, for example, proves impractical. A central authority can mobilize force more effectively, by disarming self-defense units and incorporating them into a mass army that could pursue a coordinated war plan.[28] If self-defense units no longer exist, rebellion and/or alliance with an external force by the population, or sections of it, is impractical. The result is a monopoly on organized violence: the population

---

[25] We have theorized this under an expanded concept of sovereignty; Chowdhury and Duvall 2014.

[26] E.g., Rotberg 2004; Bates 2008; Acemoglu and Robinson 2012.

[27] Tilly 1992.

[28] Mann 1993, 55, 54–63.

foregoes outside options as the scale of conflict increases.[29] As the scale of conflict increases (i.e., war becomes more costly), the central authority has to accept checks on its power and provide services like support for returning soldiers to compensate for their sacrifice. One manifestation of this is that as the costs of war increase, the central authority has to conscript previously marginalized populations, like Druze Arabs in Israel and African-Americans in the United States, who then demand equal rights for their sacrifice in war.[30] At the same time, as war becomes more costly, it cannot appear hopeless: that is, the central authority must have some positive probability of winning or forcing a stalemate; otherwise the population will be unwilling to sacrifice. Thus, costly, but winnable, war implies a process of "positive feedback," which deepens the relationship between the central authority and the population.[31] Not only would the central authority be the only provider of protection to the population given external enemies, but it can more credibly commit to accept checks on its power after war than those enemies. A self-enforcing exchange thus would become a self-reinforcing institution as the cost of war increases, as long as there remains some probability of victory. This is the logic of Tilly's famous aphorism "wars made the state, and the state made war."[32]

Positive feedback implies variation over time in the level of, on the one hand, concessions made and services provided by the central authority and, on the other hand, extraction submitted to by the population. Another way of putting this is that the demand for services and the supply of the state have changed over time. This is intuitively plausible: over the last 150 years, the centralized state has gone from providing almost no services beyond national defense to intervening in health, education, and poverty relief. The state has come to internalize costs previously externalized on individuals and groups. But the ability to deliver these services rests, in the last instance, on the population's willingness to sacrifice the resources to pay for the services themselves, and also the overhead—for example, the salaries of bureaucrats—to provide them in an institutionalized, or centralized in the case of the modern state, fashion. The population has to be willing, in short, to supply the state. For the exchange to endure over time, the demand for services and the supply of the resources needed to fund them (the supply of the state) should co-vary, forming a rough equilibrium. If, as I will show to be the case, the demand for services is rising while the supply of the state does not rise to the same degree, the state will be unable to fulfill expectations and will appear incapable of carrying out its tasks.

[29] Spruyt 1996.
[30] Krebs 2006, 16–19; Parker 2009, 5–11.
[31] Pierson 2000, 252–253.
[32] Tilly 1975, 42.

The population's willingness to supply the state in response to costly war can vary for endogenous or exogenous factors. The logic of the bellicist mechanism— "war makes states and states make war"—implies endogenous factors. That is, as war becomes more costly, the central authority must extract more taxes and conscripts for which it must grant more rights to the population and provide more services. As war becomes more costly, the population is willing to sacrifice more to the central authority but will also make claims on it. Thus, the demand for services and the supply of the state increases. However, this does not mean that the cost of war can rise in isolation from the probability of victory. The population will not be willing to make sacrifices if the war looks unwinnable, because not only will its members suffer costs during the war, they will not receive postwar benefits if the central authority is overthrown or too impoverished to compensate them. They would prefer to defect to the winning side and submit to indirect imperial rule or self-arm to protect themselves after an occupation than continue to support a losing central authority (these sorts of defections have been common in both interstate and intrastate wars). A costly war expected to end in defeat can lead the population to prefer an alternative to the central authority if that alternative could save them the costs of fighting.

Costly wars in themselves are neither necessary nor sufficient for the exchange to be self-enforcing. It is also neither necessary nor sufficient for wars to be winnable for the exchange to be self-enforcing. A war that is winnable, but not costly, like a colonial war, can be contracted out to intermediaries like a commercial company without requiring the population to supply the state. It is *jointly* necessary that wars be costly and winnable for the exchange to be self-enforcing or self-reinforcing, and for the population to supply the state at a high level. That is to say, in the absence of costly but winnable wars, we should not expect to see a self-enforcing exchange with a high level of extraction.[33]

When costly but winnable wars are rare and unlikely, we should expect to see at least the articulation of alternatives to the state, and the states that do develop should be more attenuated than the exchange that developed through costly war and empire. An example may help concretize this abstract discussion. In Chapters 6 and 7, I discuss how anti-colonial leaders promised their populations they would abjure costly wars as these were essentially unwinnable. Consequently, they expected to extract less from their populations in the form of taxes. To make up for the shortfall, they proposed a variety of alternatives to the state that would reduce transaction costs and increase efficiency by pooling functions, for example, federations in the Caribbean and South Asia.

[33] The formation of centralized states in the absence of costly but winnable war, or mobilization for such war, would falsify the analysis. While some centralized states have emerged without costly war-making, like Singapore, these are acknowledged to be anomalies.

In addition, postcolonial leaders expected to supplement their revenues with foreign aid. The European and postcolonial experiences of state formation were fundamentally different. The postcolonial state was less a two-sided exchange forged through bargaining over taxes and conscripts, and more a one-sided gamble where the state promised to develop the population. The gamble was predicated on the notion of the population as stuck in "customary" identities, like ethnicity and tribe, which disabled them from contributing to development. But these customary identities could also be used as the basis for collective protest and rebellion when development did not fructify. In the absence of costly war, these customary identities could serve as an outside option that the population could exercise against the state. This lowered the supply of the state *even as the postcolonial state spends more on the population than its European predecessors did*, and quality-of-life statistics like life expectancy have improved since independence, after stagnating in the colonial era. The postcolonial state has never been a self-enforcing exchange. Because it developed in the absence of costly war, it is constantly vulnerable to the articulation of alternatives (or the exercise of outside options), and is thus characterized by a wide gap between the demand for services and the supply of the state.

That costly but winnable wars make states is a more precise specification of the bellicist mechanism, "war made the state and the state made war." Only costly but winnable wars yield self-enforcing centralized states in which the demand for services and the supply of the state are roughly equivalent over time. Not all wars build states! As scholars have emphasized, Tilly's argument depends on a certain type of war, namely, large-scale war depending on taxation and conscription rather than debt and mercenary armies.[34] This type of war, "absolute" war in Clausewitz's term, is historically specific. With the Napoleonic wars, the population became mobilized, and popular participation raised the cost of war beyond ex ante predictions. Hitherto limited and imperial wars became affairs of state answerable to the nation,[35] and it became harder for rulers to abide by agreed upon limits on conflict, as I show in Chapter 3. As the costs of war rose, the population became increasingly willing to supply the state. The jointly necessary conditions for the exchange to self-reinforcing are that the costs of war are high enough to compel the population to disarm and submit to taxation and conscription, but there should remain some positive probability of victory such that the population is more likely to be protected from the worst effects of war by fighting rather than surrendering. There are, then, other combinations under which the exchange is not self-enforcing and/or the supply of the state

[34] Centeno 2002.
[35] Dirks 2006, 125.

is significantly lower: war could be highly costly, with very low or zero odds of victory; war could be low cost, with high odds of victory; war could be low cost, with very low or zero odds of victory. Each combination has different implications for the likelihood of war and the population's willingness to supply the state, as summarized in Table 2.2.

As discussed, when war is costly but victory is possible, both sides prefer the exchange to alternatives, and the level of extraction is high. In every other combination, the self-enforcing aspect of the exchange is either unnecessary or tenuous, and the supply of the state will be lower. When the costs of war are low and the probability of victory is positive, the population will neither be required nor willing to supply the state at a high level, and the central authority will be unwilling to make concessions. Wars in this situation are likely, but they can be prosecuted with minimal sacrifice, for example, imperial wars were often subcontracted to private actors or local intermediaries, and consequently, the population could levy fewer demands on the central authority. In sum, wars are likely, but there is no need for a self-enforcing exchange to prosecute these wars. This was the pattern of European warfare between 1648 and the Napoleonic wars. Where the probability of victory is very low or zero and the cost of war is low, wars should be unlikely because inevitable defeat just leaves the population worse off. In this situation, again, the population will be unwilling to supply the state, and there is little reason for a self-enforcing exchange to emerge. Finally, and this is the combination that is neglected in studies of state formation, there is the possibility that wars are costly and the probability of victory is very low or zero. Here, war becomes less likely. This reduces the willingness of the population to supply the state if their sacrifice leads to a costly and unwinnable war.

The jointly necessary conditions under which the exchange proves self-reinforcing—where war makes states and states make war—correspond to wars where there is some positive probability of victory and the costs of war are high. Less costly and/or unwinnable wars do not build centralized states. But this brings up a theoretical puzzle: given that war is costly, central authorities have an incentive to reach settlements prior to war that will save them the costs of fighting. As the costs of war go up, the range of possible bargains expands,

Table 2.2 **War and State-Making**

	High cost of war	*Low cost of war*
Positive probability of victory	War likely; supply of state high	War likely; supply of state low
Very low/zero probability of victory	War unlikely; supply of state low	War unlikely; supply of state low

and war should become less rather than more likely.[36] At this point, the positive feedback between war-making and state-making runs up against an internal, or endogenous, limit. As extraction increases *because of the demands of war*, the costs of war rise, raising the likelihood of a bargain that avoids war to save both sides the costs of fighting. Of course, the costs of war may rise for exogenous reasons, such as new technology that increases the lethality of weapons. I stress the endogenous origin of the rising cost of war for two reasons. First, even absent technological advancements that increase lethality, the costs of war rise as taxation and conscription rise because of war (i.e., they would not have risen in the absence of war). Second, war, and the expectation of war, often facilitates state investment that leads to technological breakthroughs: the invention of the atom bomb, for example, was driven by US investment during the Second World War. The rising costs of war are the consequence of state formation, as the population becomes increasingly willing to supply the state to provide protection from the worst aspects of war. But, paradoxically, as the population increases its supply of the state, the costs rise so that the service they demand, protection in war, becomes harder to achieve.

Thus, the possibility of negative feedback necessarily attends the "war makes states, and states make war" mechanism. As state-making increases the costs of war, the incentive to reach bargains that save the cost of fighting increases. But if such bargains endure, the population's willingness to supply the state will

---

[36] Fearon explained this logic with a simple example; Fearon 1995, 387–388. I expand on it here to concretize how as the costs of war increase, the incentives to reach a bargain increase, raising the likelihood of a settlement instead of fighting. Consider two people bargaining about how to split $100. Each has an outside option to fight, at even odds of winning everything (50 percent), and at the cost of $20. In this instance, there is a range of possible bargains between $31 and $69 which would be preferable to fighting. That is, if either side is offered anything in excess of $31, their utility is greater than if they fought, leaving $69 or less for the other side. The bargaining range is a function of the cost of fighting, as Table 2.Footnote suggests, and beyond a certain cost ($50), any bargain is preferable.

Table 2.Footnote **Bargains Given Variation in Costs of Fighting**

Cost of fighting ($)	Bargaining range ($)
10	41–59
20	31–69
30	21–79
40	11–89
50	1–99

decline over time. This does not necessarily imply that the exchange ceases to be self-enforcing, as long as the demand for services also decreases. That is, if in the absence of war, the population is satisfied with fewer services and lower taxes, the exchange will continue to be self-enforcing. Even if the population is dissatisfied, there may be no alternative, so the exchange endures, as in the case of "tyranny" in Table 2.1. For the exchange to be undermined depends on two conditions. First, there must be an alternative to the exchange, which, second, requires less sacrifice and promises a different service from war-making.

The idea that the process of war-making and state-making is not replicable beyond a certain point raises an intriguing possibility, which runs counter to extant understandings of state formation. In the early modern period, the modern state beat out alternative institutions, like empires and city-leagues, by being most efficient at war-making and driving out other types of polities.[37] But in the absence of costly war, alternatives to the centralized state should emerge, and the imperative for all polities to become states diminishes. To be precise, in the absence of costly war, the imperative for a high level of centralization and sacrifice is attenuated, creating the conditions for alternatives promising a lower level of sacrifice to gain some popular support, even if they are ultimately not institutionalized. Because the war-making state is self-undermining, *state formation itself* throws up the possibility of alternatives to the centralized state and reduces the need to emulate that institutional form, which counters the expectation that units in world politics should emulate the strongest units in order to survive.[38] The "competition" that Hendrik Spruyt suggested the centralized state had won by the early modern period has never really ended. Indeed, I show in Chapter 3 that the centralized state was an anomaly in the nineteenth century, and in Chapters 4, 6, and 8, I show that since 1945, there has been a range of proposed alternatives to the state even as the state is said to be the only unit of world politics. These alternatives have not been institutionalized, for reasons I discuss in the next section, but they have made it more difficult for the state to compel the same level of sacrifice that costly war forced on the population. Building centralized states has become more difficult because of state formation.

The articulation of alternatives to the state in reaction to overly costly war is not automatic; it is a political process. As such, it cannot be predicted by the theoretical model. For example, after 1918, there was a profound disillusionment with war in Europe. However, as John Maynard Keynes would bemoan at Versailles, policymakers like Clemenceau saw European history as a "perpetual prize" fight and sought to repeat the war-making process that had led to the Great War. War was not understood as overly costly and/or unwinnable, and

---

[37] Spruyt 1996, 178.
[38] E.g., Waltz 1979, 127–128.

policymakers expected to wage war in the future. By contrast, after 1945, there emerged a range of proposals for world government and international control of nuclear weapons, even among policymakers, that stemmed from the realization that nuclear war was too costly and unwinnable.

The limit at which war becomes too costly and/or unwinnable reflects, as much as the material cost of war, a process of learning and updating the parameters conditioning the decision to go to war.[39] These parameters are epistemological and political (that is, they are social constructions). Parameters are epistemological in that they are conditioned by existing knowledge of how wars are waged and financed, and political in that they are based on expectations of what one's own population and the enemy are likely to do. In some cases, existing knowledge is proven wrong by the course of war, because in-war extraction raises the costs beyond what was initially expected. For example, because past wars had been predominantly financed by debt and not taxation, observers like Keynes predicted the war that broke out in 1914 would be short, as the combatants would run short of funds and be unable to borrow (this is described in Chapter 5). This assessment was revised during war as taxation increased, lengthening the war and increasing its costs. More subtly, a short war financed by debt, as expected, would not have required the state to extend its provision of public goods. But as the war unexpectedly lengthened, the state had to compensate the population that was conscripted and paying taxes, doubling the number of maternity clinics in Britain, for example.[40] The parameters under which the costs of future wars were calculated shifted endogenously (i.e., because of war).

This logic applies more broadly. For any institution to be self-enforcing or self-undermining depends on the parameters within which the costs and benefits of the services it delivers are calculated, and the expectation, given those parameters, that it can deliver these services. Parameters can shift endogenously or exogenously. Consider the declining popularity of the sport of boxing. Boxing has become less popular partly because awareness has grown of brain injuries suffered by boxers and partly because fighting itself is less socially acceptable. The first cause is endogenous—boxing is losing popularity as people become more aware of its inherent, and unavoidable, dangers; the second is

[39] Strictly speaking, because they are endogenously determined and change over time, they should be called "quasi-parameters"; Greif and Laitin 2004, 633–638. I avoid the term "quasi-parameter" for two reasons. For one, it is an awkward construction. More important, the idea that parameters are fixed over long periods is an analytical convenience that may be necessary for formalization, but parameters like the rules of the game do change and often quickly.

[40] Another unexpectedly long war, the US Civil War, ended with the American state assuming, for the first time, the responsibility to count and bury the war dead. It was not anticipated before the war that a private ritual of mourning would become the responsibility of the state; Faust 2009, 260.

exogenous—boxing is losing popularity because of broader social trends that have little to do with boxing itself.

As the boxing example suggests, parametric shift is epistemological, as new knowledge develops that falsifies existing knowledge, and political, as certain types of behavior are contested and come to be seen as unacceptably costly (or just unacceptable). Consider, for example, the difference between state formation in nineteenth-century Europe, analyzed in Chapter 3, and after the 1950s in Africa, analyzed in Chapter 6. In the nineteenth century, aspiring state-builders like Mazzini wished to build their new polities through conquest of those, like Tunisians, who were seen as lacking states and being incapable of founding then. Underpinning these arguments was a hierarchy of peoples, understood in racial and civilizational terms. But the anti-colonial movements in Africa sought to reverse this hierarchy, arguing for the equality of Africans and Europeans as a reaction to—hence endogenous to—European state formation. By rejecting the racial categories that justified conquest, postcolonial leaders committed to more cooperative relationships with fellow decolonized states. The anti-colonial movements brought about a shift in the parameters within which the costs and benefits of what the postcolonial polity would provide to the population were calculated, in reaction to European state formation. This shift, by diminishing the expected benefits and/or raising the expected costs of conflict, ruled out one mechanism of state-building, the mechanism that has led, historically, to a high level of popular sacrifice.

To give another example, consider the effects of the replacement of the category "savages" with the category "indigenous peoples," analyzed in Chapters 7 and 8. The term "indigenous" has developed out of previously unconnected struggles against land displacements and other actions necessary for state formation across the world. In the nineteenth century, the category "indigenous" did not exist, and such groups were unable to form alliances and a collective movement to challenge their displacement. The category "indigenous" is epistemological (a new way of understanding groups previously understood as "savages") and political (allowing these previously disaggregated groups to form alliances). When contemporary states need land for establishing military bases or building dams or allowing mining, they now have to engage and compensate indigenous communities to a greater degree than did their predecessors. Here the parametric shift—identifying groups as indigenous rather than as savages—has internalized for the state the costs of actions that were previously externalized onto individuals and groups. These actions are thus more costly now than they were in the heyday of nineteenth-century state formation. My historical analysis of the parameters within which the costs and benefits of war, *or any other role for the state*, are calculated reveals that they are not constant over time. Shifts in these parameters, by internalizing costs that were previously externalized, can raise the

costs of actions necessary for state-building. Again, only one part of such parametric shifts—the conditions under which parameters are likely to be revised—
can be predicted by the deductive model; it takes historical analysis to reveal
when the shift occurs or what the revised parameters look like. The model cannot predict, for example, that the category "indigenous peoples" would replace
the category of "savages." I trace these shifts in the next six chapters.

To return to the costs of war, the two prior points—that rising costs of war
make future wars less likely, and that the costs of war rise endogenously to the
war-making/state-making relationship—lead to a somewhat paradoxical prediction about the exchange underpinning the modern state. The conditions
under which the exchange proves self-reinforcing—that the costs of war are high
and there is some positive probability of victory—make interstate war less likely
as the costs of war rise beyond a certain point. Given that state formation over
time makes costly war unlikely, the exchange will be subject to negative feedback, manifested in the articulation of alternatives to the state. These alternatives
reduce the population's willingness to sacrifice and render the exchange not self-
enforcing over time. Alternatives to the state that the population can prefer, at
least as an outside option, emerge as a consequence of state formation: thus the
centralized state is "self-undermining."

Essentially, I have juxtaposed the major explanation of how modern states
form, Charles Tilly's "bellicist model," with the preeminent theory of why states
go to war, the "bargaining model of war" formalized by James Fearon.[41] Both
emphasize bargaining, the first within polities, the second between polities. But
the bellicist model does not consider a possibility implied in bargaining models
of war. That is the possibility that war becomes so costly that combatants prefer
to reach and abide by agreements rather than fight. Such agreements, by reducing
the need to extract, can undermine the exchange that has developed through an
escalating process of war. That state formation can be undermined (or is "self-
undermining") introduces two non-monotonic elements to the somewhat uni-
directional narrative that centralized states form through "waves of war."[42] First,
the process of war-making is not infinitely reproducible; rather, as the costs of
war rise, war-making becomes less desirable and less likely. This is consistent with
the pattern of interstate conflict, especially between great powers: as it rose in
intensity between 1800 and 1945, it became less frequent, and after 1945 it has
declined even further.[43] The decline in warfare has a micro-foundation in popular
preferences: beyond the greater level of casualties, costly wars require taxation and

[41] Respectively, Tilly 1992; Fearon 1995.
[42] Wimmer 2013.
[43] Tilly 1992, 72–74; Holsti 1996, 21–25; Pinker 2011; Goldstein 2011.

conscription, which individuals wish to avoid. Instead of costly wars, the population should prefer limited wars that can be financed by debt and conducted by all-volunteer forces.[44] Anticipating popular opposition, leaders should be unwilling to engage in costly wars unless absolutely necessary. Consequently, wars should diminish as the scale of war-making increases, as seen in the empirical record.[45] Second, as war-making becomes less desirable, the exchange underpinning the modern state comes to be endogenously undermined or self-undermined. The exchange is undermined because the service the state delivered, protection in war, is no longer possible given the rising costs of war.

Incorporating the insights of the bargaining model of war into the bellicist framework emends the latter significantly by introducing the possibility that escalating warfare can undermine the state. By contrast, the insights of the bellicist model introduce only minor revisions to the bargaining model. The main mechanisms leading to war—private information and commitment problems—remain intact. However, the historical conditions of the nineteenth century—namely, popular participation and intense imperial competition—have a somewhat underappreciated impact on the likelihood of war. Popular participation and imperial competition led to sudden shifts in the balance of power, as mass armies were mobilized for the first time, borders shifted frequently, and polities disappeared from the map.[46] Such sudden shifts in the balance of power created commitment problems, making it harder to agree on bargains that would have avoided war or ended it quickly.[47] Further, when the population could be mobilized for war, it became more difficult for a ruler to make credible commitments to limit his own use of force, as rivals feared that the ruler would be deposed by an upstart who would renege on the agreement and mobilize the population. Nineteenth-century conditions made costly and winnable wars more likely, which facilitated state-making. However, and this is the crucial point, these conditions could not be replicated indefinitely.

[44] This is an emendation, but not a departure, from Kant's argument that when wars require the consent of the people who pay the costs of war, peace is likely to result; Kant 1983, 113. Kant's claims can be reframed as implying that the population are indifferent to or may support less costly wars that do not require sacrifice but will oppose taxation and conscription—costly wars—unless absolutely necessary.

[45] This broadly Kantian argument can be extended to the relationship between regime-type and state capacity. Democratic leaders will anticipate opposition to conscription and taxation, and so be less likely to wage costly wars, preferring to wage limited wars. Undemocratic leaders, anticipating either opposition to conscription and taxation or having to make concessions after costly war, will also prefer limited to costly wars. Whatever the regime-type, costly wars should be unlikely, which limits the ability to build centralized states extracting 25 percent or more of GDP.

[46] Zacher 2001; Fazal 2007; Davies 2012.

[47] Powell 2006.

Alternatives to the State

What would alternatives to the centralized state look like, in a schematic sense? There are three possible institutional trajectories that differ from the war-making state that developed in Europe. First, if war-making and state-making are both contested, the result could be the rise of an alternative to the state, which promises a service different from protection in war, like a regional federation set up to maximize trade, a sort of modern Hanseatic League. Second, if war-making alone is contested, the state would survive but promise a service different from protection in war, for example, a developmental or welfare state. Third, if state-making but not war-making is contested, the result could be the rise of a decentralized war-making institution that combats state power, like a militia (Table 2.3).

These institutional trajectories have been presented as independent of each other. However, in the absence of costly war, they can coexist because the population has an interest in maintaining an outside option. Alternatives to the state gain popular support by making fewer demands on the population, reducing extraction and repression. But in the event of costly war, the population prefers the centralized state's protection, despite the high level of extraction. However, as the costs of war rise beyond acceptable limits, the population will prefer alternatives to the state that seek to preclude war-making altogether and promise a service different from protection in war.[48] This raises the question of how an alternative promising a new service can be self-enforcing, and this can be divided into two further issues: the extent of popular sacrifice the alternative can compel, and the cost of the new service. I address these issues in sequence.

Let us assume for the time being that the cost of the new service is roughly similar to the cost of war-making. Given this, for an alternative to the state to be self-enforcing, those promoting it must establish a new equilibrium between the demand for services and the population's willingness to sacrifice for the alternative. To supersede the state, the population has to prefer the alternative and be

Table 2.3 **Examples of Institutional Trajectories**

	Centralized state	*Alternative to state*
War	Euro-American state	Militia
Absence of war	Developmental state	Regional federation

[48] For a suggestion of this appeal, consider that a majority of Americans polled between 1946 and 1950 supported a United Nations that would have armed forces, which is discussed further in Chapter 4.

willing to sacrifice for it as it delivers services. However, the alternative cannot compel a higher level of popular sacrifice that has already proven unpopular if it wants to gain support. Rather, it must offer a more efficient way of delivering the service, that is, require less sacrifice.[49] If this promise is not credible or the alternative actually requires more sacrifice, the alternative will not gain popular support and will fade away. Two examples, from Chapters 4 and 6, will concretize this logic. In both cases, the alternative to the state was unable to compel initial popular sacrifice, which may, in the longer term, have generated greater benefits. After 1945, there were calls for international control of atomic weapons to reduce the risk of nuclear war, and proposals that the United States give up its weapons if the Soviets and others refrained from developing them. International control would have saved both sides the costs of stockpiling nuclear weapons; it could have been an efficient way of preventing war compared to what eventually became nuclear deterrence. But these proposals foundered because, as American policymakers argued in 1950, there was a risk that the Soviets would renege on the agreement. The alternative required the population to run an unacceptable risk, and the possibility of international control of atomic weapons faded away. But the premise of the alternatives—that nuclear war should be avoided—was accepted.

Similarly, anti-colonial leaders promised to abjure war and focus on economic development, for which they needed larger economic entities to increase market size and lower transaction costs. Under this logic, a Caribbean federation was formed, which included a customs union and some shared functions like ports. But after a few years, Jamaicans voted to leave because they feared they would be subsidizing their then-poorer peers like Trinidad (ironically, while Jamaica was slightly richer in aggregate but not per capita terms than Trinidad in 1960, it now lags on both indicators). Again, the premise for federation, that economic development and not war-making should be the basis of whatever institution succeeded the colonial state, was accepted by the population, but the alternative faded away because it could not compel popular sacrifice.[50] Alternatives to the state face significant barriers if they are to be self-enforcing and supersede the state. These barriers stem from, first, the populations' initial unwillingness to disarm and pay taxes that makes the formation of centralized states extracting

---

[49] Theoretically, this would require a technological or administrative innovation, unavailable to the state, which improves efficiency such that a higher level of services can be provided with a lower level of sacrifice. Empirically, these innovations have either not seemed credible or have not delivered on their theoretical promise. For example, the open labor market in the European Union (EU) has not raised economic growth to the degree that tax rates can be cut significantly. Indeed, the EU is being challenged precisely because wealthier states are being asked to subsidize poorer ones.

[50] This problem has bedeviled efforts at European integration from the 1950s with the demise of the European Defense Community, in the last decade with the Greek economic crisis, and in 2016

25 percent to 35 percent of GDP historically anomalous; second, the need for alternatives to undercut the state by requiring less of the population. Absent some innovation that has, empirically, either not seemed credible or not fructified, we can expect to see alternatives fade away because they are unable to compel popular sacrifice.

This raises a second issue, that of the costs of the new service. Why can't the new service cost less, so it can be delivered at a lower level of popular sacrifice (especially given the reduced need to sacrifice for war)? For example, all other things being equal, development saves the costs of fighting, and so an institution promising development should be self-enforcing at a lower level of popular sacrifice. But all other things are not equal because the reaction to prior state-building through war and conquest has served to internalize costs that were previously externalized by the war-making state. War imposes significant externalities. While the state may provide collective protection through waging war, the suffering borne by individuals and families often exceeds the benefits they receive. As the costs of war rise, so do the externalities that exceed the collective benefits, and the population may prefer an alternative to the war-making state. Intuitively, we would expect this: to command popular support, the new service cannot just promise to eliminate the costs of war-making; it has to compensate in some way for prior sacrifices or excesses in the course of state formation. Consequently, the parametric shift that has precluded war-making has driven up the costs of the new service even as the willingness to sacrifice diminishes. Take the example of famines in colonial India. During the Bengal famine of 1941–1943, the colonial government diverted rice from rural to urban areas so public officials and industrial workers could be fed.[51] This continued a trend of minimal responses to famines in colonial India, where the blame for starvation was often attributed to the sloth of the natives; a rather callous way of externalizing the costs.[52] The colonial state did not promise to provide for Indian peasants, and so it externalized the costs of famines onto them. By contrast, the anti-colonial movement, *by promising to prevent the failures, like famine, of the colonial state*, promised to internalize those costs. This was costly in two ways: first, development internalized the cost of providing relief rather than leaving the peasants to their own devices; second, if peasants did starve, they had cause to challenge the institution that

---

with Britons voting to leave the EU. The so-called Brexit brings the issue into sharp relief, because many Britons voting to leave were unwilling to pay the comparatively lower costs of accepting immigrants, to the extent that they were willing to forego the greater benefits of integration. Alternatives to the state, even ones that are institutionalized like the EU, find it difficult to compel even a lower level of sacrifice because they emerge by undercutting the level of sacrifice the state demands.

[51] Bose 1990, 715–717.
[52] Davis 2001, 33–38.

had promised development. Famine in the postcolonial period would mark a failure of the institution that promised development; it could not be blamed on the peasants, leaving them to bear the costs. If the colonial state had externalized some of the costs of war—namely, the famine—onto Indian peasants, the postcolonial state sought to preclude war and internalize these costs. Therefore, development may save the costs of war-making, but it does so by necessitating a range of other costs that the war-making state did not incur. Further, these costs are more or less constant in contrast to war, which involves periodic spikes in spending. Rather than imposing temporary levies in the face of evident threats, the state must, on average, extract at a higher level than the nineteenth-century European war-making state (which mostly financed wars with debt in any event, as I show in Chapter 5). Given that contemporary developmental states rarely wage interstate wars, and they spend and tax at levels comparable to or higher than war-making European states in 1900, they should not be "weak." That they are seen as weak states speaks to expectations of what the state should do rather than material factors.

Alternatives to the state promise a new service that costs more than the population is willing to sacrifice. The alternative must either promise to internalize the difference between the cost of the service and what the population is willing to pay or reduce the cost of the service to what the population is willing to pay through some type of innovation. If they are unable to do either, alternatives will not satisfy expectations of order that they have themselves raised. This creates the possibility that the population will prefer the state, if it is reinvented to deliver the new service. Actors inside and outside the state can accept that war-making is too costly—implicitly or explicitly confirming the shifts in the parameters within which the costs of war are calculated—and accept that in the absence of war the supply of the state will wane over time, but argue that the state is best prepared to provide a new service, such as welfare or development. Because the new service internalizes many of the costs previous externalized on the population, the restaged state also finds it difficult to provide this (costly) service without compelling popular sacrifice, because when it compels sacrifice the population may prefer alternatives to the state. The postwar Euro-American state, for example, promised to deliver welfare and to secure the population from economic downturns. This new service internalized costs, such as health care and pensions, previously born by individuals, as I show in Chapter 5. Initially, these costs were paid for out of vastly increased tax receipts from the world wars. But as the threat of war diminished, the space opened for neoliberal arguments that posited market mechanisms as more effective ways of achieving the goals of welfare than state provision. More damagingly, neoliberalism showed how state provision of welfare distorted markets and lowered economic growth, endogenously undermining the ability to provide the service. The welfare state internalized significant costs that the war-making state did not, but, in the absence of costly war, the population could prefer alternatives that, even if illusorily, promised to deliver welfare at lower cost. The welfare state thus proved self-undermining, because policies designed to deliver welfare were shown to undermine that service.

The above argument—the new service is costly because it internalizes costs that were previously externalized—helps us explain why the restaged state is self-undermining. Not only is the population unwilling to sacrifice the higher costs needed to deliver the new service, in the absence of costly war, but alternatives can always be articulated that promise to deliver the new service at lower cost. The population gains from being able to support an alternative in case the state tries to compel sacrifice (here the alternative serves as an outside option in bargaining). Even if the alternative is ephemeral and fades away, because it too cannot compel the level of sacrifice necessary to provide the service, it makes it harder for the state to extract at the level necessary to provide the service. Neither the state nor alternatives to it can compel sacrifice equivalent to the high costs of new services like development or welfare; consequently, neither is self-enforcing. The outcome is a persistent gap between the demand for services and the supply of the state, accompanied by a fluctuation between the articulation of alternatives to the state and the restaging of the state. As I will show in the historical narrative, the latter drives the former: as alternatives to the state emerge promising new services, the state is restaged to provide these services, but the willingness to sacrifice—pay taxes, face coercion—does not increase.

That alternatives cannot compel the population to sacrifice helps explain the puzzle of why the state is diffused despite its inability to perform the functions expected of it. The state is a second-best option to various alternative institutions that might most efficiently deliver services other than protection in war. However, these institutions emerge by promising to reduce the level of popular sacrifice, even as they internalize costs previously externalized onto the population. When they are unable to deliver these services or impose costs on the population, the latter prefer what I have called the restaged state. But the conditions under which the population prefer the restaged state—namely, to deliver a more costly service yet compel less popular sacrifice—render the state unable to perform the functions expected of it.

The emergence of alternatives to the state, no matter how fleeting, in the historical record is not just a historical curiosity for two reasons. First, because the costs of interstate war, especially nuclear war, are so high as to make it extremely unlikely, the conditions under which the population would *never* support alternatives to the state do not hold. This is a complicated way of saying, given the general absence of costly but winnable war, that the population should periodically support one or other alternatives to the state, even if for a brief period, as an outside option to reduce the level of extraction. Second, and consequently, even if alternatives to the state fade away, they leave their mark on the state in the form of a persistent gap between the demand for services and the supply of the state. "State weakness" is only the most contemporary manifestation of this gap. The occasional emergence of alternatives makes forming "strong states" with a monopoly of violence and a high level of extraction more difficult. The paradox, of state incapability *and* centrality, derives from the development of the modern state as a self-undermining institution. The process of state formation, rather than superseding other institutions, continuously throws up the possibility of alternatives to the state.

Other Mechanisms for State Formation

Could centralized states form for reasons other than war-making? Scholars have provided different mechanisms for state formation and different periodizations of the development of the centralized state. In a nutshell, these other mechanisms do not compel the same level of popular sacrifice as war does, and they lead to a more attenuated state form than the exchange theorized above. This is because, in contrast to my explanation, they focus on bargaining with elites rather than the population.

Consider Hendrik Spruyt's important argument that the centralized state developed in France in the thirteenth and fourteenth centuries as the result of an alliance between the king and burghers seeking to avoid papal taxes.[53] As is evident, the motive for this alliance, and for bargains between the central authority and elites more generally, is to *depress* the rate of taxation and expropriation, not raise it. To raise the rate of taxation, the central authority would have to recruit from the general population to extract from elites, but in return it would have to provide a higher level of public goods and, potentially, political representation. Thus, an equilibrium exists where the central authority accepts a lower rate of extraction from elites in order to forestall direct bargaining with the population who may demand representation, and elites accept a lower level of centralized authority in order to forestall potential redistribution.[54]

This logic can be expanded to another prominent set of explanations for the rise of the state, those that emphasize the role of property rights as a credible commitment between the ruler and elites.[55] North and Weingast showed that in seventeenth-century England the constitution placed constraints on the

---

[53] Spruyt 1996, 86–105.
[54] Ansell and Samuels 2014.
[55] Root 1994.

king's power to expropriate. Given these limits, elites from England and all over Europe became more willing to lend money to the English state.[56] The greater availability and lower cost of credit gave England significant advantage in the wars against France, which did not have such commitment devices and had to pay higher borrowing costs.[57] Rather than war forcing institutional constraints on the central authority, as the bellicist account would have it, constraints on the central authority facilitated war-making. These accounts also time the origin of the modern state to about two centuries before the era I am arguing should be seen as the real period of state development, that is, after the Napoleonic wars.

But the logic of property rights, and other central authority-elite bargains like trading states, for example, leads to a more minimal state, and potentially a decentralized one, than that produced by war-making. This is the case both in the level of extraction and the level of bargaining with the population instead of elites. The protection of property rights does not require much more than basic policing and national defense; it does not require large social spending, for example. More important, the protection of property rights can be provided without bargaining with the general population. Consider such a minimal or "regalian"[58] state from the point of view of the population, most of whom own very little private property. Bargains between the central authority and elites are precisely to limit and regulate expropriation, thus putting a cap on the resources available for redistribution to the broader population and to limit the ability of the population to make claims on the central authority.[59] The population has very little to gain from such a state. If anything, the population would fear the expropriation of communally held resources like land and fisheries—what is protection of property for elites is enclosure for much of the population—and being press-ganged into forcible labor projects.[60] To protect against this threat, the population should prefer an outside option, whether that is self-defense or shifting allegiance to another armed actor who will protect them against such expropriation. Hunter-gatherers and mobile cultivators, for example, have had little need for property rights protection and have preferred to escape state power and remain stateless.[61] The protection of property rights can be achieved by a minimal state, even one where there are several wielders of violence, like an imperial state that subcontracts governance to private companies, or the Hanseatic League.[62]

---

[56] North and Weingast 1989.
[57] Root 1994, 183–194.
[58] The term is Piketty's; 2014, 475.
[59] For nineteenth-century examples, see Bayly 2004, 298–299, 417–426.
[60] Scott 2009, 4–9.
[61] Clastres 1989.
[62] Spruyt 1996, 126–128.

Costly but winnable interstate war, by contrast, generates different incentives for all parties. Should the external enemy win, it is likely it will extract at a higher level than the incumbent central authority, to punish the loser and/or compensate the enemy's own population. Because defense requires resources beyond those available at a local level, the population must give up its outside option. In the future, by sacrificing in war, the population can compel the central authority to accept constraints on its power, and can extract from elites to provide some level of public goods. Faced with costly war, elites will be more likely to pay taxes at a higher level, because this is still lower than what they expect to pay in the event of defeat. Property rights are less secure under conditions of costly war than under limited war—the threat of expropriation by the enemy is high, and so is the risk of high taxation—yet elites must accept this insecurity. Other mechanisms for state formation do not lead to this combination of the population giving up their outside option and elites submitting to high levels of taxation and insecurity of property rights.

Finally, it is worth situating this argument about the self-undermining structure of the modern state and its alternatives in relation to historical institutionalist explanations for the persistence of the state, and slow change in institutions more generally. To give three of these explanations: alternative institutional visions are inchoate and at odds with each other;[63] state bureaucracies reinvent their roles to remain viable in changed circumstances; it is overly costly to entirely replace organizations as complex as the modern state, which evolve rather than are selected out.[64] These explanations of institutional persistence in the face of changing circumstances all have merit. However, they implicitly posit that if the state survives alternatives, it does so because it fulfills its tasks or is capable of fulfilling new ones. To use an evolutionary term, the state has adapted. They do not explain why the state continues to be incapable of fulfilling its tasks (that the state may, in fact, be maladapted). That is, these explanations approach only one part—state centrality—of the paradox this book addresses.

---

[63] Hoffman 1966, 863; Legro 2005, 35–38.
[64] E.g., Thelen 2004; Mahoney and Thelen 2010; Steinmo 2010.

3

Europe as an Other

Government is but now beginning to be known.

—Thomas Paine[1]

Evaluating the absolutist state of the eighteenth century, Thomas Paine pungently asked, "From such a beginning of governments, what could be expected, but a continual system of war and extortion?"[2] The French Revolution, Paine wrote, repudiated this "continual system." Now that the people themselves, not unpopular monarchs, were in charge, Paine predicted wars would become less likely, and the state would no longer function as an extortion racket.[3]

As a prediction for the next century and a half, Paine was off the mark. By the end of the Great War, along with 16 million battle deaths, the top marginal income tax rate in the United States, the United Kingdom, and Canada exceeded 50 percent (on the eve of the war it had been under 10 percent in all three states). If state-making was comparable to organized crime, murder and shakedowns just kept rising.[4] But Paine does point us to a consequential puzzle: how did an era that began in popular revolution against the excesses of monarchs end by establishing centralized states that required ever greater levels of war and extortion?

In this chapter, I draw attention to the types of wars fought in the nineteenth century to suggest a different story of state formation. The French Revolution inaugurated a qualitative shift in war-making: interstate wars hitherto fought between rulers became wars of peoples. The cost of interstate wars increased, and their frequency diminished, consistent with the model laid out in Chapter 2.[5] Yet, despite the relative peace of the nineteenth century *in Europe*, this was the period when the state, for the first time, began to play a direct role in the lives of

---

[1] Paine 1973, 443.
[2] Paine 1973, 404.
[3] Paine 1973, 406.
[4] Tilly 1985, 169.
[5] Tilly 1992, 72–74.

the population.[6] At the same time, the nineteenth century was the age of empire, wherein European powers violently expanded their writ over large parts of the globe. Most conflicts were wars of conquest or counterinsurgency campaigns.[7] The combination of wars of the people armed and imperial wars, on the one hand, contradicted the purpose of the American and French revolutions as protests against taxation. But on the other hand, this *combination* of wars, with imperial wars being crucial, led to a new exchange in Europe between a nascent central authority, which promised protection in war and imperial conquest, and the population, who were willing to supply the state. The exchange developed quite late in the nineteenth century; hence, we should view this period differently on two dimensions. First, the nineteenth century is the period of the emergence, not the consolidation, of the state;[8] second, the state did not succeed empire but emerged alongside empire and in relation to it.[9]

Yet the conditions of its emergence made the modern state self-undermining. If Tilly argued that "states make war, and war makes states," I have specified that these wars need to be costly, but not too costly, and winnable. But the involvement of the population in war (and their willingness to supply the state), unless limited, would raise the cost of war to levels that would undermine the exchange. Empire, I suggest, was the condition under which the exchange could develop, raising the potential costs of war but limiting the cost of conflict in Europe through bargains with those who were recognized as having states. These bargains were not meant to prevent war altogether, because war was seen to be necessary and inevitable, but would limit its costs. Colonial populations, however, incapable of forming their own states, were understood as appropriate targets of coercion and denied protection. Released from limits in the colonies, European powers developed tactics from strategic bombing to concentration camps. These limits on violence were necessary for war to be costly but winnable—for war to yield states. If war in Europe was conducted as it was in Africa or Asia, the costs, given the increasing willingness of the population to sacrifice in war and the new tactics developed in colonies, would rise to unacceptable levels and undermine the exchange. In the nineteenth century, competition between Europeans, as they sought to build states through war and compile empires, meant that bargaining would break down in some instances. In those instances, agreements predicated on categories of who had a state and who did not would limit the costs of war so that the exchange would not be undermined.

---

[6] Tilly 1992, 107–117.

[7] Wimmer and Min 2009; Lyall and Wilson 2009.

[8] Bayly 2004, 247–249.

[9] Tilly 1992; Wimmer 2013.

The problem, however, was that these categories of who had a state and who did not were both recent and tenuous because the centralized state was an anomaly *in Europe* in the nineteenth century.[10] Most Europeans could reasonably be seen as lacking a state in this period and could be likened to non-Europeans. (Indeed, I will show, rigid distinctions between Europeans and savages were themselves nineteenth-century constructions.) As these categories unraveled due to their own lack of foundations, the unlimited conflict inflicted on colonial populations came to be inflicted on "Europeans." The costs of war rose, and the state was no longer able to protect the population even as the population supplied the state at unprecedented levels. The exchange proved self-undermining the moment Germans became "Huns," a defeated "Hun" in turn described the French nation as having degenerated from "race" ("the fate of the few who excel") to "mass" ("the fate of all the worst"),[11] and Europe descended into two decades of crisis, by the end of which Nazi Germany acted toward the USSR not so much as an enemy but as an empty space to be settled. Empire was constitutive of European states but also destabilizing. The emergence of the modern European state is more recent and fragile than is often appreciated.

New Wars, New Problems

In Chapter 2, I qualified Tilly's aphorism "war makes state and states make war." For war to make states, it had to be costly but winnable. Limited wars relying on debt and mercenary armies neither forced the ruler to centralize and provide services nor forced the population to supply the state. Nineteenth-century Latin America did not see total wars, nor did its polities engage in major imperial expansion. Consequently, Latin American elites did not build European-style states, focusing instead on preserving their power over their indigenous majorities, and fought limited wars exchanging territory.[12] These practices were similar to those of European states prior to the Napoleonic wars, for rulers rarely conscripted and relied on debt rather than taxation.[13] Overseas expansion was subcontracted to commercial concerns, like the East India and Hudson Bay companies.

What, then, was different between nineteenth-century European polities on the one hand, and previous European polities and nineteenth-century Latin

[10] Mann dates centralization of national administration to the nineteenth century in the UK, France, and the United States and not in Germany or Austria; Mann 1993, 472, 444–475.

[11] This was the "Decalogue" of a major in the imperial army, quoted in Theweleit 1989, 74.

[12] Centeno 2002.

[13] Kissinger 1994; Schmitt 2003, 126–130.

American polities on the other? It was not the actual scale of war, for the wars of the nineteenth century, even the Great War, did not approximate the destruction of the Thirty Years' War, in which present-day Germany saw its population reduced by a third.[14] And imperial expansion was hardly new to the nineteenth century—empires had been the dominant organizational form over history.

The primary difference was the participation of the people in interstate wars, to the extent that the new subject of war was the people themselves. Thomas Schelling wrote that "from about 1648 to the Napoleonic era, war in much of Western Europe was something superimposed on society."[15] In comparison with the exchange described in Chapter 2, sovereigns waged limited wars among themselves, borrowing to finance their undertakings, and the peasants were more or less indifferent to both the war and to the victor, trying to avoid it as best they could. But when Napoleon invaded Spain "people cared about the outcome . . . . [T]he nation was mobilized."[16] Francisco de Goya documented this shift in two of his most famous pictures (both commissioned by the Spanish government in 1814 and hanging in the Prado in Madrid). After Napoleon had vanquished the King of Spain, the citizens of Madrid rose against the French cavalry on May 2, 1808 (see Figure 3.1).

The next day, May 3, 1808, Napoleon's troops executed those patriots. The novelty that observers saw in the Spanish case was that the people themselves resisted the French invasion; they were not indifferent to the outcome of the conflict as previous generations of Europeans had been. In the past, struggles against oppressive governments, like peasant struggles, had been common but short-lived because they were disaggregated, and invading forces often found local intermediaries to govern. In Spain, however, resistance came to be coordinated because guerilla forces mobilized by elites targeted those who would collaborate with the French.[17] Aware of this threat, the Spanish army did not just not join Napoleon, as he had expected in 1808, but many generals conducted unsuccessful maneuvers just so they would not be accused of cowardice (and to the dismay of Wellington).[18] Aggregated and willing to punish intermediaries, popular participation raised the costs of war, to the point that Napoleon termed it his "Ulcer." If Goya seemed to glorify the involvement of the people in these paintings, his series of etchings *Desastres de le Guerra* (not commissioned by the government) showed a darker side. The etchings featured atrocities—hangings, decapitations, executions—committed by sides with and

[14] Pinker 2011, 142.
[15] Schelling 1966, 27.
[16] Schelling 1966, 28.
[17] Esdaile 1988.
[18] Esdaile 1988, 308–313.

Figure 3.1 Francisco de Goya, *The Second of May, 1808*

without uniforms. The people armed were capable of great brutality, and the arrangements between rulers since the end of the Thirty Years' War had sought to limit their involvement in conflict, but after the French Revolution, this task was more difficult.

The participation of the people in war transformed the parameters within which the costs of war—from the capacity to wage war to norms of combat— were understood and calculated. As Napoleon's army drove into Russia, the peasants resisted, flouting the rules of war. Tolstoy would later praise the peasants for casting aside the "rapier" of more genteel conflicts and belaboring their enemies with "the *cudgel* of the people's war [which] was lifted with all its menacing and majestic strength, and without consulting anyone's tastes or rules and regardless of anything else, it rose and fell with stupid simplicity, but consistently, and belabored the French till the whole invasion had perished."[19] This is of a piece with the resistance documented by Goya: it is *irregular*, in that it escapes both political and legal regulation.[20] By contrast with the violence that characterized the Thirty Years' War, the people were no longer fighting local conflicts but fighting the invasion on their own behalf. War became more costly because the people were mobilized and they were less likely to be contained by agreements between rulers.

[19] Tolstoy 2010, 1111, emphasis mine.
[20] Schmitt 2004, 3.

If Tolstoy suggested that the rapier had been replaced with a cudgel—marking a shift in the cost and the conduct of warfare—Clausewitz used a different metaphor to make a related point. Observing the involvement of the people in war, Clausewitz called it a "terrible *battle-sword* that a man needs both his hands and his entire strength to wield, and with which he strikes home once and no more."[21] Such a weapon was unpredictable, and it had become more difficult for rulers and subjects to predict the course and costs of war. This presented political problems, for if war was reduced to one blow (its "absolute perfection"),[22] its utility for policy diminished. A ruler could not credibly use such a disproportionate threat to coerce a rival on a minor issue (or commit to not declare war if the population was beyond his control). And once a war began, war ran the risk of exceeding political goals and becoming its own master, a situation in which "war would of its own independent will usurp the place of policy the moment policy had brought it into being."[23] The new type of war was more costly. But by virtue of being so, it risked becoming either useless in bargaining over minor issues or, worse, overwhelming the political goals motivating it. The rising cost of war elevated the importance of centralized control. This required a new exchange between the central authority and the population, who were no longer indifferent to war, but now concerned with its costs and outcome.[24]

Popular participation in conflict during this period cannot be understood without examining the role of empire. Individuals had always gone to the colonies for profit or to settle. But individuals also participated in nineteenth-century imperial campaigns for a novel reason. Hannah Arendt later dismissively characterized imperialism as "the export of superfluous men and superfluous capital."[25] She was correct that colonial functionaries were often from marginal populations—Cecil Rhodes, after all, would advocate imperialism "to settle surplus population" and thus "avoid civil war"[26]—but these marginalized individuals increasingly used their participation in colonial conflicts to make claims to

---

[21] Clausewitz 1976, 606, emphasis mine.

[22] Clausewitz 1976, 592–593.

[23] Clausewitz 1976, 87.

[24] While conservative rulers might have preferred to wage limited wars without conscription and taxation, this would leave them vulnerable in case the population in a rival state, or their own state, was mobilized by an upstart like Napoleon. This possibility, in an age of revolution, reduced the ability of rulers to credibly commit to other rulers that their population would *not* become independently involved in war under an upstart. Rulers had little choice but to incorporate their own populations in an exchange instead. Thus the exchange developed even under conservative rulers that sought to repress popular movements.

[25] Arendt 1951, 150–151.

[26] Quoted in Young 1995, 36. The concern that settlers were less than industrious had a long lineage: John Locke had complained of the Carolinas that the "planters there [were] somewhat sluggish"; quoted in Seth 2010, 93.

membership in the home nation. Scots, for example, were excluded from membership of the *English* community, but by participating in the wars against France and the empire in India, they became part of the *British* nation, increasing the war-fighting capacity of the latter (it was no coincidence, as Edward Said argued, that Kipling's *Kim* was Irish).[27] Empire was a crucial mechanism in constructing the exchange in the nineteenth century.

One manifestation of this, which I expand on below, was that as colonial functionaries made claims back home, their relations with native populations shifted to a different and more rigid differentiation, based on novel racial categories.[28] These categories developed to police, for example, sexual relations between whites and non-whites in the tropics. Eighteenth- and nineteenth-century commentators noted such interracial mixing. While there were theories of how such relationships would yield offspring best suited to tropical climates, the dominant view became one that claimed the climate of the tropics led whites to go astray—for example, that tropical heat caused "surexcitation of the sexual organs"[29]—and sought to stop such straying. As the nineteenth-century proceeded tighter boundaries drawn to place whites on one side of society and non-whites on the other, the better to prevent intermarriage and racial mixing.[30] Far from being natural and immutable, these racial divisions are of recent origin and contained ambiguities. Colonial functionaries, for example, were seen as subject to various maladies and susceptible to degeneration through exposure to natives: they were suspect *Europeans*.[31] By separating themselves from the natives, despite a history of interaction and often intimacy, colonial functionaries claimed their affinity, on the basis of race, with populations in the metropole to whom they had comparatively tenuous connections, and through that affinity, a direct relationship with the central authority in the metropole. Kipling's Kim, after all, would be a "Celtic Caliban" in England.[32] But this affinity, and how it was to be established, was not self-evident or straightforward.

The novelty of the nineteenth century was that the population began to participate in absolute and imperial wars as part of a process of establishing a new exchange with their rulers in Europe.[33] The population was no longer indifferent to wars between rulers, nor did they see wars overseas as purely

---

[27] Colley 1992, 120; Said 1993, 141.

[28] Mamdani 2012.

[29] This was the view of the American racial theorist William Ripley in 1899, quoted in Young 1995, 40.

[30] Young 1995, 142–158; McClintock 1995, 47.

[31] Stoler 2002, 66–67.

[32] McClintock 1995, 53.

[33] On the novelty of citizenship in this period and its imbrication with empire, see Burbank and Cooper 2010, 223–235.

opportunities for private enrichment. Rather, the costs of war (and the probability of victory) were a function of the exchange between central authority and
population, where it held, and where it did not. The British diplomat George
Cornewall Lewis wrote in 1841 that to understand and negotiate this required
a tripartite mode of political analysis that could identify "the nature of the relation between a sovereign government and its subjects, the relation between
the sovereign governments of independent communities, and the relation of
a dominant and dependent community."[34] I turn now to how those relations
came to be predicated on the state.

Managing Empire

If absolute war opened and imperial war typified the nineteenth century, throwing up the question of how the energies of the people were to be channeled so
that the costs of war would be limited, we must reevaluate the theory of state
formation. The nineteenth century is not the time when the modern state succeeded empires but when the modern state emerged in relation to empire. The
rising costs of war cannot be understood without considering this imperial
context: Britain drew on 2 million South Asian troops and 0.5 million African
troops during the world wars.[35] This continued a trend of the British using Indian
troops in British expeditions to "China three times between 1829 and 1856,
Persia (1856), Ethiopia and Singapore (1867), Hong Kong (1868), Afghanistan
(1878), Egypt (1882), Burma (1885), Ngasse (1893), and Sudan and Uganda
(1896)."[36] Indeed, in the nineteenth century, the Indian army was significantly
larger than Britain's standing army.[37]

Centralized states were an anomaly in the nineteenth century. In 1820, they
controlled less than 20 percent of the globe's territory.[38] The political units of
that period were, by self-definition, empires, and nineteenth-century wars were
mostly imperial wars: of 107 wars fought between 1816 and 1900, more than
half (62) were wars of conquest. This would change in the next century. Between
1901 and 2000, of 57 wars, only 10 were wars of conquest, and none after 1950.[39]
The modern state consolidated through interstate war *and* imperial conquest, as
shown in Figure 3.2.

---

[34] Quoted in Vitalis 2010, 910.
[35] Barkawi 2006, 329–331; Killingray 2010, 8, 144.
[36] Said 1993, 73.
[37] Osterhammel 2014, 453.
[38] Wimmer 2013, 1–2; Burbank and Cooper 2010.
[39] Wimmer and Min 2009.

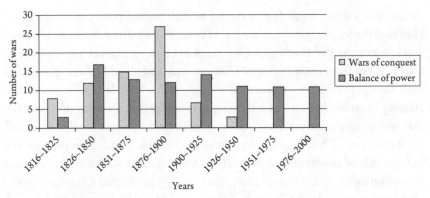

Figure 3.2 Number of interstate conflicts, 1816–2000
Source: Wimmer and Min 2009

Empires may have been the dominant political unit, but by virtue of their expansionary and violent nature, they were transient in duration and membership. Europeans educated in the classics were familiar with the demise of empires, from Rome to the more recent fall of Aragon and Etruria, which ceased to exist in 1714 and 1814, respectively.[40] Walter Bagehot noted that "in early ages all nations were destructible, and the further we go back, the more incessant was the work of destruction."[41] The transient nature of empires was made worse by the unsettling of domestic hierarchies through increased participation in war. War, in the nineteenth century, was seen as inevitable, even necessary. Observers like de Tocqueville understood war as a form of self-improvement: "War almost always enlarges the mind of a people and raises their character."[42] But the involvement of the population was new and had raised the costs of war. Empires and popular participation in war was a dangerous combination that demanded novel forms of management and political organization. Edmund Burke had worried, in his writing on the French Revolution, that colonial functionaries would return to England from India, buy political office, and inflict the moral and institutional laxity of the colonies on populations at home: "The power of the house of commons, direct or indirect, is indeed great; and long may it be able to preserve its greatness . . . and it will do so, *as long as it can keep the breakers of law in India from becoming the makers of law for England.*"[43]

The reference to India and empire in a discussion of revolutionary France reveals a significant uncertainty, at the start of the nineteenth century, about how to manage popular participation in war and imperial conquest. These

[40] Davies 2012.
[41] Bagehot 1873, 77.
[42] Quoted in Pinker 2011, 242.
[43] Burke 1973, 57, emphasis mine.

uncertainties were on full display during Burke's zealous prosecution of Warren Hastings, the former governor-general of India, in Parliament between 1788 and 1795. Burke charged Hastings with a range of offenses, from abuse of power to taking bribes from Indian princes. Hastings had made, and broken, agreements with Indian princes that illustrated a gray area: whose law governed India? Hastings justified his actions by saying that he practiced a form of despotism that was properly Indian. He could not be judged by some foreign standard, for the treaties he had signed were consistent with the divided sovereignty and indirect rule of empires more generally. In this, Hastings was correct: European expansion into North America and India had been predicated on treaties signed with local rulers and tribes because Europeans were not always powerful enough to displace those actors.[44] Hastings's trial therefore held a greater meaning. To find him guilty was to demand a new relationship between metropole and colony. This new relationship would go beyond the abrogation of treaties; rather, it was founded on the rejection of the possibility that natives could be party to bargaining with Europeans at all. That is, it rejected the view that European polities were not dissimilar to non-European polities in that both lacked centralization and direct rule, and thus both could be bargaining partners in relationships, if hierarchical, of indirect rule.

Burke's was an early effort to alter this relationship and its presumption that non-Europeans could be bargaining partners. He contested Hastings's "geographical morality," arguing instead that Hastings should have conducted himself as if he were subject to British law.[45] The existence of dual or mixed legal systems outraged "the laws of morality [which] are the same everywhere . . . . [T]here is no action which would pass for an action of extortion, of peculation, or bribery and of oppression in England, that is not an act of extortion, or peculation, of bribery and of oppression in Europe, Asia, Africa, and all the world over."[46] The Mughals and other Indian royals had proven unable to stop Hastings's excesses—indeed, they had collaborated in his despotism, rendering *them* unfit to rule—and so it was left to the British state to do so. Burke's was not, therefore, an anti-imperial argument; he was not saying that Mughal law was the ultimate arbiter, and Hastings had fallen afoul of it.[47] In contesting the divided sovereignty that Hastings was party to, Burke criticized empire as it was actually practiced but did not argue that empire itself was illegitimate.

Burke's prosecution of Hastings was unsuccessful. Its importance lies as an early salvo in the reformulation of empire in the nineteenth century. Empire had

---

[44] Williams 1997; Asch 2014.
[45] Dirks 2006, 196.
[46] Quoted in Dirks 2006, 289.
[47] E.g., Buckler 1922.

historically been a public-private partnership, not "an affair of state answerable to the nation."[48] While explorers were authorized by European rulers through charters and papal bulls, they had some degree of autonomy from the metropole.[49] Further, the laws and customs of the natives were often recognized and codified in plural legal orders and treaty diplomacy.[50] These plural legal orders were not dissimilar from systems of divided sovereignty or indirect rule *present in eighteenth-century Europe* where the centralized state was rare.[51] These systems increasingly came under fire in the colonies and in Europe.[52] Just like Burke's concern about breakers of law in India making law in England, Alexis de Tocqueville worried about French soldiers in Algeria who might "pick up the practices and tastes of a hard, violent, and arbitrary, and coarse government," raising the problem of "what we would do with a large number of such men, if they returned home."[53] Faced with an "arbitrary and coarse" government in Algeria, de Tocqueville urged the settlement of a French population.[54] But prospective settlers were dissuaded from moving to Algeria by a situation of near-anarchy. To fix this, de Tocqueville urged not just military colonization, but centralization of "the administration in Algiers in the hands of a single official in charge of giving a common direction to all the department heads."[55] Similar to Burke's demands on Indian governance, de Tocqueville saw empire as necessary for French greatness. It took some more decades for this vision to be realized, but eventually, French colonial possessions went from 1 million square kilometers in 1880 to 9.5 million square kilometers in 1885.[56]

A few years after de Tocqueville's appeals to the Assembly, Burke's demands were belatedly fulfilled in India. The Indian Mutiny of 1857 had come as a shock

[48] Dirks 2006, 125.

[49] Mudimbe 1988, 45.

[50] The basis for recognition could vary. For example, treaties were sometimes predicated on indigenous people's ability to declare and terminate war, rather than their claim to property; Pocock 2000, 31–32. Indigenous peoples could still be recognized as participants in the law of nations (*jus gentium*) without formally claiming the land. Contradictory as it sounds, a territory could contain a group capable of declaring war over it and hence a participant to a treaty *and* be an uncultivated, and hence empty, space: *jus gentium* and *terra nullius* could coincide.

[51] Tilly dates the transition to direct rule after 1750, but accelerating after the French Revolution; Tilly 1992, 107.

[52] Although there were exceptions to this centralizing intent: the French prime minister said of Tunisia in 1884 that maintaining the bey's rule "frees us from installing a French administration in this country . . . . [I]t allows us to supervise from above, to govern from above, to avoid taking on, in spite of ourselves, responsibility for all the details of administration"; quoted in Lewis 2013, 64.

[53] de Tocqueville 2001, 78.

[54] de Tocqueville 2001, 90, 111.

[55] de Tocqueville 2001, 107.

[56] Said 1993, 169.

to British audiences used to quiescent colonial subjects. Concerned that a loss of power in India would diminish Britain as a world power, massive force—invoked in terms like "extermination" and "race war"—was authorized to subdue the rebellion.[57] Then, observers turned to the culpability of the East India Company in the Mutiny. The Company, in particular the divided sovereignty it exercised, was blamed for the unrest in India. As the London *Times* editorialized:

> We may say that as a nation that India is ours. Its government has long been our affair, and it has been administered in effect by the CROWN and the Parliament of this country. The second government of the India-house [East India Company] is an effete tradition; its own action, as far as it was left to itself, an avoidance of responsibility.[58]

To address this problem, a resolution prefiguring the 1858 India Bill read, "It is expedient that there be established for India a responsible form of Government in the name of the Crown."[59] On November 1, 1858, the East India Company was dissolved, and India came under the "undivided" rule of the Crown.[60] Just as Burke had evaluated Hastings's behavior according to British law, Viscount Palmerston emphasized that the India Bill was purely an internal matter for Britain: "Again, as regards our interests in India, I may state at once that the Bill which I am about to propose to the House *is confined entirely and solely to a change in the administrative organization at home, and that we do not intend to make any alteration in the existing arrangements in India*."[61] The India Bill, the extension of direct rule, was properly about Britain because it addressed the anomaly of an essentially ungoverned space, where neither the private company nor the native monarchs had any right to rule. The India Bill established the proper place of India, and Indian history as "an entire, and highly interesting, portion of the British history," in James Mill's formulation from 1817.[62] Mill's son, John Stuart, would later make a similar point about Britain's Caribbean possessions:

> Our West Indian colonies, for example, cannot be regarded as countries with a productive capital of their own . . . [but are rather] the place where England finds it convenient to carry on the production of sugar, coffee and a few other tropical commodities . . . . [*T*]*he trade with the*

---

[57] Chowdhury 2012, 29.

[58] *Times*, "Editorials," February 13, 1858, 9.

[59] *Times*, "India Reform," December 18, 1857, 7.

[60] Metcalf 1990, xviii.

[61] Viscount Palmerston, "Speech to the House of Commons," February 12, 1858, *Hansard*, Vol. 148: c 1282, emphasis mine.

[62] Quoted in Guha 1997, 79.

West Indies is hardly to be considered an external trade, but more resembles
the traffic between town and country.[63]

Here, as elsewhere, the state did not succeed empire. The state emerged within
the taken-for-granted context of empire, to better manage empire. As late as
1946, Charles de Gaulle could say that the reborn French state would "reestab-
lish national unity and imperial unity."[64]

What of those *Europeans* without a state? In 1802, Hegel was blunt: "Germany
is no longer a state."[65] The division of Germany into estates had created centrif-
ugal tendencies wherein the people had prioritized their own interests over
resisting enemies like Napoleonic France.[66] Admiring Napoleon as he marched
through Jena, Hegel called for a "conqueror" who would unify Germans by
force. The irony, of course, was not that Germany was no longer a state, but *it
was that Germany had never been a state*. In another century, Germany would
be a great power, but at the beginning of the nineteenth century, there was no
such thing as Germany, "merely a muddle in Europe's middle."[67] The lack of
German "national attitude" had been lamented by Johann Gottfried Herder and
the nobleman Carl von Moser.[68] To address this, Hegel was calling on a French
emperor to unite Germans in a state *for the first time*. By Hegel's own standards,
from his lectures on world history, Germans were closer to Orientals, outside of
history. (Hegel had argued that Asiatics and Africans were "lacking the essential
self-consciousness of the concept of freedom" which was the precondition for
forming a state and being truly historical subjects.)[69] Similarly, North America,
although it was "the land of the future," lacked "firm coherence in the political
structure" because it was in the process of expanding: the North American state
was still to come.[70] In this world-historical context, in which pretty much everyone lacked a state, Hegel was calling on a *French* emperor to bring *Germans* into
world history (which was by definition European) and elevate them above the
Asiatics and Africans that Hegel claimed had no history. In the nineteenth century, most "Europeans" did not exist as such. They had to become European by
waging war to build a state.

Thus, Massimo d'Azegelio's statement—"We have made Italy, now we must
make Italians"—was more representative of nineteenth-century Europe than

[63] Quoted in Said 1993, 90, emphasis mine.
[64] Quoted in Cooper 2005, 153.
[65] Hegel 1999, 6, 7, 15.
[66] Hegel 1999, 57.
[67] Krebs 2011, 20–21.
[68] Krebs 2011, 163, 178–179.
[69] Guha 2002, 37–38.
[70] Hegel 1988, 89–90.

the British and French anomalies. Mazzini had demanded, and his successor Count Cavour had in fact enlisted foreign support (from Napoleon's nephew Louis Bonaparte) in supporting, the liberation of northern Italy from Austria.[71] The reader will note the absence or weakness, in the nineteenth century, of what are now represented as enduring European polities (and models for contemporary weak states!). Centralized states, what we would now call strong states, were the anomaly. Those seeking to build new states in nineteenth-century Europe were doing so by appealing for foreign assistance in wars. And the ascension to statehood involved colonization outside Europe (this, I will show in Chapter 8, is the opposite of current state-building that is meant to *prevent* interstate and intrastate conflict). In the same text in which he wrote, "Italy is a new fact of international politics, a new people, a *life* that only yesterday did not exist,"[72] Mazzini emphasized the link between war-making and state-making. He noted that "Italy's resurgence would indeed not have been possible without going to war" against the papacy and the Austrian empire, and he urged the colonization of Tunisia as part of "an inevitable trend (which) is calling for Europe to civilize the African regions."[73]

Yet others could reasonably argue that Italy was not a state and hence could be treated just like Tunisia or India, which Churchill would later mock as a "geographical statement." Churchill was preceded by Metternich, who had called Italy merely a "geographical expression."[74] Today, in a sardonic reminder of the novelty and the tenuous nature of European state formation, consider that the racists of the Italian Northern League party claim that the Risorgimento did not unite Italy; it divided Africa. This distasteful jab nonetheless illustrates the centrality of race and war in European state formation. However, this centrality has been neglected by otherwise perceptive scholars. This neglect, I will now show, has led us to miss the self-undermining nature of European state formation.

Spiriting War Away

Napoleon did not march just to Russia. He also went to Egypt, and those looking to his example, like Mazzini, aspired to similarly engage in war and empire to build the states they did not have. But as the Napoleonic wars had unleashed war in its absolute perfection, statesmen also spent much of the next few decades trying to limit the cost of conflict *in Europe*. As the cost of war increased, Europeans

---

[71] Kissinger 1994, 110–111.
[72] Mazzini 2009, 234, emphasis in original.
[73] Mazzini 2009, 235, 239; Ziblatt 2006, 96–98.
[74] Davies 2012, 420.

sought bargains that would limit these costs even if they could not eliminate war. An absurd but revealing example was a proposal by the German scholar Lorenz von Stein to treat rail transport, even that passing through hostile territory, as neutral in times of war.[75] The reader will note that von Stein is trying to limit war but more or less accepting that it would occur. War drove the exchange between central authority and population, and wars of conquest made balance of power wars between Europeans more likely. The expansion of European empires—the land area controlled by them expanded from 35 percent in 1800 to 85 percent in 1914—created problems of credible commitment and increased uncertainty about relative power. As European powers scrambled to gain land, the balance of power was subject to sudden shifts, undermining bargains struck at earlier periods.[76] Maintaining peace in Europe became more difficult because of European state formation.

The "Hundred Years' Peace" makes it appear that the period of war-making and state-making was over and that the nineteenth century was a period of state consolidation in Europe (this is the conclusion Tilly draws).[77] I have suggested instead that the nineteenth century was the period when states emerged, but in relation to empires, not succeeding them. Even the "stronger" states were in flux at this time: late nineteenth-century British thinkers, for example, envisioned a Greater Britain combining England, Australia, and Canada—a sort of United States of Britain that the English historian Charles Oman wished "might control the whole world."[78] The state was situated within transnational themes of civilizational cooperation and imperial competition.[79] I will now argue that the relationship between empire and state was to limit war along the borders of the state: war was to be conducted according to rules restricting the use of force against those populations that had states (and fighting whom would be very costly), while those rules were relaxed in wars against those without a state. The expectation was that bargaining between Europeans would break down in some instances into war. In those instances, agreements would limit the costs of war so that the central authority could protect the population during war and the exchange would be self-enforcing. Bargaining, whether about who was subject to the rules or what the rules would be, was restricted to those who had states and increasingly excluded those who did not. But the very recent emergence of

[75] Schmitt 2003, 214.

[76] The corollary is that periods with fewer wars of conquest and less territorial change should, because the balance of power does not shift suddenly, see fewer commitment problems and thus a lower risk of balance of power wars.

[77] Tilly 1992, 190.

[78] Quoted in Bell 2007, 1, 92–98.

[79] On the seventeenth–century origin of civilization as an object—e.g., Egyptian civilization—rather than a process, see Mazlish 2001.

the state meant the parameters determining who had a state and who did not were shaky at their foundation (they could justifiably be said to lack foundation). Most "Europeans" could quite reasonably be represented as lacking states, and hence could be targets just like Asians or Africans. Not only did empire make wars between Europeans more likely, but when these wars broke out, the agreements that would limit the costs were based on shaky foundations and as a consequence often broke down.

The move to direct rule in the colonies took place as European rulers placed informal and formal limits on conflict within Europe. The nineteenth-century congresses and the Hague and Geneva conferences saw ongoing efforts between European states to develop norms regulating conduct within war, including the protection of civilians and prisoners of war.[80] These bargains did not eliminate war but defined where limits to it applied and where they did not. These bargains were predicated on parameters that could limit the costs of (inevitable) war. Racial differences, inseparable from membership in a state, constituted these parameters.[81] The imbrication of racial and civilizational notions with the ability to found a state can be seen, for example, in how the Scottish jurist James Lorimer mapped the world in concentric circles, with civilized nations in the inner circle, barbarous nations in the middle, and savage nations on the outside.[82] Lorimer drew on anthropology and ethnology for his understanding of "indelible" "ethnical differences."[83] These indelible differences meant that the savage did not just lack a state but that he could never found one.[84] Not belonging to a community deserving recognition in the present or future, the individual savage did need not to be recognized as having rights.[85] Russian Chancellor Aleksandr Gorchakov expressed this view in justifying Russia's right to expand in Central Asia: "The situation of Russia in Central Asia is similar to that of all civilized states that come into contact with half-savage nomadic tribes without a firm social organization . . . . [I]n such cases, the interests of border security and trade relations always require that the more civilized state have certain authority over its neighbors."[86]

Like the Italians looking at Tunisia, Gorchakov argued that the Russians, in contrast to the savages of Central Asia, were European. But, illustrating the

---

[80] Mazower 2012, 68.

[81] Foucault suggested that racial difference justified war in the nineteenth century; Foucault 2003. I am suggesting that racial *similarity* allowed the limitation of war, by allowing whites to see themselves within one civilization.

[82] Simpson 2004, 238–242.

[83] Quoted in Grovogui 1996, 71–72.

[84] Grovogui 1996, 72.

[85] Mbembe 2001, 188.

[86] Quoted in Kissinger 1994, 141.

tenuousness of these distinctions, the European view of Russia has fluctuated between Russia as the exemplar of Oriental despotism—in one of the more colorful descriptions, a French traveler wrote that between France and Russia was "a Chinese wall—the Slavonic language and character"[87]—and Russia as a liberalizing late entrant to Europe.[88] Russians themselves acknowledged and resisted this classification; Dostoevsky noted that "in Europe we were Asiatics, whereas in Asia we, too, are Europeans."[89] Nineteenth-century understandings of who was European and who was not were novel. Even though "Europe" had come to be seen as a single historical entity by the early nineteenth century, there were several different and contradictory ways of drawing its borders.[90] Further, the concepts through which some were classified as Europeans and others not were shifting; race and nation, for example, were sometimes conflated, as when Renan wrote "if it be permitted us to assign sex to *nations* as to individuals, we should have to say without hesitance that the Celtic *race* . . . is an essentially feminine *race*."[91]

Non-European populations were represented as unequal to Europeans because they lacked states and were incapable of forming them. But this was not always the European view, for the very good reason that only the French and the British could be said to have centralized states prior to the nineteenth century, and most continued not to have them right through this period. The idea of the centralized state that developed in Europe between the seventeenth and nineteenth centuries, much like the notion of "strong states" today, was more an object of desire than an empirical reality. Liebniz in 1677 had said of the theories of Hobbes and Pufendorf, theorists of centralized power, that no known political society *anywhere* exhibited the institutional uniformity and centralization they "took for granted."[92] Most Europeans lived in decentralized polities not dissimilar to the New World or parts of Asia.[93] Liebniz's near-contemporaries Vitoria and Montaigne had compared European peasants and menial workers to indigenous Americans.[94] Mudimbe contrasts two missionary views of West Africa to show when this view changed. In the seventeenth century, Giovanni Romano described "an African version of a Christian European

[87] Quoted in Wolff 1994, 365.

[88] Kissinger's statement that "Russia belonged partly to Europe, partly to Asia" indicates the endurance of this trope; Kissinger 1994, 173.

[89] Quoted in Judt 2005, 749.

[90] Osterhammel 2014, 87–88.

[91] Quoted in Young 1995, 70, emphasis mine, 82–84. On this conflation in British arguments, see Bell 2007, 113–119. In India, colonial anthropologists, especially H. H. Risley, conflated caste with race; Dirks 2001, 206–207, 224–227, 246–247.

[92] Tully 1995, 83.

[93] Bayly 2004, 30–33.

[94] Seth 2010, 57.

kingdom with its dukes, earls and barons" where poor pagans were not dissimilar to European peasants.[95] Two hundred years later, the former slave Samuel Ajayi Crowther advocated conversion of Africans that he described with the characteristics—"paganism, nakedness, and cannibalism"—of savages, that is, *not* comparable to European peasants.[96] That Crowther referred to cannibalism is particularly apposite, because in the nineteenth century, historians of the Crusades stopped referring to cannibalism by Frankish knights, even though previous accounts noted the practice.[97] Cannibalism, which desperate European sailors were said to practice in the nineteenth century, came to be seen as the exclusive preserve of non-Europeans: a map of Liberia issued by the US government marked the unknown interior as just "cannibals."[98] Conversely, just as pre-nineteenth-century European thinkers could see their own peasants as pagans, so could they understand some non-Europeans, like the Chinese or Mughals, as civilized.[99]

But this shifted in the nineteenth century, when non-Europeans began to be seen as different, unequal, and unable to attain civilization due to immutable racial differences.[100] Due to this, previously sanctioned treaties between local leaders and entities, from Indian princes to Native American tribes, came to be voided.[101] The novelty of this process, I suggest, derives from the fact that previous agreements had been between two representatives of decentralized polities, but the rise of the centralized state in Europe negated these agreements. For example, a representative of the East India Company exercised a divided sovereignty similar to that of an Indian prince and could recognize the prince's jurisdiction (and see him as equal). But as the British state, aspiring toward centralized and unitary rule (the "universal center" that Hegel called for), came to deal with the Indian prince, it did not recognize his jurisdiction as equal—recall Burke's criticism of a geographical morality that would have implied equality—and thus voided the prior arrangements made by the East India Company as its representative. An analogous process was the exclusion, in the late nineteenth century, of Egyptian and Ottoman rulers from European conferences to which they had been invited as late as 1856.[102] Put differently, while empires had

---

[95] Mudimbe 1988, 48.

[96] Mudimbe 1988, 49.

[97] Said 1993, 16.

[98] McClintock 1995, 25–27

[99] Seth 2010, 116.

[100] Hunt 2007, 190.

[101] For example, between 1776 and the War of 1812, the new American state's treaties with Native American groups recognized these groups' original claim on the land, that is, the land was not "undiscovered" as later versions of the "doctrine of discovery" put it; Wilkins and Lomawaima 2001, 42–47.

[102] Mazower 2012, 71–72; Simpson 2004, 244.

historically recognized the principle of difference,[103] the colonial state increasingly came to subordinate difference. The key difference, inseparable from racial and civilizational notions, was the idea that while European polities were states, non-Europeans did not have states and hence were not due recognition as bargaining partners or equals under newly emergent international law.

This lack of recognition meant that savages were not due the protections extended to Europeans. As laws of war developed to limit the costs of war—to protect civilians, allow humanitarian workers access to battlefields, and grant rights to prisoners of war—these laws did not apply in the colonies. In 1868, the St. Petersburg Declaration restricted the development of bullets to avoid unnecessary injury, but by 1895, the British military was using the soft-point, dum-dum bullet in the Chitral campaign in what is now northern Pakistan, and then its successor the Mark IV in Omdurman,[104] which battle Churchill would acclaim as "the most signal triumph of the arms of science over the barbarians."[105] The concentration camp emerged in southern Africa during the Boer War.[106] Deportations and famines were used to subjugate groups in India, China, and southwest Africa.[107] Aerial bombing was first used in Libya in 1911, and then against recalcitrant tribes in Iraq, despite objections of "immorality" from the British army and navy.[108]

The costs of war could thus rise without undermining the exchange developing in Europe. This was because the exchange was predicated on limiting the costs of war between those with states and removing those limits when war was declared against the stateless. The bargaining that yielded states in Europe, within European states and between them, was predicated on not bargaining with non-Europeans, which enabled the rise of novel, and ever deadlier, tactics. De Tocqueville, otherwise a critic of Marshall Bugeaud, governor-general of Algeria, still noted that "today we can say that war in Africa is a science whose laws are known to everyone and that can be applied almost with certainty.... [O]ne of the greatest services that Marshal Bugeaud has rendered his country is to have extended this new science, perfected it, and made it clear to all."[109]

The "new science" held that the natives could be subjugated through excessive shows of force: "half-civilized peoples have difficulty understanding forbearance and indulgence; they understand nothing but justice ... exact, but rigorous, justice

---

[103] Burbank and Cooper 2010.

[104] Spiers 1992, 288.

[105] Winston Churchill, "The Battle of Omdurman, 1898." Available at http://www.fordham.edu/halsall/mod/1898churchill-omdurman.asp.

[106] Spiers 1992, 311.

[107] Davis 2001; Hull 2005.

[108] Mazower 2012, 76; Biddle 2002, 82.

[109] de Tocqueville 2001, 135.

should be our sole rule of conduct toward the indigenous population when they act reprehensibly towards us."[110] That natives reacted differently than Europeans did to force was a staple of nineteenth-century counterinsurgency theory. C. E. Callwell, author of *Small Wars*, asserted that "colonial victories had come . . . by making the 'lower races,' who were 'profoundly impressionable,' feel a 'moral inferiority throughout.'"[111] Such 'moral inferiority,' as the American counterinsurgency theorist Eldridge Colby put it in 1927, meant that a Frenchman seeing a shell strike Rheims cathedral, and a "fanatical savage" seeing a bomb striking his temple would react differently. The Frenchman would perceive the act as "lawless" and be enraged, but the savage would perceive it as a sign that "God has withdrawn his favor" and surrender.[112] Tactics that led to swift victory in the colonies would have the opposite effect in Europe (an acknowledgment that the costs of war in Europe, given the involvement of the population, might be too high). Smoking the recalcitrant out of caves in Algeria or burning farms in the Boer conflict are to be understood within this paradigm of warfare targeted at a population (although the Hague convention had also proscribed collective punishment). The same logic was eventually applied to aerial bombing. In Afghanistan, a Royal Air Force memo on using the new weapon ticked the usual boxes: "hesitation or delay in dealing with uncivilized enemies are invariably interpreted as signs of weakness," and "in warfare against savage tribes who do not conform to codes of civilized warfare . . . aerial bombardment is not necessarily limited in its methods or objectives by rules agreed upon in international law."[113]

The need for the state to limit the costs of war had begun with the problem of the Spanish guerillas in the Napoleonic wars. They, according to Tolstoy and Clausewitz, were epitomes of the people armed, but their tactics were *irregular*.[114] When these types of irregular fighters could be brought under state control, Clausewitz argued, their energies could be best channeled in the aim of policy. This could be done in two ways: through self-armed militias that would mobilize in the event of invasion, or by standing armies controlled by the state.[115] In 1813, Prussia passed a decree requiring every Prussian citizen to resist invading armies with available weapons, including pitchforks and knives.[116] But three months after it was passed, the decree was changed to proscribe guerilla warfare in

---

[110] de Tocqueville 2001, 141.

[111] Quoted in Spiers 1992, 298.

[112] Quoted in Mazower 2012, 78.

[113] Quoted in Graham Chandler, "The Bombing of Waziristan," *Air and Space Magazine*, July 2011. Available at http://www.airspacemag.com/military-aviation/The-Bombing-of-Waziristan.html.

[114] Schmitt 2004, 3.

[115] There was popular opposition to standing armies from the eighteenth century onward. On the American case, see Bailyn 1992, 35–36.

[116] This edict was based on a Spanish model; Schmitt 2004, 29–30.

national defense and to restrict warfare to regular armies. The short-lived decree seems insignificant, but its repeal suggests an important shift in war-making and state-making. The people armed were an essential, indeed unavoidable, component of war, but they had to be under the centralized control of the state. This would limit the costs of war and enable bargaining so that political ends could be achieved, as Clausewitz had urged.

What of the tactics of those without a state, who could not, by definition, have a regular army, like the Herero in southwest Africa fighting the Germans? How could *they* defend themselves? Not only were the Herero not due recognition as bargaining partners, but under international law as it had emerged in the nineteenth century, the Herero's use of force, such as making bullets out of shards of glass, was considered illegal. Insofar as the Germans were rightful sovereigns of southwest Africa, the Herero were their subjects and did not have the right to resist.[117] This was not European hypocrisy or a rule selectively applied, but was how nineteenth-century international law functioned by excluding certain populations, even when they tried to defend themselves, from the status of combatants due rights of protection.[118] It was not hypocritical because when French or Belgian citizens resisted German soldiers in the Great War, they too were not treated as regular fighters and were subject to collective punishment much like the Herero were.[119] Here, the behavior of these "European" populations cast them as unworthy of protection. The distinctions between Europeans and others were unstable, and this instability meant that limits on conflict could break down during war. The expected costs of war were based on shifting parameters and were subject to quite significant errors.[120]

Limiting conflict to the colonies was both a geographical phenomenon and an effort to spirit away tactics of irregular warfare and justifications for colonization that had been used in Europe as well. This was why the repeal of the 1813 decree requiring Prussians to resist an occupier is significant: such militia mobilization was not under the control of the state, and therefore it was not to be recognized as part of combat. As these tactics had been used in Europe

[117] Hull 2005, 10–11, 49–52.

[118] "Extermination" or "race war" came to be used on European populations but had previously been considered appropriate means of quelling restive non-white populations. On how Theodore Roosevelt evoked "extermination" when blacks or Indians rebelled, see Lake and Reynolds 2008, 103.

[119] Hull 2005, 226, 316.

[120] This instability was characteristic of nineteenth-century racial thinking, which was neither scientific nor, and this is the important point, consistent. Race inflected the discussion of class in Europe, especially the representations of the underclass and marginal populations. This meant that, on the one hand, the underclass would work to "become white" and differentiate themselves from savages, and on the other, that the threat of racial degeneration existed at home; McClintock 1995, 104–122.

they could always potentially be used again, on "Europeans," itself a novel and unstable category in the nineteenth century. Just as John Locke had seen native peoples as undeserving of their land because they did not add value to it, the English official John Barrow described Dutch frontiersmen in southern Africa as lacking the "spirit of improvement and experiment" that had led them to neither survey nor cultivate the Cape."[121] Later, Ludendorff would state that Russia had not *used* the ports of Windau and Libau (now Ventspils and Liepaja in Latvia) and thus did not deserve to control them.[122] If colonial theorists claimed that natives were particularly susceptible to shows of force, advocates of air power could extrapolate from success in the colonies to advocate bombing European cities. John Salmond, eventually chief of air staff in the Royal Air Force, did just this in Quetta in 1922, avowing that civilians *everywhere* could eventually be cowed by strategic bombing.[123] Completing the circle, a British Air Staff paper in 1941 explained aerial attacks on German morale as "an adaptation, though on a greatly magnified scale, of the policy of air control which has proven so successful in recent years in the small wars in which the air force has been continuously engaged."[124] The modern state emerged to protect the population that participated in conflict as that participation increased the scale of conflict, but it did so by subjecting another population to violence without limits. Yet the basis of these distinctions lacked foundation, and once war began, they broke down. When Europeans were represented as lacking social organization and a state—a not unreasonable position given how recently and tenuously European states had developed—the costs of war could no longer be contained.

Colonial tactics were not without critics, but these critics did not offer an alternative to the war-making/state-making process. Rather, they either urged that the colonial state protect the colonized or that the colonized go to war for themselves. The Quaker Emily Hobhouse revealed the conditions of the concentration camps during the Boer War, leading to censure back in England.[125] The British diplomat (and eventual Irish nationalist) Roger Casement traveled to the Congo, accompanied by Joseph Conrad, to investigate allegations of atrocities against the natives.[126] The accountant Edmund Morel had discovered that the Congolese were exporting rubber so that Belgian soldiers could buy rifles. Casement found that the rubber was extracted by coercion, including taking whole villages hostage—a version of collective punishment that de Tocqueville noted was the great discovery the French had made in Algeria—and forcing the

[121] Comaroff and Comaroff 1991, 95.
[122] Liulevicius 2000, 97.
[123] Omissi 1990, 110–111.
[124] Quoted in Biddle 2002, 83.
[125] Spiers 1992, 311.
[126] Taussig 1987, 11–17.

men into the jungle to tap rubber. His findings shocked audiences in Europe, and in response, the Belgian state took over the governance of the Congo from King Leopold (but committed to pay him 50 million francs from the Congo). The solution to excesses of empire was not independence for the colonies. Instead, it remained the responsibility of the European state to bring law to the colonies and protect the colonized.[127] The takeover by the Belgian state, like the assertion of direct rule in India, marked a paradox in the relationship between racial difference and the establishment of the state. Racial difference authorized violence against the Congolese population, but the establishment of the Belgian state implied some responsibility to protect that population against violence. At the turn of the century, liberals like Morel held out the hope that the colonial state could protect the natives even as it subjugated them.[128]

By 1913, Roger Casement broke with Morel. He had lost faith in the colonial state and declared the paradox of protection from the colonizer by the colonizer insoluble. His missions in Putumayo and the Congo had taught him that the natives would not be protected by their European masters. Instead, he came to self-knowledge as an Irish nationalist; "in these lonely Congo forests, where I found Leopold, I found also myself, an incorrigible Irishman."[129] The British, he went on to argue, did not care as much for the well-being of the natives as they did for their control of the sea lanes. They would run the risk of war in Europe to maintain this advantage.[130] Growing unrest in Ireland had led the British government to propose a form of Home Rule that Casement mocked as "a curse and a crime."[131] Instead of Home Rule, he urged an alliance between Irish nationalists and the Kaiser's Germany to overthrow British rule (Casement tried unsuccessfully to recruit Irish prisoners of war to fight for Germany). Eventually, Casement was captured and executed for running guns to the rebels in 1916. The reader will note the similarity with Hegel and the Italian nationalists appealing to Napoleon and his nephew, respectively, for assistance in forming a modern German and an Italian state, and the expectation that empire would only be ended when the colonized went to war for themselves. In Chapter 6, I will show that the anti-colonial movements rejected Casement's strategy, with important consequences on state formation in the postcolonial world.

We are left with the paradox I have called the self-undermining state. The modern state was not developed to prevent war. Nineteenth-century observers saw war as inevitable, a part of the human condition. Popular participation

---

[127] Hochschild 1999, 257–259.
[128] Hochschild 1999, 257.
[129] Quoted in Taussig 1987, 19.
[130] Casement 1915.
[131] Casement 1915, 70.

in war would therefore make wars more costly as they tended toward absolute war in planning.[132] This necessitated efforts to limit the cost of war, to the extent that the state could only be self-enforcing and self-reinforcing as long as these limits held. But the effort to limit conflict was based on shaky (or non-existent) foundations. Casement's disillusionment indicated a realization among some Europeans that empire had not benefited colonized peoples. The Great War revealed that empire, and the modern state that managed it, did not protect Europeans either.

"Never Such Innocence Again"

The activism of Hobhouse and Casement marked the tenuous nature of the effort to keep the colonies separate from Europe. After 1900, this frayed further, first in the cultural realm. Picasso's *Desmoisilles d'Avignon* (1907) was part of an emerging tendency in the art world to internalize the savage, the child-like, and the animal within Europe.[133] When first performed in 1913, Stravinsky's *Rite of Spring* provoked a scandal by unleashing these naturalistic elements on the Parisian stage, leading a critic to call it "refined Hottentot music."[134] The scandal was that savage artifacts or people were no longer merely to be represented at arms length, as in the idealized Oriental harems of Ingres, or to be ogled by Europeans from the outside in a sanitized exhibition like the World's Fair.[135] They had come to constitute Europeans themselves.

But it took another type of symphony, that of "shells, gas clouds, and flotillas of tanks" to drive that lesson home.[136] The Great War shocked Europeans— quite literally, as the term "shell shock" came into usage in 1915 as a result of the war.[137] In 1926, Carl Jung interpreted a dream of being shelled on his way back from the frontlines as an indication that "the war, which in the outer world had taken place some years before, was not yet over but was continuing to be fought within the psyche."[138] More prosaically, then British foreign secretary Austen Chamberlain put it in 1925, "The old Europe was consumed in the fires of the Great War and the new Europe has yet to be built on foundations that may give

---

[132] Kissinger 1994, 203; Hull 2005.

[133] Previously, artists like J. M. Whistler had sought to learn from the most sophisticated non-European arts, like Japanese prints, not the "simple" art of tribal societies; Gombrich 2006, 434–463.

[134] Eksteins 1989, 50.

[135] Mitchell 1988, 1–13.

[136] Remarque 1982, 283.

[137] Kaes 2009, 10.

[138] Quoted in Fussell 2009, 137.

peace and security to the nations of the old world."[139] It is to the "battle within the psyche" and "the inability to build new foundations" that I now turn.

Immediately after Versailles, John Maynard Keynes argued that "the forces of the nineteenth century have run their course and are exhausted."[140] Keynes wanted to use the Great War as a lesson to force Europeans to confront the tenuous basis of European state formation. Racial categories had proven necessary for limiting conflict but had broken down under the weight of their own ambiguities (or lack of foundation). On the one hand, "white men's countries" could be seen to form a racial bloc around what the American political scientist John Burgess called the superiority of the "Teutonic" race, the first to establish "national states" which then bestowed on them the duty to "organize the world politically."[141] The view that American political institutions derived from a Teutonic model and were part of a broader Aryan civilization was widely held before the Great War, including by Woodrow Wilson, but its proponents disavowed it as tensions with Germany rose.[142] (In the more anxious formulations of the day, "white men's countries" needed to mobilize against the "rising tide of color" and stave off civilizational decay.)[143] On the other hand, as Burgess's example suggests, "white men" could be further subdivided because the term itself was ambiguous: Russians, Burgess wrote, were "Slavs" who could only be politically organized under a foreign power, such as the Teutonic Romanovs or Hapsburgs.[144] Indeed, Hitler would argue that Russia must have been built by a Germanic racial core as the lower races of the East were incapable of such feats.[145] As states were new in Europe, many "Europeans" could reasonably be represented as lacking states.

In one of the founding texts of the discipline of international relations, E. H. Carr, like Roger Casement and Keynes, said this system of limiting conflict to protect European populations had ceased to work:

> For more than a hundred years, the reality of conflict had been spirited out of sight by the political thinkers of Western civilization . . . . [T]he men of the nineteen-thirties returned shocked and bewildered to the state of nature . . . . [T]he brutalities which, in the eighteenth and

[139] Quoted in Steiner 2007, 387.

[140] Keynes 1920, 238.

[141] Burgess 1890, 37, 48. On similar views of the origin of British institutions, see Bell 2007, 191–193.

[142] Oren 2003, 33–46.

[143] Baum 2006, 170; Lake and Reynolds 2008, 314–315.

[144] Burgess 1890, 31–32.

[145] Liulevicius 2000, 257.

nineteenth centuries were confined to dealings between civilized and uncivilized peoples were turned by civilized peoples against one another."[146]

The Great War indicated that war was now too costly, because the parameters on which bargaining was predicated and the costs of war could be limited—the recognition of fellow "Europeans" as different from "uncivilized peoples"— had broken down. Germans slaughtered Frenchmen as they had slaughtered Hereros—indicating that conquered Frenchmen were not just and equal enemies (*justi hostes*)[147] because they no longer had a state. In Polanyi's words, in the Great War, "nineteenth century civilization . . . collapsed."[148] In 1917, W. E. B. Du Bois had preempted Carr: "As we saw the dead dimly through rifts of battlesmoke and heard faintly the cursing and accusations of blood brothers, we darker men said: this is not Europe gone mad; this is not aberration nor insanity; this *is* Europe."[149] Du Bois's analysis, we will see in Chapter 6, had much in common with that of anti-colonial leaders.

Observers saw three aspects constitutive of nineteenth-century European civilization that was now undermining it. First, Keynes argued, the nineteenth century use of force had become untenable. However, policymakers were not acting as if it was. Instead, the participants at Versailles continued to understand "European history (as) a perpetual prize-fight."[150] They could not propose alternatives to the pattern of inevitable war, even as they acknowledged this type of war as too costly. If Clemenceau took a hard line aimed at punishing Germany, it was because of this way of thinking, which Keynes bemoaned as both outmoded and dangerous. It would impoverish Germany and would provoke in Central Europe a civil war "before which the horrors of the late German war will fade into nothing, and which will destroy, whoever is victor, the civilization and the progress of our generation."[151] Now that the population were involved in war, they had come to demand revenge, and leaders had to accommodate these demands. Lloyd George, for example, altered his political platform to emphasize pursuing indemnities from Germany and punishing the Kaiser.[152] Roman Jakobson noted that this sort of "zoological nationalism" affected even scientific inquiry, pointing to the Royal Society's denial of a medal for Albert Einstein

---

[146] Carr 2001, 225.
[147] Schmitt 2003, 124.
[148] Polanyi 1944, 3.
[149] Du Bois 1917, 437.
[150] Keynes 1920, 31.
[151] Keynes 1920, 251.
[152] Keynes 1920, 127–133

because it would have involved exporting gold to Germany![153] The popular willingness to supply the state through conscription and taxation now undermined the state's ability to limit the costs of war.

Second, the racial and civilizational categories on which the bracketing of conflict was predicated had been shown to lack foundations and prove not binding. The shifting status of Russia in and out of Europe exemplified this. In the Great War, the Germans viewed the East as a vast, uninhabited land to be cultivated, its people to be colonized and improved through *Kultur*. In the Second World War, the Nazis viewed the East as just space (*Raum*) for growing food for Germans, at the cost of starving millions of Soviet citizens.[154] Hitler aimed to "direct the gaze towards the land of the East . . . . [W]e finally close the politics of colonialism and trade and go over to the politics of soil of the future."[155] Carr argued that the "harmony of interests"—the liberal notion that the interests of states were not in conflict but could be achieved by working in concert—only appeared as such because it had been "established through the sacrifice of 'unfit' Africans and Asiatics."[156] In the nineteenth century, war had proven productive—that is, it was costly but winnable—for Europeans only because its costs had been limited by categories specifying who possessed a state and were thus due protection in war. The failure to limit war-making to those who did not possess a state meant that war in Europe could compromise European order. But, worryingly to European observers, war *still* seemed inevitable. In 1917, Sigmund Freud acknowledged the devastation of the Great War but did not see an end: "But war cannot be abolished; so long as the conditions of existence among the nations are so different and their mutual repulsion so violent, there are bound to be wars."[157] This was the crisis of European civilization: war, necessary to spread that civilization, had now come to undermine it.

If war now threatened to undermine European civilization, it meant, third, that the central authority could no longer protect the population from the

---

[153] Jakobson 1987, 40. The politicization of science would intensify. The Nobel Laureates Philipp Lenard and Johannes Stark developed "German physics" or "Aryan physics" as a counter to Einstein's theory of relativity, disdained as "Jewish physics." George Orwell would write that for the Nazis there "was no such thing as 'science' . . . there is only 'German science,' 'Jewish science' etc."; Orwell 2009, 170. To identify the "provinciality" of concepts that distinguished Europeans from others—the state, science—is not relativism, but essential to understanding how these concepts functioned through excluding certain groups. Consider that Edmund Husserl, himself marginalized because he was a Jew, still wrote that Eskimos, Indians, and Gypsies were not of Europe because they lacked the orientation of *theoria*, or philosophy for its own sake; Husserl 1970, 275.

[154] Tribe 1995, 154.

[155] Quoted in Liulevicius 2000, 257.

[156] Carr 2001, 49.

[157] Quoted in Kaes 2009, 97.

ravages of war. A period that had begun with peasants being indifferent to war ended with the population potentially being sacrificed in the war. This would be taken to the extreme by the Nazis. As the Soviets advanced, the Nazi leadership ordered the destruction of its own population's war supply and other basic needs, with the line, "If the war is lost, let the nation perish." According to Albert Speer, the impending defeat indicated that "the Volk [had] shown itself to be weaker" and did not deserve to survive the war.[158] The state could no longer deliver on the promise of protection through which it had emerged. As the Dadaist Hugo Ball articulated in 1927, "The state is like a giant slaughterhouse or cemetery; there, in the shadow and on the pretext of representing the general interest, all the real aspirations, all the living forces of a country give themselves willingly to the slaughter."[159] If the state had failed to protect the population, they might prefer alternatives, and the exchange might no longer be self-enforcing.

Yet, after the Great War, the state was providing more for its population than ever before (and the trend would only accelerate, as I will show in Chapter 5). In Britain, for example, public spending on health in 1918 exceeded private spending for the first time.[160] That the state was becoming responsible for more aspects of everyday life even as it was proving incapable of protecting the population in war reveals its self-undermining basis. Wars of the people required coordination and limits in order for the exchange between central authority and population to be self-enforcing. The modern state emerged as both condition for limits on conflict and enforcer of those limits. The state channeled the energies of the people in war and empire, increasing the potential cost of all conflicts; but it also promised to protect the population from its worst ravages, by limiting actual conflicts within Europe. But the limits were predicated on unstable racial and civilizational categories that came apart as a result of state formation through war. Once tactics developed in the colonies were actualized in Europe—that is, Europeans became targets of colonization—the state could no longer provide that protection.[161] Truly "absolute war" revealed that the modern state—the type of government that Thomas Paine had said was just becoming to be known in 1789—was a self-undermining institution.

---

[158] Schwendemann 2003, 607; Foucault 2003, 258–260.

[159] Quoted in Demos 2003, 155.

[160] Porter 1994, 182.

[161] Hitler's war plan to combat Britain's control of the sea lanes involved colonizing the western Soviet Union, with a potential death toll of 31 million to 45 million people; Snyder 2010, 160, 157–160.

4

Restaging the State

One must—and this is not an exaggeration—keep in mind that we are living in the atomic age, where everything material and physical could disappear from one day to another, to be replaced by nothing but the ultimate abstraction imaginable.

Yves Klein[1]

In his 1961 picture "Hiroshima," the artist Yves Klein traced a ghostly silhouette or "void" onto a canvas as a representation of the shadow burned onto a door-step by the atomic blast (Figure 4.1). According to Klein, this "void" was the new subject of postwar art.

Klein's "void" could be understood, on the one hand, as a logical progression of the prior century's efforts to break down the representation of the world into its component parts (and then reassemble it). But on the other hand, the void was a step beyond, for there was no physical object to take apart anymore. Not only had the subject of art changed from the physical to the abstraction; so had its techniques. Jackson Pollock explained his own innovation of dripping paint over canvases as a response to his historical moment: "It seems to me that the modern painter cannot express this age, the airplane, the atom bomb, the radio, in the old forms of the Renaissance or of any other past culture."[2]

A new subject of art, requiring new forms of art. In this chapter, I will argue that the atomic age raised the specter of a new subject of politics, different from the state, and the need for new forms of politics, different from the war-making/state-making process of the past. Just as Hiroshima forced Klein and Pollock to create alternatives to previous artistic practice, a variety of alternatives to the state were proposed after 1945. These alternatives were premised on the idea that the state was no longer in a position to protect the population in the event of war. Rather than aggrandizing through costly war, the state had proven to be

[1] Quoted in Peterson 2004, 579.
[2] Quoted in Peterson 2004, 587.

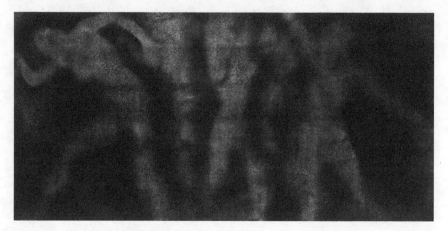

Figure 4.1 Yves Klein, *Hiroshima*

self-undermining as wartime extraction had driven the cost of war to its "absolute perfection." The parameters within which the costs of war were estimated had shifted. Updating to the new parameters, most observers came to the conclusion that war was too costly and was no longer winnable. This realization raised the question of what sort of exchange, and what polity, could prevent war after 1945. Pointing out the risks of establishing new polities, intellectuals and policymakers articulated ways in which the state could ensure "security"—the prevention of war through nuclear deterrence and intervention in the economy. Yet, this new function, requiring permanent state presence rather than a temporary wartime expansion, paradoxically expanded expectations of order at the same time that it bound the state from war-fighting.

Alternatives to the State

The interwar years, as the last chapter showed, were characterized by stasis. The devastation of the Great War informed a sense that Europe faced an existential crisis. Yet there seemed no other way of conducting international politics; recall, for example, Keynes lamenting that Clemenceau and other leaders at Versailles could not see the world in any other way than that of nineteenth-century competition with its expectation of inevitable conflict. While war had proven overly costly to most observers in the 1920s, there were no proposed alternatives to the state, and hence the war-making/state-making process continued. After 1945, however, the latter criticism did not hold, for there was an efflorescence of alternative visions of ordering the world. As one observer put it in 1948, "If we compare the general mood of 1919, when everybody was keen to get back to what had gone on before, with the mood of 1948 one generation later . . . the need for an active international society is almost universally taken for granted."[3]

To some degree, this should have been expected. Stanley Hoffman would write later that "the conditions seemed ideal [to supersede the nation-state in Western Europe] . . . [O]n the one hand, nationalism seemed at its lowest ebb; on the other, an adequate formula and method for building a substitute had apparently been devised."[4] Europe was in ruins; three quarters of buildings in Berlin, for example, were no longer fit for habitation.[5] The emergence of the state after 1789 had been a dizzying period when states, especially in Eastern Europe, appeared and disappeared from the map. For example, after an independence movement had emerged against the declining tsar's rule, Estonia became independent and joined the League of Nations in 1920, then faced a Soviet-backed insurrection in 1924, and alternated between being controlled by Germany and the USSR between 1939 and 1945 (with a brief interlude of five days in 1944 when Estonian politicians declared an independent government before Soviet tanks arrived).[6] Contra the idea that modern European states were enduring polities, Europe had lived through a period in which many states were fleeting, and where they existed, were unable to protect their populations. War had proven costly and unwinnable, and unmade more states than it had made in this period. The conditions seemed ideal for establishing alternatives to the state. For a fragmentary sense of the open possibilities of the time, consider that in 1945, 81 percent of respondents to a Gallup poll in America favored American entry into a "world organization with the military power to enforce world peace."[7] In fact, in surveys from 1946 to 1950, more than 50 percent of Americans responded affirmatively to the question, "Do you think the U.N. should be strengthened to make it a world government with power to control the armed forces of all nations, including the U.S."[8] Europeans similarly would "look for solutions to their problems in a framework larger than the discredited nation-state . . . . [T]he nation-state seemed unable to guarantee economic welfare, military security, or the enjoyment of democracy and human rights."[9]

While a variety of alternative visions of world order emerged, they were motivated by the overwhelming imperative to avoid a future, nuclear, war. Mark Mazower points out that "in the 1940's, world government momentarily

[3] Mitrany 1948, 350.

[4] Hoffman 1966, 863.

[5] Judt 2005, 16.

[6] Davies 2012, 705–715.

[7] Mazower 2012, 208, 233.

[8] Roper Center, "Seventy Years of U.S. Public Opinion on the United Nations," June 22, 2015. Available at http://ropercenter.cornell.edu/seventy-years-us-public-opinion-united-nations/.

[9] Haas 1967, 321.

seized the imagination of an astonishingly large number of people . . . . [T]he reason was simple: the atomic bomb and how to control its use."[10] The urgency reflected a fundamental shift in the parameters within which the costs of war were calculated. Previously, war was seen to be inevitable. But with atomic weapons, as Harold Laswell argued, that *expectation* of inevitable war, a staple of nineteenth-century thought, was itself dangerous.[11] Even the idea that war, though inevitable, could be limited had been repudiated by the world wars, during which the distinction between civilian and combatant had been viti-ated.[12] Given the constant erosion of nineteenth-century efforts to limit (but not eliminate) conflict built on interstate agreements and norms, the effort to prevent war needed to be ambitious, even revolutionary, if it was to reverse 150 years of historical experience. And as the escalating costs of war were endogenous to the promise of state protection—as the population sacrificed more to win the war—it followed that proposals to prevent war would chal-lenge the primacy of the state.

The first class of alternatives to the state was international organizations serv-ing as a world government. In 1945, group of twenty prominent Americans, including Senator William Fulbright and Albert Einstein, wrote an open letter urging a world constitution. In similar vein, the University of Chicago chancel-lor, Robert Hutchins, went on the radio to argue that nuclear war was inevitable unless "the monopoly of atomic force by a world organization" was established.[13] He commissioned members of his faculty to devise a World Constitution, which was published in 1948 to varying reviews (including, from the right-wing *Chicago Tribune*, the verdict that it combined the ravings of Franklin Roosevelt and Karl Marx).[14] E. H. Carr wrote in 1946 that "international security in the modern world is likely to demand the maintenance of some standing interna-tional forces made up of different national units; and such a system calls for an institutional framework."[15] Even policymakers entertained the possibility of a supra-national organization with military functions.[16] In 1948, the US Senate passed the Vandenberg Resolution whose Article 5 called for "maximum effort to obtain agreements to provide the United Nations with armed forces as provided

---

[10] Mazower 2012, 231.

[11] Lasswell 1949. The view at the time that nuclear war was inevitable or highly likely was recalled by Thomas Schelling in 2008: "The most astonishing development during these more than forty years—a development that no one I have known could have imagined—is that during the rest of the twentieth century . . . not a single nuclear weapon was exploded in warfare"; Schelling 2008, vii.

[12] The distinction was itself a modern idea; Arendt 1963, 5.

[13] Quoted in Boyer 1995.

[14] Boyer 1995.

[15] Carr 2001, 54.

[16] Bundy 1988, 145–161.

by the Charter."[17] In his Fulton, Missouri, speech where he used the term "iron curtain," Winston Churchill also asserted that "the United Nations Organization must immediately begin to be equipped with an international armed force."[18] More revealing was what he said about the parameters within which the costs of war had come to be understood:

> On the other hand, ladies and gentlemen, I repulse the idea that a new war is *inevitable*; still more that it is imminent. It is because I am sure that our fortunes are still in our own hands and that we hold the power to save the future, that I feel the duty to speak out now that I have the occasion and the opportunity to do so. I do not believe that Soviet Russia desires war. What they desire is the fruits of war and the indefinite expansion of their power and doctrines. But what we have to consider here today while time remains, is the *permanent prevention of war* and the establishment of conditions of freedom and democracy as rapidly as possible in all countries.

Despite arguing that the Soviet Union desired to dominate Europe, Churchill suggested that the costs of war made that desire moot. War was not inevitable, but it was questionable, given the breakdown in previous efforts to limit war that relied on state enforcement, whether states could prevent war without third-party involvement. For a brief period, even state actors entertained the possibility of supra-state organizations because as, Bertrand Russell put it, "the great majority of those who have considered the conditions for secure peace are persuaded that the most important of these conditions is the creation of an International Authority with power to enforce its decisions."[19]

The second class of alternatives involved the delegation of nuclear weapons to an international organization and the commitment from states not to develop nuclear weapons.[20] Rather than establish a world government, technical cooperation would eventually reduce tension between states, and, in the views of its proponents, lead to "federalism by installments."[21] Robert Oppenheimer and Albert Einstein called for atomic materiel to be brought under the control of the United Nations, what the latter called "the denationalization of military

---

[17] US Senate Resolution 239, 80th Congress, 2nd Session, available at http://www.nato.int/cps/en/natohq/official_texts_17054.htm?.

[18] Winston Churchill, speech at Westminster College, Fulton, Missouri, March 5, 1946, emphasis mine. Available at http://www.historyguide.org/europe/churchill.html.

[19] Russell 2009, 47.

[20] Mitrany 1948, 358; Haas 1964.

[21] Quoted in Haas 1964, 13, 11,

power."[22] This proposal had some odd bedfellows. It had been made in 1945 by John Foster Dulles, who would later decry the "nuclear taboo" and advocate the policy of massive retaliation, and by Henry Stimson, the US secretary of war.[23] Similarly, the inaugural editorial of the *Bulletin of the Atomic Scientists* "appeal(ed) to the American people to work unceasingly for the establishment of international control of atomic weapons, as a first step towards permanent peace."[24] Parts of this general idea were extended into a proposal, the Baruch Plan, under which nuclear secrets would be shared through a UN agency but individual states would forego developing nuclear weapons (the plan was rejected in 1946, largely because the USSR was unwilling to give up its nuclear program).[25] In 1948, the UN Atomic Energy Commission would summarize the assumption behind international control as "all Members of the United Nations share the conviction that, unless effective international control is established, there can be no lasting security against atomic weapons for any nation, whatever its size, location, or power," and "past experience has shown that unless there is a novel approach to the problem of controlling a force so readily adaptable to warfare, atomic weapons . . . will continue just as uncontrolled as other weapons have been and still are, and the threat of atomic war will remain."[26] There were two choices—international control or atomic war—because historical experience suggested that states armed with atomic weapons would use them in wars.

These alternatives did not come to be institutionalized, and the state persisted. There are several reasons for this, from the contingent to the structural. Contingent factors that undermined world government or a more robust UN include the reliance on legal instruments, like the UN, that could be obstructed by the great powers. At a more fundamental level, alternatives to the state must either promise more to or expect less from the population in order to gain popular support. Alternatives like world government and a strengthened United Nations did not do the latter. For alternatives to come into being, the population had to run the risk that if they gave up their own nuclear weapons (in the case of the United States), or did not acquire them (in the case of non-nuclear powers), the alternative would credibly monopolize these weapons and prevent their use. If there was any likelihood of another state reneging, the population would be existentially vulnerable. As articulated in the key US Cold War document NSC-68 in its objection to international control of atomic weapons, "For

[22] Quoted in Iriye 2004, 54.

[23] Kaplan 1983, 179.

[24] Atomic Scientists of Chicago 1945, 1.

[25] Bundy 1988, 161–168.

[26] Third Report of the Atomic Energy Commission to the Security Council, May 17, 1948. Available at http://avalon.law.yale.edu/20th_century/decad242.asp.

such an arrangement to be in the interest of the United States, it is essential that the agreement be entered into in good faith by both sides and the probability against its violation high."[27] The population was being asked to run an existential risk, which they were unwilling to do. Thus, acknowledging that nuclear war was too costly and unwinnable was not enough, Reinhold Niebuhr, a critic of international control, would write, "Virtually all arguments for world government rest upon the simple presupposition that the desirability of world order proves the attainability of world government."[28] And, as I will describe below, there was another choice beyond atomic war or world government, as state actors promised to prevent war by marshalling a large nuclear force. Harry Truman put the choice simply: "I am of the opinion we'll never obtain international control. . . . [S]ince we can't obtain international control, we must be strongest in atomic weapons."[29] But the real impact of the alternatives lies in their underlying logic, namely, the insight that the war-making/state-making relationship was no longer tenable. Once this logic was accepted, the process of costly war through which alternatives to the state had been selected out was no longer operative, and the stage was set for future articulations of alternatives to the state.

Parametric Shift (or Why War No Longer Makes States, Part 1)

In Chapter 2, I suggested that for war to make states, it had to be costly but winnable. Wars of the people armed fit these conditions: they required the population to supply the state through taxes and conscription, yet they could conceivably end in victory. However, this process could only continue up a certain point, after which the costs of war would be too excessive, and/or war would be unwinnable. At this point, bargains would be preferable to fighting in virtually all circumstances. Nuclear weapons, observers agreed, marked this inflection point. Instead, wars had to be limited by avoiding direct confrontation between the superpowers, and truly costly wars—the types of war that had led the population to supply the state—had to be avoided altogether. This led observers, including the initial realist thinkers of international relations, to question the relevance of the state.

To theorize this inflection point, I return to Clausewitz. Clausewitz theorized the new type of war—"absolute war"—as raising the costs of war beyond ex ante

[27] National Security Council 1950, 41.
[28] Niebuhr 1949, 380.
[29] Quoted in Rosenberg 1983, 21–22.

estimates by involving the population. The population was motivated to sacrifice given the threat, and this created the opportunity for a central authority to develop a direct exchange by promising protection from the worst aspects of war. The exchange developed insofar as the central authority could protect the population, yet mobilize it as if their survival was at stake. War had to be winnable—or could not be unwinnable—and the expected costs could not be so high that the population itself could be eliminated in defeat. But in Clausewitz's time, no war ever approximated, much less achieved, absolute status, threatening the survival of the population.[30] Absolute war was a purely theoretical construction, because for war to be absolute, it could have to be conducted in one blow, and the result would be final, ending in the elimination of the enemy.[31] These theoretical conditions—war conducted in one blow, war capable of eliminating the enemy—did not hold in reality. Rather, it took time to mobilize the resources of a state, and states could rarely eliminate each other. Hence Clausewitz argued that in reality,

> warfare thus eludes the strict theoretical requirement that extremes of force be applied. Once the extreme is no longer feared or aimed at, it becomes a matter of judgment what degree of effort should be made; and this can only be based on the phenomena of the real world, and the *laws of probability*.[32]

It was because war could *not* be waged to an extreme that it could function as a political instrument: it was costly, but could never be suicidal. Yet to mobilize the population for absolute war would increase the costs.

This was because the new type of war had to be waged *as if it were absolute*. It was the sense that war threatened them directly that had compelled the population to prefer the exchange with the central authority over alternatives like self-defense through militias. In response, the central authority had to "put the largest possible army into the field."[33] Doing so raised the costs of war because it required extending the promise of protection to more members of the population who then became willing to sacrifice more. (Yet, given prior experience of war, the population could not fully anticipate the costs of the new type of war.) The threat of absolute war enabled greater extraction, which in turn increased the likelihood that war would be absolute.

But how could war be waged as absolute, even though this was impossible in reality? In this paradox, Clausewitz suggested, lay war's political utility. Secure

---

[30] Clausewitz 1976, 78–80.
[31] Clausewitz 1976, 79–81.
[32] Clausewitz 1976, 80, emphasis in original.
[33] Clausewitz 1976, 195.

in the knowledge that war would occur over a period of time, making it possible to bargain in case the costs exceeded ex ante calculations, and that the outcome, while costly, was unlikely to be final, policymakers could, and should, expend all the resources they could to achieve a favorable outcome, whether through fighting or at the negotiating table.[34] If the initial course of battle went against their calculations, they could sue for a peace without having expended all their capabilities. In the context of limited war (or war that could not be unlimited), the nineteenth-century idea that war was inevitable did not contradict or compromise political goals. Indeed, it enabled bargaining because the shadow of warfare allowed credible threats to be made. The costs of war were high enough that a threat would impose significant damage if carried out, but not so high as to not be credible. As Raymond Aron explained, "Clausewitz compared diplomacy to a business transaction on credit, in which war is the ultimate cash settlement; all outstanding obligations must be honored on the battlefield and all debts paid."[35] Wars were seen as inevitable in theory because they could not be absolute in practice. Such wars built the modern state.

Nuclear weapons made the extreme of theory possible in reality. This was an inflection point, reversing the relationship between war-making and state-making. The costs of a nuclear war exceeded any political benefits and could undermine the promise of protection. A nuclear war could be conducted, if not in one blow, in a series of quick blows that would dramatically shrink the duration of war. This combination of speed and scale of destruction limited both interstate and intrastate bargaining: as Robert Dahl noted in 1953, atomic power challenged basic democratic processes.[36] Finally, a nuclear war would result in the near-elimination of each side; it would be "final." This made moot the concept of "victory"; hence Eisenhower would claim "the only thing worse than losing a global war was winning one."[37] Nuclear weapons essentially negated Clausewitz's thesis that war was an instrument of politics, and by implication, of state-making. The impossibility of absolute war in the nineteenth century—that war could be costly but winnable—had created the space in which political goals could be pursued through fighting or bargaining through mobilizing maximum force.[38] With the advent of nuclear weapons, absolute war was possible in reality, transforming the relationship between the theory and reality of war. Before 1945, war could be waged as if it were absolute, precisely *because* it could not be absolute in reality: war was costly, but not too costly, and winnable. As nuclear

---

[34] Wagner 2007, 133–137.

[35] Aron 1965, 207.

[36] Dahl 1953, 6.

[37] Trachtenberg 1989, 40.

[38] Aron 1965, 207.

weapons made war absolute in reality, war could not be waged except in theory. As Stanley Hoffman put it in 1966, "international politics today is more a stage on which one can parade than a battlefield that seals one's fate."[39]

War-making, noted observers in 1945, was at an inflection point. But analyses of state formation have not theorized the impact of nuclear weapons on the exchange between central authority and population.[40] Given that the costly and winnable wars that built states were a recent development, it behooves us to explore how quickly this type of war became outmoded. The military theorist Basil Liddell Hart argued in 1946 that "warfare as we have known it in the last thirty years is not compatible with the atomic age."[41] Liddell Hart directly countered Clausewitz: "Total warfare implies that the aim, the effort, and degree of violence are unlimited . . . . [A]ny unlimited war waged with atomic power would be worse than nonsense; it would be mutually suicidal."[42] The state's ability to protect its population had been predicated on a combination of defensive and offensive strategies to disarm the opponent. Nuclear weapons made both moot: a state could neither defend against nuclear weapons nor win a nuclear exchange.[43] Liddell Hart advocated steps from norms limiting conflict to disarmament, eventually leading to "the establishment of the United States of the World."[44] The assessment that war was too costly and unwinnable drove the calls for the obsolescence of the state. As Carr put it, "The small independent nation-state is obsolete or obsolescent" and "no workable international organization can be built on a membership of a multiplicity of nation-states."[45]

Observers understood the advent of atomic weapons to render other forms of statecraft unusable. Previously, bargaining between states was facilitated because war could *not* be absolute. This made threats credible because as long as both sides had some expectation of winning, they could conceivably declare war. That war could not be absolute enabled bargaining between states, and within, by compelling individual and collective sacrifice so that the population as a whole could survive the war. Nuclear war, observers from De Gaulle in 1960 to Gorbachev in 1985 agreed, was not winnable.[46] Therefore, both superpowers gained from avoiding nuclear war *in all circumstances*. As Oppenheimer

---

[39] Hoffman 1966, 908.

[40] Tilly mentions nuclear weapons once, and Wimmer not at all; Tilly 1992, 202–203; Wimmer 2013.

[41] Hart 1946, 98.

[42] Quoted in Freedman 1989, 99.

[43] Hart 1946, 98–99.

[44] Hart 1946, 118–119.

[45] Carr 2001, viii.

[46] Quoted in Jervis 1989, 1. To use contemporary concepts, when both sides have nuclear weapons (or at least secure second-strike forces), neither major mechanism for war is operative because of

articulated this view, "The common interest of all in the prevention of atomic warfare would seem immensely to overshadow any purely national interest."[47] For Raymond Aron this meant that the age of enmity between nuclear powers had passed; nuclear weapons had made the superpowers "enemy partners."[48] "Enemy partners" always lost more in nuclear war than they could gain from it.[49] A nuclear war would leave the responsibility for rebuilding much of the world to the superpowers.[50] Before Aron theorized "enemy partners," Eisenhower had exemplified its logic. In rejecting a proposal to wage a preventive war on the USSR before the latter achieved second-strike deterrence, Eisenhower asked his advisors, "What do you do with the world after you have won victory in such a catastrophic nuclear war?"[51]

Along with the prospect of military victory, other aspects of statecraft like external and internal balancing were rendered ineffective by nuclear weapons. Hans Morgenthau noted the irony that the superpowers simultaneously negotiated arms limitation talks as they accumulated nuclear weapons and targets: in 1976, the US Single Integrated Operational Plan identified 40,000 potential targets in the Soviet Union.[52] The cost of war due to such strategies was so high as to make any threat non-credible, and superpower bargaining was about limiting the likelihood of war through arms control and improved communication like the Hot Line rather than threatening war. Nuclear weapons made the powerful "impotent in the fullness of their power."[53] Morgenthau's statement echoes even more today in the cases of North Korea and Pakistan, who face much stronger conventional adversaries who nevertheless are unable to use that advantage to compel concessions.[54]

Now that war could be absolute and the extant tools of statecraft ineffective in the absence of the ability to make credible threats, the exchange underpinning

---

the mutual understanding that nuclear wars are unwinnable. There is no private information either side can possess that would suggest a nuclear war is winnable. Even if there are significant commitment problems, the expectation that a war is unwinnable makes initiating it unlikely.

[47] Quoted in Iriye 2004, 54.

[48] Aron 1966, 536–572.

[49] Aron 1966, 546.

[50] Aron 1966, 547.

[51] Quoted in Trachtenberg 1989, 40.

[52] Ball 1982, 36.

[53] Morgenthau 1964, 25.

[54] When two nuclear-armed states bargain, the range of possible settlements increases but the need to reach an agreement diminishes because states will prefer the absence of an agreement to fighting. States may ultimately neither resolve their disputes nor fight. Hence the resolution of disputes depends on changes within the states in question, such as the economic collapse in the Soviet Union. Such changes, and thus the resolution of the dispute, are independent of the bargaining dynamic between the states in question.

the modern state was in question. John Herz, the formulator of the security dilemma, noted that airpower and nuclear weapons challenged the modern state's main benefit to its population: the impermeability of its territory.[55] Given the vulnerability of the population to nuclear attack, "the chief external function of the state seems to have vanished."[56] Herz, like authors of several of the accounts above, called for agreements between states, including no-first-use policies, delimited spheres of influence, in a transition to a "universalism" built on "a sense of concern which will urge us to be alert to chances to prevent extinction."[57] Herz's espousal of "universalism" exemplifies that the alternatives to the state were driven by pragmatic considerations. It is somewhat ironic that those now remembered as the early formulators of realism in international relations— Carr, Morgenthau, and Herz—were concerned about the viability of the main unit of realism, the state, and the patterns of power politics that had constituted it.[58] But if we consider that the modern state had developed in a short span of time and its development had proved self-undermining, this irony becomes understandable.

We can now qualify a bit further the statement that it takes costly but winnable wars to build states. As Centeno has argued, limited wars do not force the exchange that typifies "strong" states because the population does not feel the need for protection, and hence they may prefer alternatives or stay indifferent to wars so they do not have to supply the state.[59] To make states, wars must be costly. However, if war is too costly, as nuclear war can be, the exchange is voided because protection is impossible. Wars in which a large section of the population are at actual mortal risk do not make states. Indeed, such would-be states are often absorbed into conquerors and cease to exist, like the Baltic states in the early twentieth century, or the Mahdist state in Sudan. For this reason, I specified that wars need to be winnable as well as costly.

Yet there is no reason inherent to the exchange itself—rather than the parameters that condition it, as I argued in Chapter 3—that the costs of war necessarily escalate to "absolute" levels to threaten the survival of the population. Clausewitz provides the theoretical reason that the war-making/state-making relationship increases the costs of war to the point of being self-undermining. Only wars fought as if they are absolute *without actually being absolute* can make states. Only such paradoxical wars compel the level of sacrifice that builds centralized states. Yet their costs are often underestimated in advance because the

[55] Herz 1959, 5, 13.
[56] Herz 1959, 22.
[57] Herz 1959, 309–310.
[58] Scheuerman 2011.
[59] Centeno 2002, 21–24.

full extent of mobilization is not fully anticipated. (Put differently, existing knowledge of wars fought without full mobilization leads the population to underestimate the costs of future wars.) Other interstate wars, from limited wars that do not require taxation and conscription to actually absolute wars like a nuclear war that can kill a large section of the population, do not facilitate the exchange between a central authority and a population or the level of extraction that typifies the modern state.

To see the logic of how contemporary limited wars do not facilitate state formation, consider the sometimes bloody wars that the superpowers have engaged in since 1945. These wars fall into one of two categories, neither of which facilitates state-building. These wars are not "absolute" in the sense that the population's survival is not at stake—indeed, they must stop short of risking escalation into nuclear war—and invariably begin with the expectation of low costs.[60] When these expectations are correct, like the Soviet invasion of Hungary in 1956 and the US-Iraq war of 1991, the great power wins quickly (low costs and high probability of victory), and the war does not require major sacrifices. But if the expectations are incorrect and the costs of war rise and/or lead to a stalemate, as occurred in Vietnam, Afghanistan (for both superpowers), and Iraq since 2003, the population is eventually disillusioned with the war because its' survival is not at stake even if the opponent wins, and it becomes unwilling to sacrifice for it. This is consistent with the initial model, which specified that both a positive probability of victory and a high cost of war are necessary for the population to supply the state. Great powers can, and do, wage limited wars despite diminishment in popular willingness to supply the state. In Table 4.1, I adapt the schematic from Chapter 2 to give examples of the types of interstate war that yield states, and the many types of interstate war that do not.

Most wars either do not make states or can unmake them. It is only a paradoxical, historically brief, and now unlikely type of war that facilitated the formation of the European state.

If nineteenth-century conditions, namely, popular involvement in war and empire, made costly and winnable war more likely, the advent of nuclear weapons made such wars less likely and diminished the imperative to build centralized states. There were two possible mechanisms for this outcome. The first, which did not really transpire, was widespread proliferation after China obtained nuclear weapons in the 1960s.[61] Nuclear proliferation would make costly but winnable war less likely by creating bilateral relationships of deterrence. However, US policymakers feared that proliferation would make it more difficult for the

---

[60] Jervis 1989, 79.
[61] Brands 2006, 85–91; Gavin 2012, 78–79.

Table 4.1 **War and State-Making after 1945**

	High cost of war	Low cost of war
Positive probability of victory	Wars of the people armed; supply of state high	Limited war; supply of state low
Very low/zero probability of victory	Nuclear war; supply of state low	War unlikely; supply of state low

superpowers to project force and raised the risk of accidental nuclear war.[62] Both superpowers were wary of proliferation and sought to prevent it.[63]

The second mechanism, which did transpire, was the combination of non-proliferation efforts and superpower commitments to prevent escalation of conflicts in Asia and Africa. Non-proliferation efforts took various forms, some of which seem contradictory in retrospect. In 1961, the United States proposed to the Soviets a joint strike on Chinese nuclear facilities.[64] The superpowers also pursued legalistic strategies like the Test Ban Treaty. At the very least, this suggests that policymakers were uncomfortable with the logic of deterrence—that more nuclear-armed states should lead to more stability—to the consternation of scholars.[65] Instead of disseminating nuclear weapons to prevent war outright, the superpowers would intervene during wars elsewhere in the world to prevent absolute victory.[66] When they could not prevent war—for example, when Brezhnev tried and failed to prevent Anwar Sadat from initiating war on Israel in 1973—the superpowers sought to prevent wars from escalating.[67] (By contrast, where the risk of escalation was low, as in southern Africa, the superpowers made no such efforts.) The expectation of superpower intervention to limit war and prevent absolute outcomes like territorial absorption and state death affected state-building decisions by postcolonial leaders. Even in areas where the risk of war was high, postcolonial leaders did not have to extract at the level European states did in the first half of the twentieth century because they could rely on superpower mediation to end conflicts short of absolute outcomes.[68] Postcolonial states, for reasons I discuss in Chapter 6, were in any case less likely

[62] Gavin 2015, 20–23.

[63] Gavin 2012, 27–28; Gavin 2015.

[64] Chang 1988.

[65] Kull has called this "the problem of adapting to nuclear reality"; Kull 1988, 3–29.

[66] Trachtenberg 1999, 383.

[67] Grynaviski 2014, 74–85.

[68] Consider that after a border war with China escalated, Indian prime minister Jawaharlal Nehru requested President Kennedy to provide twelve squadrons of fighter aircraft to protect Indian cities and two squadrons of bombers to target Chinese airfields.

to emulate the European process of state formation through conflict; super-power efforts to limit war put a further ceiling on the extent to which they could emulate the process should they have tried.[69]

Restaging

The reader will object that, if anything, after 1945, the state was disseminated worldwide rather than replaced. The alternatives, as Harry Truman scoffed of world government, were no more than a "theory" that might become reality, but not for a "thousand years."[70] However, to dismiss the alternatives as mere theory is to obscure two transformations to the exchange between the central authority and the population. First, the parameters within which the costs of war and the probability of victory were calculated had shifted to make prevention of war the service demanded by the population. Second, consequently, the state after 1945 was no longer expected to wage absolute war but to prevent it through deterrence and economic intervention. This expanded expectations of the state, but could over time reduce the necessity for the population to supply the state.

At the center of the transformation in the role of the state was an epistemological shift away from the notions that war was inevitable, and the best way to protect the population from such wars was to win them. Accepting Liddell Hart's premise, the American strategist Bernard Brodie wrote that same year (1946) that while atomic weapons had transformed conflict, the absolute weapon need not imply a crisis of the state: "Thus far the chief purpose of our military establishment has been to win wars . . . . [F]rom now on its chief purpose must be to avert them."[71] This shift in military strategy was the basis of a new exchange between the state and the population, from protection through war-fighting to the more amorphous (and expansive) promise of "security." The state survived its alternatives because a multiplicity of actors proposed that the state could prevent war by taking on an expanded and permanent deterrence role. Deterrence was not an inevitable and self-evident response to the advent of nuclear weapons: as the previous section suggests, there were other ways of preventing war than stockpiling nuclear weapons and rendering populations existentially vulnerable.

I have suggested that calls for alternatives to the state were motivated by the necessity to prevent war; those espousing alternatives asserted that the state,

---

[69] Even in regions where bellicist strategies were most likely, like the Middle East, superpower intervention mostly limited the costs of war, with the exception of the Iran-Iraq war.

[70] Quoted in Bundy 1988, 175.

[71] Brodie 1946, 76.

a war-making entity by nature, had not and could not fulfill this task. One response could have been that this time was not different, and the old patterns of war-making and state-making were appropriate for the atomic age. In contrast with the situation after 1918, policymakers and intellectuals did *not* respond this way. Policymakers conceded that large-scale interstate war was too costly and not winnable. However, they also asserted that there remained a role for the state in preparing for war and holding unthinkable force in reserve, *while acknowledging that force could not be used anyway*. These arguments embodied Hoffman's statement that "the decline of the state's capacity to defend its citizens is neither total nor sufficient to force the nation-state itself into decline."[72] Henry Kissinger had summed up this logic in 1957:

> The enormity of modern weapons makes the thought of all-out war repugnant, but the refusal to run any risks would amount to handing the Soviet leaders a blank check. We can overcome the paralysis induced by such prospects only if our strategy can pose less absolute alternatives to our policy-makers. To be sure, *we require at all times a capability for all-out war so great that by no calculation could an aggressor hope to destroy us by a surprise attack*. But we must also realize that a capacity for all-out thermonuclear war can only avert disaster. *It cannot be implied to achieve positive ends.*[73]

This statement summarizes the epistemological and political novelty of nuclear deterrence. The costs of war were so high that "all-out thermonuclear war" could not be inevitable, in contrast with the fatalistic post–Great War sense that war, despite its costs, continued to be inevitable. Further, the need to avoid such wars made nuclear threats less credible, and hence nuclear weapons could not be used to aggrandize state power and incorporate citizens, as war had in the era of European state formation. Politically, therefore, the war-making/state-making relationship was disarticulated: the state's role was to prevent, not prosecute, war by marshalling "a capability for absolute war" to deter surprise attack, but never to use this capability.

To trace how the state went from being placed in question by nuclear weapons to being the central unit of the atomic age, consider the shift in three statements, over a period of fourteen years. The first statement is speculative in the sense that the speaker is trying to establish a parametric shift in thinking about the use of force in an era when the costs of war are too high; the second performative, when the speaker is advocating a novel policy for using force; the third constative, when the

[72] Hoffman 1966, 909.
[73] Kissinger 1957, 131, emphasis mine.

author is stating as fact how force is used in the new era.[74] Speaking at the Air War College in 1952, Brodie addressed the possibility of deterrence breaking down and having to fight a war

> I've been toying with an idea about that. *If I had heard it from anyone else I should have called it a crackpot idea*, but I offer it to you for what it may be worth. The atomic bomb thus far has achieved really great successes; it helped end the Pacific War, and it has so far deterred the Soviet Union from aggression. At least, there is nothing visible to us, that is, nothing physical, that has deterred the Soviet Union from aggression. *Notice that the deterrent value has resulted from the threat value.* I submit that even the ending of the Pacific War resulted not from the cities we destroyed, but *rather from the threat value of the nonexistent additional bombs which the Japanese did not know we didn't have*—from the threat of more to come.[75]

Actual physical force—the destruction of two cities—was not what had compelled the Japanese to surrender, Brodie speculated; it was the threat that was not used (indeed, may not even have existed). The costs of war were so high that war-fighting served no purpose, just like the alternatives to the state implied. Yet, and this was the parametric shift, preparing for wars that one wanted to avoid could prevent war by deterring the opponent. For this, one did not need alternatives to the state. Rather, one needed to invest in precisely the war-making capacity of the state but to hold that capacity in reserve.

In 1955, back as prime minister and nine years after he had spoken of an international police force for the United Nations, Winston Churchill explained to the House of Commons why Britain needed to develop its own hydrogen bomb.[76] He explained that "the best defense would of course be *bona fide* disarmament . . . . [T]his is in all our hearts."[77] But Soviet expansionism and intransigence compromised this goal, leading Churchill to advocate the following course:

> Unless a trustworthy and universal agreement upon disarmament, conventional and nuclear alike, can be reached . . . there is only one sane policy for the free world for the next few years. This is what we call defense through deterrents.

---

[74] On the distinction between performative and constative utterances, see Austin 1975, 1–11.

[75] Quoted in Trachtenberg 1989, 306, emphasis mine.

[76] John Foster Dulles made a similar move away from disarmament/international control in the 1940s to massive retaliation in the 1950s.

[77] Winston Churchill, "Never Despair," March 1, 1955. Available at https://www.winston-churchill.org/learn/speeches/speeches-of-winston-churchill/102-never-despair.

If, for Brodie, deterrence was a speculative idea in 1952, for Churchill three years later it was positively distasteful. No shrinking violet when it came to colonial coercion of entire populations, Churchill called the period when the British population could not be protected from Soviet bombardment a "hideous epoch." In an ideal world, disarmament would remove the threat of nuclear war, but to enable this, the states of the free world had to invest in their nuclear and conventional war-fighting capacity. Churchill advocated a purportedly "temporary" policy to prevent war, necessary for disarmament in the long run, which required the state to marshal maximum destructive force.

By 1966, what was variously derided as the "crackpot idea" (Brodie) and the "hideous epoch" (Churchill) came to be seen as normal. What had previously appeared novel and unsettling—the impossibility of winning war, the state's inability to protect in the event of nuclear war—had become the central component of statecraft. Deterrence acknowledged that essential components of war-making and state-making—military victory, the possibility of defense, the protection of the population—were now obsolete. Schelling put as a matter of fact what had appeared "crackpot" to Brodie and "hideous" to Churchill: in the nuclear age, "victory inadequately expresses what a nation wants from its military forces . . . . [M]ostly it wants, in these time, the influence that resides in latent force . . . . [It] wants the bargaining power that comes from its capacity to hurt, not just the direct consequence of successful military action."[78] For another example of how the terms of nuclear deterrence swiftly became part of everyday vocabulary, consider the term "escalation," a word that was not used in a military context in dictionaries of 1961.[79] If Yves Klein had placed the abstraction at the center of the picture, deterrence placed the threat of the use of force at the center of what strategy had become: "strategy . . . is not concerned with the efficient *application* of force but with the *exploitation of potential force*."[80] Yet it was the actual "application of force" that had driven the exchange between central authority and population.

In the immediate term, deterrence required more, not less, centralization and extraction. In 1950, National Security Council Report 68 (NSC-68) recommended a defense budget of 20 percent of GNP; in 1940, the revenues of all levels of government in the United States were below this number.[81] Hence, the recommendation was followed by a succinct bullet point: "increased taxes."[82] At this point, the highest marginal rates of income tax and inheritance

---

[78] Schelling 1966, 31.
[79] Kahn 1965, 3, 275–276.
[80] Schelling 1960, 5, emphasis in original.
[81] Wallis 2000, 65.
[82] Yergin 1977, 402; National Security Council 1950, 57.

in the United States were over 70 percent. George Kennan futilely dissented that increased military expenditures constituted "uneconomic and regrettable diversion of effort." But US military expenditures rose: spending on military research and development in 1949 exceeded the entire military budget of 1924.[83] In the 1950s, Kissinger, Herman Kahn, and Albert Wohlstetter were among those to urge the United States to come up with a strategic doctrine that would constitute "the mode of survival of a society,"[84] build more bombers to deter the Soviets (Wohlstetter), and plan for survival after nuclear war (Kahn).[85] Kahn's was the most extreme but also revealing formulation of the increased role of the state: "If the government has made even moderate postwar preparations . . . then people will probably rally around."[86] Both superpowers would develop deterrent forces and conventional war strategies, even when they acknowledged that the latter could not be used without risking nuclear war—what Brodie called "a common recognition . . . that thermonuclear war between [the superpowers] is simply forbidden, and thus also lesser wars that might too easily lead up to the large-scale thermonuclear variety."[87] Yet this initially required the population to supply the state, because, as Brodie argued "if deterrence fails, we shall want enough forces to fight a total war effectively."[88] The logic of nuclear and conventional buildup would persist, even if the former ruled out the full exercise of the latter. Two decades later, US Secretary of the Air Force Verne Orr would write that "if deterrence does fail, we must be able to win to survive."[89]

The irony, of course, is that if nuclear war occurred, deterrence, the purpose of the state, had failed, and all the centralization and extraction would have been in vain. As many policymakers conceded, nuclear war was unwinnable. The demands of deterrence created a paradox:

> Deterrence now means something as a strategic policy only when we are fairly confident that the retaliatory instrument on which it relies will not be called upon to function at all. Nevertheless, that instrument has to be maintained at a high pitch of efficiency and readiness and constantly improved, which can be done only at high cost to the community . . . . In short, we expect the system to be always ready to spring

[83] Yergin 1977, 390, 362.
[84] Kissinger 1957, 428.
[85] Wohlstetter 1958; Kahn 1960.
[86] Kahn 1960, 90, 10.
[87] Brodie 1973, 425–426; Jervis 1989, 79–82.
[88] Brodie 1959, 277.
[89] Quoted in Chaloupka 1992, 30. For other examples, see Kull 1988, 156–176.

while going permanently unused. Surely there is something almost unreal about all this.[90]

Making War "Materially Impossible"

The prevention of conflict required intervention in the economy. Hyperinflation had destabilized the Weimar regime and created the ground for the rise of fascism. Downturns in the business cycle were not just economic problems; impoverishment could compromise political stability. From 1900 onward, there had been several prominent arguments linking economic competition to imperialism and interstate war. These arguments—from Hobson to Lenin to the less-prominent economist Eugene Staley in the 1930s—pointed to different solutions, of course, but one class of solutions (exemplified by Staley's) involved delegating investment to "various agencies representing the world community and having a world-wide jurisdiction."[91] In 1940, the German economics minister Walter Funk proposed a plan to coordinate prices throughout a "united" Europe, using the Deutschmark as the currency. Keynes was asked to prepare a response, and while opposed to the German plan, he found much to commend in a stable currency system. Both proposals shared the premise that the laissez-faire system had, in Keynes's terms, "led to chaos."[92]

The economic and political were thus imbricated in postwar economic thinking. A member of the American delegation to Bretton Woods, Ansel Luxford, explained the purpose of the International Monetary Fund (IMF) thus:

> You have a question here, too, of an international body that has both political and economic phases. In other words, this document is an attempt to marry, to mingle and to blend the political aspects of this agency with the practical business aspects of the agency, the economic aspects. Institutions in the past have been established on more or less completely commercial lines. Others have been established on completely political lines. This whole document is an attempt to blend those two concepts.[93]

Economic arguments were analogous to the arguments about war-making made above. Unrestrained economic competition embodied the same logic that Keynes

---

[90] Brodie 1959, 272–273.
[91] Quoted in Frieden 2006, 258.
[92] Tribe 1995, 241–243.
[93] Quoted in Schuler and Rosenberg 2013, 2.

had bemoaned at Versailles. US Treasury Secretary Henry Morgenthau made this problem clear at the conference's opening ceremony: "We came here to work out methods which would do away with the economic evils—the competitive currency devaluation and destructive impediments to trade—which preceded the present war."[94]

Just like the effort to take atomic weapons out of the hands of states, Bretton Woods sought to deny states the ability to manipulate investment and trade in ways that would lead to conflict. Keynes and US diplomat Harry Dexter White had independently of each other articulated such a plan before the war ended. American bankers, and their supporters in Congress, questioned the viability of the Fund and the World Bank because they threatened the private sector's monopoly on issuing sovereign loans.[95] In response, Treasury Department officials made public presentations to build support for Bretton Woods. These presentations downplayed economic arguments to instead emphasize, in the words of one participant, that "virtually every speech touted stable monetary conditions and exchange rates as defenses against future dictators and World War III . . . . [I]nternational monetary cooperation would somehow guarantee world peace."[96]

Bretton Woods was one manifestation of the articulation of economic and political considerations to prevent war rather than let economics serve as the tool of states. The Marshall Plan and the Schuman Plan that laid the framework for the European Coal and Steel Community were efforts to incorporate a disarmed West Germany within Europe without disrupting the economies of the other European states. Without development, Germany could neither be a stable partner against the Soviets nor would it remain peaceful in its own right. In retrospect, the Marshall Plan in particular looks like a state-building exercise: indeed, a recent study of US "nation-building" efforts highlights occupied Germany as a success story.[97] There are two reasons not to see the outcome, strengthened states in Europe, as the inevitable culmination of the process. First, in the intentions of some of its American authors, these efforts were the first step in constructing a new European community because just rebuilding independent European states would not prevent war. For example, Charles Kindleberger, then on the State Department staff, advised that the United States pursue a policy of "trying to unify all of Europe" rather than treat the French and Germans separately on the issue of sharing economic resources in the Ruhr.[98] Paul Hoffman, head of the Economic Cooperation Administration, the

---

[94] Quoted in Coggan 2012, 99–100.
[95] Steil 2013, 258–259.
[96] Mikesell 1994, 45.
[97] Dobbins et al. 2003.
[98] Kindleberger 1947, 1. This view was repeated by Eisenhower in 1952; Trachtenberg 1999, 149.

main body administering the Marshall Plan, advocated a common European market in 1949.[99] Behind the push to a common market was a sense that statist planning, especially price controls in France, was squeezing the recovery.[100] The same logic underpinned American efforts to constitute a European Defense Community.[101]

Second, these efforts aimed to transform Germany into a very different polity from its recent past in order to remove the possibility of war in Western Europe. For example, Allen Dulles wrote in *Foreign Affairs* that "historically, the German people made their best contribution to western civilization in a *decentralized confederation* . . . . [T]his was a time for them of relative contentment, *of peace*, and cultural progress . . . . [W]hen Germany was a *unitary Prussianized state*, she repeatedly brought *war and catastrophe* to herself and Europe."[102] Kennan made a similar point when he advocated that "if there is no real European federation and if Germany is restored as a strong and independent country, we must expect another attempt at German domination."[103] The reader will note that Germany had damaged Western civilization by becoming a unitary state or strong and independent country; it could rejoin Western civilization by not being one. This was the opposite of what prior American observers like John Burgess and Woodrow Wilson, who had seen the unitary German state as the model for American institutions, had suggested![104] In a sense, Dulles was right and Wilson was wrong: Germany had really only been a unitary state for seven decades and had been involved in wars for almost half that period. American policymakers sought to limit German power, especially military power, to help build a German state to avoid it forming through war again.[105]

This effort—to disarticulate the war-making/state-making relationship in Europe to prevent war altogether—can be contrasted with the aftermath of the Great War. While the victors at Versailles sought to punish the defeated societies at the risk of provoking a future war, the victors in 1945 sought to develop even the defeated societies to avoid future war. This was not inevitable. Treasury Secretary Henry Morgenthau initially devised the Morgenthau Plan, to divide and impoverish German industry, so that "no matter how savage her aggressive aims may be, she cannot make war."[106] But others were wary of repeating the problem of Versailles; Dean Acheson wanted to "reverse incipient divisive

[99] Hoffman 1949, 3.
[100] Steil 2013, 311–312.
[101] Trachtenberg 1999, 122.
[102] Quoted in Jackson 2006, 159, emphasis mine.
[103] Quoted in Ikenberry 2001, 207.
[104] Oren 2003, 39, 41–42.
[105] Trachtenberg 1999, 141–143.
[106] Quoted in Jackson 2006, 116.

nationalist trends on the continent."[107] After the Soviets proved intransigent on the reparations issue at the Moscow Conference in 1947, US policy decisively shifted to the latter position.[108] In 1947, Acheson and Marshall explained the rationale for the Marshall Plan by saying that "the war will not be over until the people of the world can feed and clothe themselves and face the future with some degree of confidence" and "it is logical that the United States should do whatever it is able to do to assist in the return to normal economic health in the world, without which there can be no political stability and no assured peace."[109]

Just like deterrence, economic reconstruction disarticulated war-making, but not preparation for war, from state-making. The reconstruction of European states occurred in a context where they would *not* be primarily responsible for their defense—NATO from the mid-1950s relied on a policy of massive nuclear war to deter the Soviets[110]—and hence the basis of any future exchange could *not* be war-making. In the early 1950s, John Foster Dulles had worried that the Europeans would reject this guarantee for lack of credibility, withdraw from NATO, and rebuild their own militaries.[111] With the exception of the French, who acquired a deterrent but still stayed in NATO, this did not happen. Rather, European policymakers echoed the logic of the Americans; in introducing his scheme to pool coal and steel between France and Germany, French foreign minister Robert Schuman stated that its goal was to make conflict between the two states "not simply unthinkable, but materially impossible" by sharing resources that were essential to warfare.[112] Adenauer would agree that "the significance of the Schuman proposal was first and foremost political and not economic . . . . [T]his Plan was to be the beginning of a federal structure in Europe."[113] Contrast this with Lorenz von Stein's proposal, described in the previous chapter, to deem railway lines neutral during war, or interwar visions of a "federal" Europe to counterbalance the United States and the USSR, or even the Nazi "spatial" model for uniting Europe.[114] The former efforts typified nineteenth-century efforts to limit inevitable wars or wage them better; Schuman, by aiming to prevent wars altogether, denied that they were inevitable. The parameters within which the costs of war were to be calculated had shifted to preclude war: this now raised the question of a new exchange, and possibly a new polity or institutionalization of that exchange. For the state to survive its

[107] Quoted in Ikenberry 2001, 208.
[108] Judt 2005, 124–125.
[109] Department of State 1947, 13.
[110] Trachtenberg 1999, 158–160.
[111] Trachtenberg 1988, 40; Trachtenberg 1999, 190.
[112] Quoted in Kupchan 2010, 205.
[113] Quoted in Kupchan 2010, 205.
[114] Haas 1967, 321–322.

alternatives, it had to provide to the population something other than protection in inevitable war.

The biggest shift in the basis of the exchange occurred in Germany. There, the defeat had been described in apocalyptic terms– by one observer, "physical, political, and moral suicide"[115]—and it was clear to the population that future war was unwinnable or excessively costly. A wartime joke, "better enjoy the war—the peace will be terrible," was a premonition of a period when daily calorie intake dropped from 2,445 calories in 1940–1941 to between 860 and 1,412 in parts of occupied Germany in 1945–1946.[116] Yet the German state from the wars of unification onward had been predicated on war-making. The state itself required transformation, and here the German Ordoliberals made a radical proposal. These thinkers, from the politician Ludwig Erhard to the academics Walter Eucken and Wilhelm Ropke, saw the Nazi state as *not* an aberration from the process of German state-making since 1871. They theorized more explicitly the American argument, made by Allen Dulles and Kennan, that Nazism was the outcome of a process of centralization that developed for and from war. Ropke provided the most explicit formulation:

> The centralized unitary state, created for power politics, was the very thing that was utterly in conflict with the nature of Germany. It had therefore to be brought into existence with a violence corresponding to the strength of the resistance to it, a violence that made this Germany really a disturber of the peace in Europe.[117]

This was hardly unique to Germany for "none of the great nations came into existence through spontaneous generation or parthenogenesis, none by any other means than war and violence and diplomatic intrigue."[118] But to counter this disastrous history of centralization and war, it was necessary to found the state on a new basis. For Erhard, this required "free(ing) the economy from state control."[119] Ordoliberals provided an alternative basis for the exchange: the new state would reject its war-making past and focus entirely on economic growth.[120]

In his lectures, Michel Foucault would put this new basis of the exchange in Germany as follows:

---

[115] Ropke 1947, xi.
[116] Judt 2005, 21.
[117] Ropke 1947, 180.
[118] Ropke 1947, 177–178.
[119] Quoted in Foucault 2008, 80–81; Ropke 1947, 203–206.
[120] Foucault 2008, 85–86.

A strong Deutschmark, a satisfactory rate of growth, an expanding pur-
chasing power, and a favorable balance of payments are, of course, the
effects of good government in contemporary Germany, but to a certain
extent this is even more the way in which the founding consensus of
a state—which history, defeat, or the decision of the victors had just
outlawed—is constantly manifested and reinforced.[121]

For the European state to, essentially, outsource its defense to the United States and
focus on economic affairs was a fundamental change whose effects have not been
theorized because scholars assume the European state that formed through war is
self-enforcing once and for all. But the war-making state was self-undermining, and
in this restaging lay the potential for a centralized state to prove self-undermining
again, *if its policies could be shown to choke the economy*. At least initially, even for the
Ordoliberals, this involved a role for the state in managing the currency and stabi-
lizing prices so that markets could clear, and providing services like social insurance
(what was called the "social market economy" in Germany).[122] Yet the problem of
war had been caused by state control of the economy, and hence Ordoliberals like
Ropke argued that free trade in Europe, not state intervention, would in time solve
the "German Problem."[123] Ultimately, Ropke would argue, in a 1950 text with a
preface by Adenauer, that the goal of German economic policy should be "shifting
the center of gravity of governmental action downwards."[124]

State intervention in the economy, if not checked, ran the risk of repeating the
centralization of power that the Nazis had taken to the extreme. Ordoliberals thus
cautioned against exactly the instruments designed to stabilize postwar Europe.
In 1943, Eucken had rejected the Keynesian proposal for a currency clearing system as "part of a comprehensive, monopolistic, centrally administered plan."[125]
Regarding the Beveridge plan for the welfare state, Ropke wrote in 1944 that
"it is a gigantic machine for pumping the national income about . . . . [I]t is the
extreme logical result of a proletarianized society."[126] In 1948, Eucken would
argue that it was impossible for a centrally administered economy to achieve
equilibrium between demand and supply because it marginalized—he used
the term "dethroned"—the consumer, and did not allow the price mechanism
to function.[127] If state policies—taxation, welfare, investment—undermined

---

[121] Foucault 2008, 85.
[122] E.g., Eucken and Meyer 1948, 60; Tribe 1995, 230–240.
[123] Ropke 1947, 258.
[124] Quoted in Foucault 2008, 148.
[125] Quoted in Tribe 1995, 231.
[126] Quoted in Tribe 1995, 240; Foucault 2008, 110.
[127] Eucken 1948, 176.

economic growth, the restaged state could be represented as self-undermining. Foucault incisively notes that for Ordoliberals, the market is simultaneously the basis of the state and the mechanism that keeps state power in check: "a state under the supervision of the market rather than a market supervised by the state."[128] Another Ordoliberal said as much, writing, "The competitive order possesses the quality of nearly ideal social substructure for a democratic political order . . . . [A] purified competitive order will have to go much further in admitting coercion and governmental control than was done in the past."[129] Such a state, *by design*, would find it difficult to coerce and compel popular sacrifice, especially if, as I show in Chapter 5, there was an alternative articulated that could better ensure economic growth.

That the demand for services had increased can be seen in the basis of the new exchange: "security."[130] Yergin noted the suddenness with which "national security" became a key word in American policymaking after 1944:

> "Our national security can only be assured on a very broad and compre-
> hensive front," argued the most forceful advocate of the concept, Navy
> Secretary James Forrestal. "I am using the word 'security' here consis-
> tently and continuously rather than 'defense.'"
>
> "I like your words 'national security,'" Senator Edward Johnson told
> him.[131]

The National Security Act followed in 1947, establishing the National Security Council, and merging the War and Navy Departments into the Department of Defense. Security is more capacious than war—involving intervention in the economy, for example—but also indefinite in duration. Wars, after all, end, armies are disbanded, and tax rates fall. But in its early formulations, "security" went beyond war-fighting: "'security policy' can be construed to cover the total preparation for war as well as the waging of it . . . . [I]t would thus deal—though with clearly defined and limited objectives—with political, social, and economic as well as military matters in both domestic and foreign contexts."[132] As *Fortune* magazine put it in 1948, "The only way to avoid American policy dominated by crisis is to live in crisis—prepared for war."[133] Preparation for war can be a more or less permanent condition, *especially when these wars are not to be*

---

[128] Foucault 2008, 116–117.
[129] Franz Bohm, quoted in Friedrich 1955, 511–512.
[130] Yergin 1977, 193–201.
[131] Yergin 1977, 194.
[132] Brodie 1949, 477.
[133] Quoted in Yergin 1977, 336.

fought. The consequence would be an expanded role for the state. Nuclear deterrence required a high level of centralization; to protect the population from the business cycle involved state intervention in ever more aspects of life to provide what Keynes called the postwar "craving for social and personal *security*."[134] The restaged state promised a lot, and it required a high level of sacrifice.

An example illustrates this dynamic. As a result of the Employment Act of 1946, the US Congress established the Council of Economic Advisers and charged it with preparing an annual report. In 1950, the council released a report titled "The Economics of National Defense" which took on the challenge of increasing defense spending to deter the Soviets. Two conclusions are worth highlighting. The first was the push to centralization: "The logic of the situation requires that the Government must accept and exercise the primary responsibility for defining almost all of the broad phases of the new pattern of resource utilization in a defense emergency."[135] This involved state involvement in boosting production, and potentially imposing controls on consumption goods: essentially wartime measures. The second was the need to maintain a high level of taxation to maintain this expanded role for the state: "The prospect that the defense effort will be prolonged makes it particularly important to cover the cost through taxes.... [B]orrowing has its place in the financing of a short, intensive effort; but it is dangerous for a long-drawn out effort."[136] The report, however, left as a question whether Americans who had sacrificed in an actual war would accept lesser, economic hardships in an indefinite effort to prevent war.[137]

Security: Self-Enforcing or Self-Undermining?

In 1972, Leon Keyserling, one of the authors of the 1950 document, unhappily reported that the level of sacrifice had fallen due to the 1963 tax reform.[138] But the role of the state—to cushion against economic crises and ensure growth as well as prevent war—had expanded significantly. This begs the question: Was the national security state self-enforcing or self-undermining? Or more precisely, under what conditions would the national security state be self-enforcing or self-undermining?

Deterrence and economic intervention—"security"—required centralization and extraction. The population was expected to supply the state at a high level.

[134] Quoted in Judt 2005, 73, emphasis in original.
[135] Council of Economic Advisers 1950, 8.
[136] Council of Economic Advisers 1950, 15.
[137] Council of Economic Advisers 1950, 31.
[138] Keyserling 1972, 136–137.

But this continued willingness was conditional on two factors. First, the cost of preventing war had to remain high, requiring more or less permanent mobilization. But nuclear weapons, by their very nature, could be used to lower the cost of mobilization, through reducing spending on conventional forces, as was articulated in the 1950s.[139] Second, state intervention in the economy had to be successful, or at least preferable to alternative means of providing services. For the national security state to be self-enforcing—that is, preferable to alternatives—it was not sufficient to prevent war. The state's role had expanded, and it needed more resources than its nineteenth-century predecessor.

By contrast, for the national security state to be undermined by a gap between the demand for services and the supply of the state, two conditions had to hold. First, the cost of preventing war would diminish over time, and those wars that occurred would not be costly *and* winnable. Deterrence, over time, would cost less than the highly costly wars of the long nineteenth century. As Brodie would write in 1973, countering his assessment in 1959 that large nuclear *and* conventional forces were needed, "nuclear weapons do by their very existence make obsolete the use of hence need for conventional forces on anything like the scale of either world war," precisely the conflicts that, I will show in the next chapter, had massively increased the supply of the state.[140] Second, state intervention in the economy would come to be contested by alternative means of provision that would still promise a high level of services. This combination was facilitated by the restaging of the state—the restaged state was self-undermining—because the nature of deterrence required nuclear weapons to go unused, hence the cost of deterrence would diminish over time. The very purpose of deterrence—to prevent war—meant that if deterrence worked, the population would have to sacrifice less over time. Equally, state intervention in the economy would create distortions that frustrated the demand for services. The combination of the falling cost of deterrence as it proved successful in preventing war and the rise of neoliberalism, I show in the next chapter, would undermine popular willingness to supply the state in the 1970s and beyond.

Yves Klein and other artists linked atomic weapons with a new subject of art, the void. I have suggested that a similar process was at work in politics. Atomic weapons marked a void at the heart of the modern state: it could no longer protect its population in the event of war; indeed, the continuation of the war-making/state-making relationship placed the population at existential risk. Just like the new artistic techniques the Abstract Expressionists and others were developing, new techniques of statecraft were needed if war was to be prevented,

---

[139] Freedman 1989, 78–88.
[140] Brodie 1973, 412.

hence the efflorescence of interest in world government, international control of atomic weapons, and other alternatives to the state. But the imperative of preventing war could lead in another direction, to the transformation of the state away from its war-fighting function. Through parametric shifts in thinking about war—marshalling the "power to hurt" and controlling economic crises—wars could be avoided. The irony, as Hannah Arendt pointed out, was that this indicated the failure of the central authority to deliver on the promise that had motivated the popular sacrifices underpinning the modern state:

> The history of warfare in our century could almost be told as the story of the growing incapacity of the army to fulfill this basic function [to protect and defend the civilian population], until today the strategy of deterrence has openly changed the role of the military from that of a protector into that of a belated and essentially futile avenger.[141]

[141] Arendt 1963, 5.

5

Sympathy for the Neoliberal

> Government is not the solution to our problems. Government is the
> problem.
>
> —Milton Friedman[1]

In 1958, Gunnar Myrdal told an audience at Yale University that the time had
come to extend the welfare state beyond national borders.[2] He advocated a
"Welfare World" through planning by experts housed in international organizations. In one sense, this argument echoed the calls for a world state discussed in
the last chapter. In another sense, it testified to the shifting expectations of the
state, from a war-making entity to a war-preventing entity. To fulfill this new role,
the state needed to play a greater role in the economy and provide more services
(whether it was called a "welfare state" or not). Myrdal took for granted the latter expectation and planned to extend it to the world at large, a more ambitious
formulation than most.[3] But the expectation that the state would intervene in
the economy and provide services was accepted more broadly. A British Labor
politician put it in 1956: "Any Government that tampered seriously with the full
employment welfare state would meet with a sharp reversal at the polls."[4]

Just twenty-five years later, the OECD would release a volume titled *The Crisis
of the Welfare State.* This "crisis" went beyond a shortfall in funding to a deeper
unease. In 1973, Jurgen Habermas had described this unease as a "legitimation
crisis" where what he called the "political system" was losing the ability to command popular support.[5] In the next decade, the unease became linked explicitly
to the state. In his 1979 public lectures, Michel Foucault noted the emergence
of a sentiment he called "state-phobia."[6] In the mid-1980s, Habermas would also

---

[1] Friedman wrote this sentence, made famous by Ronald Reagan, in *Newsweek* in 1972.
[2] Haas 1964, 461–464.
[3] E. H. Carr had made a similar argument after the Second World War; Carr 2001, 237–239.
[4] Quoted in Korpi 2003, 509.
[5] Habermas 1975, 46.
[6] Foucault 2008, 75–77.

locate general social unease squarely on shortcomings of the state: "The program of the social welfare state, which still feeds on the utopian image of a laboring society, is losing its capacity to project future possibilities for a collectively
better and less endangered way of life."[7] The British cultural theorist Stuart Hall
challenged his allies on the left to acknowledge that Thatcherism had "successfully identified itself with the popular struggle against a bureaucratically central-
ist form of the capitalist state."[8] How did the welfare state go from dreams of
worldwide expansion to "crisis" in a mere three decades?

One might argue that the crisis of the welfare state was overblown, and
indeed, the anticipated retrenchment has not occurred. On the surface, this is
accurate: Euro-American states continue to provide a high level of services to
their populations. But this is a contingent and unstable development. It is contingent in that state provision of welfare and social spending more generally is
a recent development—until 1880, there was barely any social spending—that
was made possible by a novel and unrepeatable combination of events, namely,
the sudden increase in tax revenues from the world wars. To understand this,
I will analyze, first, the recent origin and expansion of social spending to supply goods that were previously either externalized onto the population or not
supplied at all; second, the sudden expansion in the state's ability to spend, on
social services or otherwise, due to the expansion in taxation during the world
wars; and third, the unraveling of the contingent relationship between the two.
When considered as one historical process linking war-making with welfare
through the mechanism of taxation, we can reject the idea that the welfare state
manifests some grand self-enforcing exchange that places it above economic
fluctuations. Rather, the expansion of state intervention to provide welfare was
underpinned by a *prior* willingness to sacrifice in costly war, which was now
less likely.

World War I and World War II saw the supply of the state and the demand
for services increase together. The exchange was self-enforcing, and as long as
taxation could be maintained, the demand for services and the supply of the
state would be in equilibrium. However, as I argued in Chapter 4, this presumed a high level of taxation in the absence of costly war. But as the likelihood
of war diminished, an alternative to the state predicated on the argument that
the welfare state was incapable, by dint of its own policies, of delivering welfare and promising services for a lower cost could be articulated. This alternative was neoliberalism, and its success was to undermine the state's ability to
compel popular sacrifice, even as it promised to deliver a high level of services.
Rather than see neoliberalism as bringing forth a crisis of the state in the 1980s

[7] Habermas 1986, 5.
[8] Hall 1980, 27.

by deregulation and tax-cutting, I will suggest that neoliberalism proposed an alternative—the market—that could deliver welfare better than the state by rais-ing economic growth. This was an epistemological and political shift from the views of classical liberals, who saw markets as important but unable to provide some goods, for which state provision was necessary. Neoliberalism's episte-mological innovation—or parametric shift—lay in theorizing the detrimental effects of the expanded role of the state in the economy and everyday life, a role that did not exist in the world of classical liberals.

The Contingency of "Welfare"

The peripheries of Euro-American states exemplify how recent the penetration of the state into society has been even in Europe. Visiting a Corsican graveyard in the 1980s, the author W. G. Sebald was struck by the fact that none of the dates on the gravestones went back beyond the early twentieth century. On investiga-tion, he learned that Corsicans had historically buried their dead on their own land to affirm their inalienable rights to that land (or, if landless, tied the corpse into a sack and flung it down a shaft). The French state established official grave-yards in the mid-nineteenth century, but another five decades would pass before central burying grounds became the rule.[9] Burying their dead in graveyards after 1900 marked the acceptance, by the Corsicans, that the French state could enforce their property rights and resolve disputes, previously settled through blood feuds. Corsica was not anomalous. George Orwell characterized much of the Spanish countryside as "feudal" during the Spanish Civil War, and right into the 1960s, parts of Appalachia and Nova Scotia had very little state presence.

Corsica was an extreme manifestation of a broader trend: only late in the nineteenth century did the Euro-American state begin to provide services that had been the province of the private sector or local governments, like educa-tion, or had not been supplied at all, like social insurance and urban sanitation. In the mid-nineteenth century, the bourgeois in Britain came to "the realization that millions of English men, women and children were virtually living in shit" because, as Engels averred of Manchester, "over two hundred people shared a single privy."[10] After 1850 the state began to intervene in public health, for exam-ple, by improving sanitation, and the benefits are borne out by life expectancy figures: essentially unchanged between 1550 and 1850, life expectancy rose by nearly 50 percent in most European states during the next century.[11] I noted

---

[9] Sebald 2005, 21.
[10] Quoted in Davis 2006, 137.
[11] Deaton 2013, 87–97.

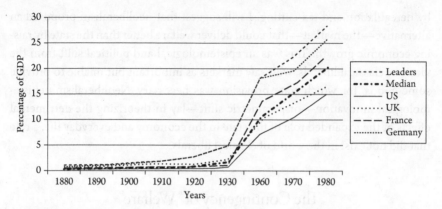

Figure 5.1 Social transfers in selected OECD states as percentage of GDP
Source: Lindert 2004

above that the welfare state had come to be taken for granted in the 1950s. Yet the provision of diverse services that would be aggregated as welfare, and the process of aggregation itself, was relatively recent. T. H. Marshall wrote in 1965 that "twenty years ago the Welfare State was a novelty, and there was much that could be said, in general terms, about the genesis and the nature of the rights to which it gave effect . . . . [*T*]*oday all this can be taken for granted.*"[12] The demand for services and the supply of the state had increased dramatically in a short span of time and had almost as quickly come to be taken for granted.

The state's responsibility for welfare can be seen in three phenomena: funding, centralization, and intervention in hitherto private areas of everyday life. The increase in spending shows three distinct phases from 1880, as shown in Figure 5.1. There was barely any social spending prior to that date, and while it increased till 1920, it did not exceed 3 percent of GDP in any OECD state. In the next forty years, however, social spending skyrocketed, to then increase more gradually until 1980. The median of social spending among OECD states went from 0.78 percent of GDP in 1920, to 10.4 percent in 1960 (after 1980, social spending has plateaued).

Along with the increase in spending came a qualitative transformation. In the mid-nineteenth century, with the exception of support to the very indigent and disabled, the central authority had no role providing welfare. Relief was provided by private agencies and local authorities, or not at all. The poor had always been with us, and individuals were expected to provide for their families by working. Put differently, poverty was seen as a natural condition, not a social problem. Its costs were to be borne by the population, not internalized by the state.[13] To this

[12] Marshall 1965, 261, emphasis mine.
[13] Himmelfarb 1984; Gay 1994, 462–465; Osterhammel 2014, 216–217.

end, the Commission on the Poor Laws in Britain recommended in 1834 that relief to a pauper should be less than the wages of a laborer, to compel the pauper to join the labor force. But very shortly thereafter, the idea that the market would support a decent standard of living came to be contested. From the 1840s, it became clear that a large number of the poor worked, but their wages were inadequate to support a decent standard of living.[14] The documentation of the plight of the poor, in new mediums like novels and early statistical investigations—Charles Booth's voluminous survey established that 30 percent of London's population was poor—came to inform a broader realization that, as the British feminist Eleanor Rathbone summarized in 1924, "before education and medical inspection were provided free, the working class did not supply them out of wages; broadly speaking, they went without."[15]

But for this realization to lead to state-provided social programs was not inevitable. There were two other responses. First, there could be no response at all, for the nature-like laws of political economy determined who would be rewarded and who would go hungry.[16] Second, one could expropriate the means of production, as the emerging communist movement urged. Despite their different solutions, the logic of both positions anticipated some degree of impoverishment and class conflict as inevitable. As older social arrangements of barter and subsistence broke down and were replaced by wage labor, nineteenth-century intellectuals feared that the market would not provide for the bulk of the population. David Ricardo saw machines as replacing individual workers—"the substitution of machinery for human labor is often very injurious to the class of laborers"—but justified machinery as necessary for the competitiveness of Britain's manufacturers.[17] Marx also saw the dangers of machinery for workers because machines sundered workers from the ability to support themselves, but he thought it enabled a new form of cooperation among workers, a precursor to the downfall of capitalism.[18] Those developing the new theories of political economy were pessimistic, worrying that, in Malthus's words, "the increasing wealth of the nation has had little or no tendency to better the condition of the laboring poor."[19]

Neither ideal-type materialized in policy. There were responses to poverty, but on a piecemeal rather than a radical basis. On the labor side, workers formed collectives to insure themselves and lobby for higher wages, like the Friendly

[14] Freedgood 1995, 43.
[15] Quoted in Pedersen 1993, 52.
[16] Polanyi 1944, 84–85, 117.
[17] Ricardo 1821, 468.
[18] Marx 1973, 700–706.
[19] Quoted in Gallagher 1986, 93.

Societies in Britain; these collectives often articulated ideals of thrift and in fact were skeptical of state intervention.[20] On the moneyed side (and supported by many free-trade liberals opposed to mercantilism), ad hoc measures provided some relief for the multiplying poor. Implicit in such measures was a realization, which I will show in the last section is consistent with classical liberalism, that markets sometimes failed to supply certain goods when the population was left to its own devices to purchase them, and this failure required non-market mechanisms to compensate.

As these ad hoc measures were implemented at the end of the nineteenth century, Herbert Spencer decried them for restricting the play of market forces. Market forces were nothing more than the manifestation of nature's "stern discipline, which is a little cruel so it may be very kind,"[21] and to restrict them was tantamount to promoting socialism. Karl Polanyi would later mock Spencer's concerns: "Most of those who carried these measures were convinced supporters of laissez-faire, and certainly did not wish their consent to the establishment of a fire brigade in London to imply a protest against the principles of economic liberalism."[22] Rather, Polanyi argued, social programs were designed to prevent socialism and facilitate the market economy.[23] Polanyi's broader point, echoing one Marx made in his analysis of "primitive accumulation," was that it was the state that had coerced the market into being by enclosing land and separating individuals from the means of production.[24]

Polanyi's mocking, however, obscures a subtle point Spencer made about the future. While individual legislators may have made pragmatic choices to provide protection against market forces on a case-by-case basis, they could not foresee that the outcome would be to put forward "the State" (Spencer's caps) as the solution to all ills.[25] Put differently, ad hoc approaches to social ills would come to be centralized and crowd out other "agencies" that could provide succor. On this point, Spencer was correct. Fifty years after his warning, the Beveridge Report, surveying existing social insurance schemes, aspired to do just what he had feared:

> Apart from the Poor Law, which dates from the time of Elizabeth, the schemes surveyed are the product of the last 45 years beginning with the Workmen's Compensation Act, 1897. That Act, applying in the first instance to a limited number of occupations, was made general in 1906.

[20] Pedersen 1993, 51.
[21] Quoted in Gay 1994, 41.
[22] Polanyi 1944, 146.
[23] Polanyi 1944, 68.
[24] Polanyi 1944, 140–141.
[25] Spencer 1892, 32–34.

Compulsory health insurance began in 1912. Unemployment insurance began for a few industries in 1912 and was made general in 1920. The first Pensions Act, giving non-contributory pensions subject to a means test at the age of 70, was passed in 1908.[26]

Beveridge went on to praise Britain as being ahead of its peers in all aspects of social insurance bar medical services, but averred that the provision of services by local authorities had been too "piecemeal" to adequately address the needs of the population. Thus he recommended that these services be centralized to fulfill the ambitions of previous schemes: "the scheme proposed here is a revolution, but in more important ways it is a natural development from the past."[27] Here was a self-professed world leader in the provision of social insurance noting just how recently these services had originated, and how they needed to be provided by the state in centralized rather than ad hoc fashion.

There are two other explanations for the rise of social spending. Rather than a sudden and contingent shift where the state became responsible for welfare, the commitment to welfare could be the result of an incremental process driven by democratization and left-labor mobilization,[28] or the forging of a new "solidarity" through the wars that united those previously divided on class lines. Neither is persuasive. Countering the first explanation is the sense at the time that the centralization of previously ad hoc policies marked a parametric shift in the understanding of the role of the state and the expectation that the state would bear, for the first time, costs previously externalized on the population. Observers saw the rise of social programs as novel, sudden, not the culmination of a trend. Further, if this was part of a long-run process, whether of increases in the franchise or a new sense of social solidarity, we should observe a sustained commitment to funding it for reasons of social equity or redistribution. I now turn to showing how the resources to fund these programs—the underlying ability to supply welfare—were extracted. Increased extraction was not the product of sustained commitment to maintain welfare, responding to expansion of the franchise or a new social solidarity, but a contingent compromise to sacrifice in the face of costly war.

Paying for the New Services

A riddle for the reader: what would compel Friedrich Hayek to write that John Maynard Keynes's tax proposals were insufficiently extractive? In 1940, writing

---

[26] Beveridge 1942, 5.
[27] Beveridge 1942, 17.
[28] Lindert 2004; Acemoglu and Robinson 2006.

a review of Keynes's pamphlet, *How to Pay for the War*, Hayek noted unanimity among economists that a higher level of taxation was necessary to pay for the war.[29] The only question was how. Keynes had argued that high tax rates on the rich would be insufficient to raise the required funds. But he balked at directly taxing middle- and low-income groups, proposing instead a "deferred pay" levy, which would take money from middle- and low-income groups and repay them after the war out of higher taxes on the rich.[30] Hayek said this would be insufficient: the costs of the war had escalated to such a degree that Keynes's scheme had to be supplemented with a sales tax and an income tax on middle and low incomes. Comparing the various proposals, Hayek noted that "these are probably no longer alternatives .... [W]e shall probably have to employ all, or at least most, of these methods simultaneously."[31]

The rising cost of war had outstripped the supply of the state. As shown above, the median OECD state was spending 10 percent of its GDP on social transfers by 1960 (defense, overhead, and debt servicing increased total spending to 20–25 percent of GDP). But state revenues around 1900 were nothing near this figure: the most advanced extractive state (Britain) had revenues of 10 percent of GDP in 1900 with which to pay for *everything*. By 1950, the corresponding figure in Britain was 50 percent.[32] Any question of the stability or crisis of the welfare state must examine not just the demand for welfare, and not even the willingness to supply it at particular times (because short-term promises can be paid for with debt), but the long-run ability to tax enough to pay for it. The last is a function of popular willingness to supply the state. So Hayek's agreement with Keynes is the beginning of the answer to the question: how could the sudden increase in social spending be paid for? The exigency of fighting the world wars created an unlikely coalition behind a sudden and massive expansion in taxation. The increase in taxation was not just an increase in the resources available to the state; it marked a shift in war financing (and by implication, financing the state). Even high-stakes nineteenth-century wars were financed through debt and the printing of money, with mass taxation a rarity. In the nineteenth century, only Britain instituted an income tax on a permanent basis, and the US northern states briefly enacted one during the American Civil War.[33] During the Franco-Prussian War, with Paris itself in danger, the French relied on a "National Defense" loan and did not institute an income

[29] Hayek 1940, 322.

[30] Keynes 1939.

[31] Hayek 1940, 325.

[32] Clark and Dilnot 2002, 2. Comparable numbers in the United States for all levels of government were 7.8 percent in 1902 and 28.5 percent in 1952; Wallis 2000, 65.

[33] Pollack 2009, 226–227.

tax.[34] And the rates were low: in no state did the highest rate of income tax exceed 10 percent.[35]

As discussed in Chapter 2, sources of finance were central to the parameters within which the costs of war were estimated and were part of why the costs were underestimated. As taxation rose as a consequence of war, the parameters were revised. Wars financed by debt should be limited in scope and duration, as was the case in Latin America.[36] Creditors should over time become unwilling to lend to the losing side as it is likely to default, as Philip II of Spain did after losing the Armada.[37] Alternatively, interest rates on both sides should creep up as the fighting went on because the war diminished the ability to repay in future. In 1914, Keynes applied this logic to forecast how long the war would last. Responding to a seizing up of credit and difficulties of foreign debtors to remit their dues to Britain (Brazil, for example, defaulted) in London after the declaration of war, Keynes anticipated that soon the combatants would have to finance the war through their gold reserves (the *New York Times* reported in 1914 that the European powers were hoarding gold to avoid paying for the war by printing money).[38] As the destruction of the war proceeded and gold production expanded, there would be a surfeit of gold chasing a diminishing stock of goods. Consequently, the combatants would face difficulties raising money on the debt markets or finding willing trade partners. Because of such financing difficulties, Keynes expected the war would be limited in scope and length: "the world will be cold and hungry this winter . . . but we must not argue from this that we are ruined for life, or suppose that *even a war of three years* can destroy, for the years which succeed it, the material benefits of the last twenty."[39]

Keynes, like most of his contemporaries, underestimated the length and cost of the war. But his error reflected contemporaneous understandings of how wars were financed and how much they cost. "Absolute wars" had never been anywhere near absolute in the sense of threatening the lives of large sections of the population. The parameters within which the costs of war were calculated made it very difficult for observers to predict how devastating the Great War would actually be. To Keynes, for example, the costs of war were limited because extraction was limited to current income; Keynes could not see how assets,

---

[34] Tomz 2007, 65.

[35] Piketty 2014, 502.

[36] Centeno 2002.

[37] Drelichman and Voth 2008.

[38] Charles Conant, "How Financial Europe Prepared for the Great War," *New York Times*, August 30, 1914.

[39] Keynes 1914, 486, emphasis mine.

which were much larger than current income, could be converted into current income to pay for the war:

> It was said in some of the German papers soon after war broke out, in answer to the question how the German army could maintain itself in being for a long a period, that the savings of the people amounted to 15,000 milliards and the Government would begin with these. The savings of the people . . . are houses and railways and the like. Luckily for the material future of their country, not even the Prussian army can eat rails and embankments or clothe itself in bricks and mortar.[40]

Keynes's analysis reflected prevailing knowledge of how wars were financed. Tax rates on assets were low (the highest marginal rate on estates was 7 percent, in the United Kingdom).[41] Income taxes were also limited in 1914: the highest marginal rates were under 10 percent in most combatant states, if they existed at all.[42] For observers in 1914, the costs of war were limited by how long credit would be available to pay for those costs. As taxation and with it the costs of war rose, the parameters would shift endogenously.

Indeed, advocates of higher taxation during the world wars were quite aware how novel their solution was to the problem of war financing. As the United States entered the war, the American economists Edwin Seligman and Robert Haig wrote:

> It is . . . of importance to recall that the policy of meeting all war expenses by taxation is *entirely new* in the United States. Indeed, the question here has rather been whether taxes could be made sufficiently high to meet merely the interest charges on the money borrowed without any allowance even for amortization . . . . Not only would it be a *novelty* to American finance to levy war taxes in larger amount than required for interest on the debt, but it would be almost as much as a *novelty* in European countries. Germany, during the present war, refrained for a long time from imposing any war taxes at all . . . . The policies of England and France have been essentially the same except that England began to tax for interest purposes somewhat earlier than the others.[43]

Previous wars had caused spikes in public debt: Britain for example, saw debt levels at 185 percent of GDP after the Napoleonic wars (i.e., comparable to

---

[40] Keynes 1914, 486.
[41] Scheve and Stasavage 2012.
[42] Scheve and Stasavage 2010; Piketty 2014.
[43] Seligman and Haig 1917, 25, emphasis mine.

Greece during its debt crisis in 2012).[44] But, faced with high public debt, sovereigns had alternatives to mass taxation: rescheduling debt or defaulting, and financial repression, the lowering of interest rates and capital controls to force citizens to lend money to the state at below-market rates. The latter were not uncommon; it was taxation that was rare. Spain defaulted on its sovereign debt thirteen times between 1500 and 1900, and France eight times between 1500 and 1788, its last default.[45] Britain in the eighteenth century restricted the ability of its citizens to invest in private markets under a range of usury laws, thus maintaining a cheap flow of credit to service a high level of public debt.[46] Wars were costly, but they had been paid for primarily through debt, with taxation being irregular and not centralized. Further, debt restructuring/default and financial repression offered postwar options to manage the debt burden. Both, however, had economic downsides. Default would raise future borrowing costs. Financial repression would cause inflation. Financing wars through debt was a form of intertemporal substitution, reducing short-term sacrifice by foregoing taxation during the war, but creating risks of higher interest rates or inflation in the future, or a form of intergenerational transfer in which future generations were left to pay the costs of war. Either way, the dominant mode of financing wars prior to 1914 reduced the need for the population to sacrifice in the present, and thus limited what the population could claim in the future from the central authority.[47] The supply of the state was low, but because the demand for services was also low, the exchange could be self-enforcing.

Until the twentieth century, mass taxation had not been a significant source of war finance and, by implication, total state spending, given that social spending was low and bureaucracies were small. In Chapter 2, I refined extant analyses to specify that costly but winnable wars made the modern state self-enforcing— war driving popular willingness to supply the state that then allowed the establishment of state institutions to satisfy the demand for services.[48] As the costs of war increased, the exchange between the central authority and the population intensified, manifested in increased services. But even in the Great War, systems of extraction were relatively rudimentary, and the bulk of spending was financed through debt: from 75 percent of war spending in the United States to almost 100 percent in France and Germany.[49] Some of this borrowing had been through

---

[44] Barro 1987, 238–239.

[45] Drelichman and Voth 2008.

[46] Drelichman and Voth 2008.

[47] In particular, minorities like African Americans who were either not allowed to serve or played limited roles were denied a pathway to claim rights as long as the scale of war stayed limited; Krebs 2006.

[48] Tilly 1992.

[49] MacDonald 2003, 402, 408.

bond drives in the combatant states, which reduced reliance on foreign debt and allowed states to borrow over longer periods.[50] One contemporary estimate had the Great Powers using taxation to pay for 20 percent or less of their war costs.[51] The capacity to tax also varied. Britain had a relatively well-developed system, but in Wilhelmine Germany, income taxes were the prerogative of the states that had resisted increased defense budgets prior to 1914.[52] The French and Russians relied mostly on indirect taxes, consumption taxes, and debt, not income taxes.[53]

This requires us to revisit the periodization and the stability of state formation, as I argued in Chapter 3: rather than a process unfolding in the early modern era and consolidating after 1800, the state-making/war-making nexus really unfolded in a period of about 150 years after 1800, accelerating after the wars of German unification and the high point of imperial expansion. At the moment at which the potential for absolute destruction was realized, it became clear that the costs of war were too high, and so war—which had compelled popular sacrifice—was to be avoided in the future.

Why does it matter that until the Great War, taxation was limited? Taxation affected both the course of war and the exchange between central authority and population. Taxation increased the cost and duration of wars beyond the expectations of prewar observers. Equally, taxation and military service was the means through which the population could make demands on the central authority. The sudden expansion in extraction and spending was self-undermining in that the costs of absolute war came to be seen as excessive even as those absolute wars expanded expectations of what the state owed the population. Historically, that wars were financed by debt (and default) until very recently is a corrective to extant accounts. It is really only after World War I that the social functions we now take for granted as the modern state's to provide came to be entrenched and the means to pay for these emerged. Cultural historians have argued that this war marked the initial experience of modernity for most Europeans, just as Europe descended into its civilizational crisis.[54] This insight could be extended to the relationship of most Europeans with the state: just as they began to make claims and receive services from the state, the wars through which these claims were made were proving too costly to be repeated. As I argued in Chapter 2, once costly wars are proscribed, alternatives to the state become possible as the population gains from an outside option that can reduce the central authority's

[50] MacDonald 2003, 407–413.
[51] Seligman 1918, 81.
[52] N. Ferguson 1994.
[53] Pollack 2009.
[54] E.g., Fussell 2009; Eksteins 1989.

extraction. The exchange, even in so-called strong states, was far more contingent and unstable than appreciated.

In this context, proposals for mass taxation were novel and had to be justified. There were three such justifications: equality of sacrifice, the cost of the war, and inflationary concerns. Given that older people were likely to be wealthier and would not be conscripted, fairness demanded that they pay while their younger counterparts served. As Britain's Trade Union Congress resolved in 1916,

> as the manhood of the nation has been conscripted to resist foreign aggression, the maintenance of freedom, and the protection of capital, this Congress demands that such a proportion of the accumulated wealth of the country shall immediately be conscripted as is necessary to defray the financial liability incurred by the prosecution of the war, and thus avoid borrowing huge loans upon which enormous sums will have to be paid in interest by further generations.[55]

Almost the same language was used from the other side of the political spectrum, with the economist Arthur Pigou arguing for a "special levy" on capital that would equalize sacrifice between the penurious young who served and the wealthy aged who were exempt from military service.[56] In peacetime, Pigou would strongly criticize Keynes's general economic theory, but his position on taxation during the Great War was echoed by Keynes twenty years later.[57] These unlikely bedfellows drove spectacular increases in marginal tax rates, evidenced by examining the burden of taxation in Britain, a state that entered the twentieth century with a developed tax capacity (Table 5.1).

In 1903, the tax burden was similar across income levels at about 5 percent of income. Taxes were not progressive and consequently did not raise much revenue.[58] In the next few decades, direct taxes on everyone increased by at least 300 percent, but those on the wealthy increased at a greater rate, providing significantly more revenue.[59] This "conscription of wealth" marked the move from a voluntaristic approach for financing war (the choice to purchase war bonds, which was limited to those with means) to a compulsory one (where sacrifice was obligatory for a larger segment of the population). A war bond was inequitable

---

[55] Quoted in Daunton 1996, 890.

[56] Pigou 1918, 145–146.

[57] Pigou 1936.

[58] Steinmo 1993, 22.

[59] Even after reductions in the highest rate of marginal tax, the top quintile of Americans (those earning more than $134,000) in 2014, paid 84 percent of all income taxes, almost 40 percent of US federal revenues and 7 percent of GDP; Laura Saunders, "Top 20 Percent of Earners Pay 84 Percent of Income Tax," *Wall Street Journal*, April 10, 2015.

Table 5.1 **Tax Burden (% of Income) in the United Kingdom, including Direct and Indirect Taxes**

Income (£)	1903	1913	1918	1923	1925	1930	1937	1941	Increase (%)
100	5.6	5.4	9.9	14.1	11.9	11.0	10.4	19.1	341
200	4.8	4.0	7.9	11.8	10.2	9.6	8.4	14.8	308
500	5.3	4.4	10.2	8.0	6.2	4.5	5.6	18.4	347
1,000	6.1	5.2	16.9	14.1	11.0	9.7	11.8	32.2	527
5,000	5.5	6.7	36.6	28.5	23.2	26.3	29.2	56.1	1020
10,000	5.0	8.0	42.5	37.1	31.2	35.8	39.1	68.3	1366
50,000	4.8	8.4	50.6	48.0	44.4	51.4	56.7	90.7	1889

Source: Scheve and Stasavage 2012, 96

because a wealthy older person exempt from military service might buy a bond, accruing interest, while the poorer, younger conscript came back from war having foregone the income he would have earned in the interim, plus he incurred the risk of injury or death.[60] The compulsory relationship that developed was not always intended by proponents of taxation to be permanent: Pigou urged a "special levy" to pay for the Great War under the logic that "wars being short, taxes levied in war time are not expected to continue as ordinary taxes."[61] This was a reasonable expectation based on nineteenth-century government spending, which had seen spikes for war-fighting, but because service provision was low, peacetime expenditures were minimal.[62] When they did increase, due to spending by local authorities, this was largely financed through debt.[63] Taxes levied in war could be rescinded, as had occurred in the US Civil War when an income tax was introduced in 1861 and repealed in 1872. But tax rates and the new practices of taxation never returned to prewar levels because the demand for services had risen, meaning that peacetime expenditures were consistently higher than in the nineteenth-century state. Milton Friedman, who had participated in the Treasury Department's design of tax withholding in 1943, recalled that effort with regret five decades later:

> We concentrated single-mindedly on promoting the war effort.... [W]e gave next to no consideration to any longer-term consequences.... [I]t

[60] Sprague 1918, 204.
[61] Pigou 1919, 255.
[62] Barro 1987.
[63] MacDonald 2003, 374–375.

never occurred to me at the time that I was helping to make possible a government that I would come to criticize severely as too large, too intrusive, and too destructive of freedom.[64]

The support for high taxes from Pigou, Friedman, and Hayek was a temporary exigency. It was not a commitment to perpetual extraction to finance the redistributive dreams of leftist reformers. The supply of the state had increased as a result of absolute war, but this occurred over a relatively short period and, when we look at the coalition behind it, was quite fragile.

The cost of the wars exceeded expectations. Now it is true that high levels of public debt had followed nineteenth-century wars, but there was a sense that "modern wars" were qualitatively different.[65] This led those who would be expected to extract from the wealthy, like Keynes, to advocate more broad-based taxes.[66] The consequence was to dramatically broaden the tax base: in 1939, 3.9 million Americans filed returns and paid $2.2 billion to the exchequer; in 1945, the corresponding numbers were 42.6 million and $35 billion.[67] But public debt also rose, from $43 billion in 1940 (less than 50 percent of GDP) to $259 billion in 1945 (about 120 percent of GDP).[68] The posters shown in Figure 5.2 indicate both trends—for example, that even lower-income individuals now had to file returns ($500 in 1944 is about $7,000 in 2016 dollars).

The numbers from other countries indicate a similar increase in government revenues, and a broadening of the tax base. In Canada, the number of taxpayers rose from 293,000 in 1938 to 2.2 million in 1945; federal income tax revenue increased from about $60 million to $642 million (both 1945 prices).[69] Even in neutral Sweden, the fear of war drove increases in marginal tax rates and corporate taxation in a short span of time, revenues going from 20 percent of GDP in 1941 to 35 percent in 1945.[70] The deepening and broadening of the tax base indicates that concerns about fairness were subordinated to the sheer cost of the wars in an effort to extract as much revenue as possible. After the war, as we saw in Chapter 4, the US Council of Economic Advisers urged that taxes continue to form the basis for defense spending under the logic that "borrowing has its place in the financing of a short, intensive effort; but it is dangerous for a long-drawn

---

[64] Friedman and Friedman 1998, 123.

[65] Sprague 1918, 204.

[66] Treasury Secretary Henry Morgenthau proclaimed that "for the first time in our history, the income tax is becoming a people's tax"; quoted in Pollack 2009, 261.

[67] Engerman and Sokoloff 2012, 195.

[68] Pollack 2009, 262.

[69] Treff and Perry 2003.

[70] Steinmo 1993, 24–27.

out effort."[71] This was completely counter to received wisdom about war finance a mere four decades prior and reflects profound parametric shifts.

Finally, there were concerns about the inflationary effects of debt. As war destroyed the means of production, the supply of consumer goods would shrink and prices would rise.[72] Debt would intensify this problem because it left money in the hands of the consumer. Compared to debt, taxation would take money out of the hands of the consumer and curb spending. Further, revenue in the hands of the state would lead to the most efficient allocation to defense production rather than consumer goods. But the effect went beyond the wartime exigency.

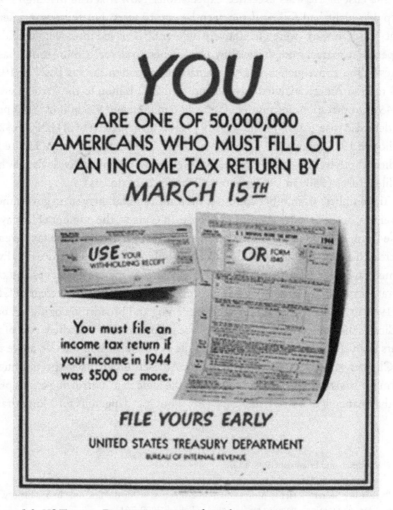

Figure 5.2 US Treasury Department posters from the 1940s

[71] Council of Economic Advisers 1950, 15.
[72] Seligman 1918, 75–76.

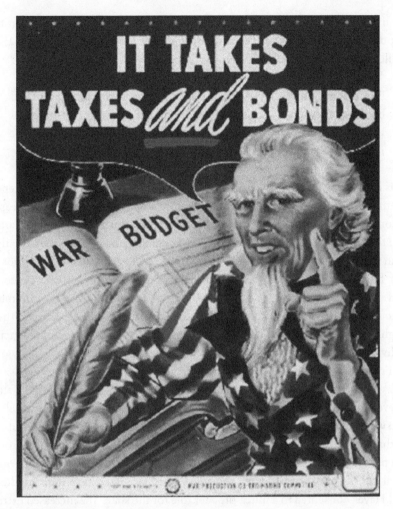

Figure 5.2 Continued

Suddenly, the state had a new lever—taxation—with which to intervene in the economy. Taxation was not just a means of paying for the war but a means of altering investment and consumption decisions for individuals. Unless an effort was made to restrict the money in the hands of consumers, rising prices for consumer goods would create incentives for producers to move capital over to making consumer goods rather than vital military goods.[73] As a National Bureau of Economic Research (NBER) study put it in 1942, "the immediate task of war financing consists largely in reducing civilian use of resources needed for the military program and in preventing the inflation that might develop because

[73] Keynes 1939; Friedman 1943.

civilians have more money to spend on fewer goods."[74] Keynes pointed out the importance of altering the consumption of lower-income individuals in 1939 while arguing for his "deferred payment" plan:

> The income group between £3 and £10 a week is scarcely touched by direct taxation and cannot be relied on to restrict its consumption when its incomes are rising. Some method must therefore be found for restricting the use of purchasing power on present consumption.[75]

This logic was echoed by a surprising contemporary. In 1942, Friedman, representing the Treasury Department, went before Congress to argue for increased income taxes rather than sales taxes, because "both the prevention of inflation and the fair distribution of the cost of the war demand that the income tax rather than the sales tax be used."[76] Reminiscent of Hayek's sense that all methods of war finance would have to be used, Friedman argued a year later for income and progressive "spending taxes" on consumption above a certain minimum amount.[77] Friedman would recall his wartime efforts five decades later as "thoroughly Keynesian," in that he was advocating a role for the state in influencing individual consumption and investment decisions.[78]

Friedman (and Hayek and Pigou) was on the same side as Keynes: an unlikely coalition. Deepening and broadening the tax base and giving the state a lever to influence consumer and investment decisions made sense whether you were concerned about inflation, winning the war, or distributing the burden of the war fairly. But being a member of this coalition meant losing control of the process in a typical logrolling process. This produced deviations from one's ideal course of action: Keynes conceded to broad-based taxation; Friedman and Hayek consented to a much broader role for the state. The increased extraction raised the supply of the state, created a powerful lever for state intervention in the economy, and forged a self-enforcing exchange with a larger number of citizens. However, driving the increased revenues was not a concern for redistribution per se but a concern with winning the war—Pigou and Friedman[79] would make clear the exceptional nature of their support for taxation—and subordinate to that end, distributing its burdens equitably. Absent the temporary

[74] Quoted in MacDonald 2003, 438.

[75] Keynes 1939, 10.

[76] Milton Friedman, "Statement," May 7, 1942. Available at http://0055d26.netsolhost.com/friedman/pdfs/congress/Gov.05.07.1942.pdf.

[77] Friedman 1943, 51–52.

[78] Friedman 1998, 112–113.

[79] E.g., Friedman 1943, 50.

exigency of absolute war, popular willingness to submit to such high tax rates could be expected to wane over time, undermining the exchange which had intensified as a consequence of costly, but now unrepeatable, war. If progressive taxation, in which a higher tax rate on the wealthy provides the bulk of revenue, was the result of "equality of sacrifice," in which the old and rich gave money to be protected by the young and poor, we can expect, in the absence of war when the old and rich need that protection, they will prove unwilling to sacrifice for the young and poor.

Paying for the Long Term

Recent scholarship on inequality has drawn attention to the role of the tax system, namely, a postwar shift in the burden of taxation which is seen, to varying degrees, in three indicators across Europe and North America: a fall in inheritance taxation, a fall in marginal rates of income tax, and a fall in taxes on capital.[80] The tax burden has been shifted to a combination of broadly distributed income tax, social insurance contributions, and consumption taxes (the combination varies from state to state). In this section, I will suggest that just as a coalition formed behind increased extraction during the wars, so a coalition formed behind lowering the highest tax rates from the 1960s onward, culminating in the "decade of tax reform" that was the 1980s. I will show that the logic of tax reform was consistent with the emerging logic that drove tax increases: high taxation in peacetime could distort investment decisions and reduce economic growth.

Tax reform reveals that the exigencies of war, not a commitment to redistribution, drove the supply of the state necessary to satisfy the increased demand for services. As the Second World War ended and the tensions of the Cold War stabilized, it followed that there would be a call to cut taxes. But along with the quantitative increase in taxation was a qualitative shift in which the state had moved from having a negligible role in welfare around 1850 to supplementing market-based incomes at the margin around 1900 to ensuring "freedom from want" in Beveridge's admittedly ambitious formulation. There was no expectation that spending would be cut, so could the taxes raised during the wars be cut but social spending continue to rise? Put differently, could social spending proceed on a basis other than redistribution, given that the popular willingness to sacrifice was limited to prosecuting the war?

The focus on lowering tax rates and removing loopholes called "tax reform" did provide an argument wherein social spending could be sustained, but not

---

[80] Piketty and Saez 2007; Piketty 2014.

on the moral (e.g., fairness) or political (e.g., preventing social unrest) grounds of redistribution. Rather, tax reform would raise economic growth, increasing government revenues and thus allowing an increase in services. This shift implied that social programs, and the desirability of state intervention in the economy, would become a gamble on economic growth rather than a sustained commitment to redistribution. If economic growth fell, social programs would be threatened. But if economic growth could be shown to fall *as a result of state intervention in the economy*, then it was not just social programs but also the role of the state itself that would come into question. That is, if the purpose of the state was to ensure economic growth, as the Ordoliberals of the last chapter presaged, and state policies could be shown to diminish economic growth, the restaged state would be seen as self-undermining.

In the United States, those committed to redistribution testified to the prioritization of growth with either acceptance of the inevitable or dismay. One such was the New Dealer Stanley Surrey, who wrote in 1961: "Very high rates of individual income taxation have come to be recognized as bad, *even by those who in the past have favored virtually confiscatory tax rates on ethical grounds*."[81] Surrey's argument shows that the logic behind the increase in taxation during war (to manipulate investment away from consumer goods so that defense production could be supported) was the same as the logic behind peacetime tax decreases (to allow investment to pursue the highest returns to maximize growth). John Kenneth Galbraith, like Leon Keyserling in the last chapter, was less sanguine, but he too testified to the same belief of those otherwise sympathetic to redistribution:

> It is the increase in output in recent decades, *not the redistribution of income*, which has brought the great material increase in the well-being of the average man. And, however suspiciously, the liberal has come to accept the fact. As a result, the goal of an expanding economy has also become deeply embedded in the conventional wisdom of the American left.[82]

So if the unlikely figure of Milton Friedman backed "confiscatory" taxation in the 1940s, New Dealers like Surrey mostly accepted that taxes had to be cut in the 1960s. The logic of tax reform to maximize economic growth, as opposed to its wartime opposite, was highlighted by John Kennedy: "We have a tax system that was written, in a sense, during wartime to restrain growth."[83] Facing

---

[81] Quoted in Zelizer 1998, 169, emphasis mine.

[82] Galbraith 1969, 92–93, emphasis mine.

[83] John F. Kennedy, "The President's News Conference," February 14, 1963. Available at http://www.presidency.ucsb.edu/ws/index.php?pid=9562&st=&st1=#axzz2fXtYw3Gq.

opposition from those concerned about broadening deficits, Kennedy acknowledged that his tax cut would reduce revenues in the near term.[84] But he argued that in the long term, increased economic growth would eventually raise revenues and reduce deficits. Contra his opponents, who wanted to maintain high taxes or cut spending to reduce the deficit, Kennedy argued that it was high taxes that reduced economic growth, and consequently the revenues that would pay off the deficit:

> History teaches us that the public debt unexpectedly rises when public revenues fall unexpectedly short. And they have been consistently falling short, precisely because our tax rates which were originally designed to meet wartime and post-wartime conditions are now imposing a restrictive brake on national growth and income.[85]

After the initial dip in revenues, tax cuts were expected to stimulate the economy, increasing revenues over the long term and allowing social spending programs to continue. This was a tenuous basis—neither moral ("this is the right thing to do even if it compromises growth") nor political ("this will prevent riots in poor communities")—for the impressive expansion of social spending detailed in the second section of this chapter. Indeed, there were hiccups. Kennedy spoke of restricting government expenditures in 1963, and when Lyndon Johnson required budget authorization for the Vietnam War in 1968, he had to accept cuts to his Great Society programs.[86] Social spending was, on the one hand, expanding and had come to be taken for granted. On the other hand, the means to pay for it were quickly devolving to a gamble on economic growth, not a sustained commitment to moral principles of equity or political exigencies of preventing unrest.

The link between tax policy and growth was seen elsewhere as well and transcended left/right divides. In Britain, Conservative Chancellor of the Exchequer, Reginald Maulding, proposed cutting the top level of income tax and reducing corporate taxes "as this is the method best calculated both to stimulate the economy and to encourage individual effort" even though it would reduce revenues in the short run.[87] In Canada, the Carter Commission was charged with

[84] In his 1963 State of the Union speech, Kennedy estimated a revenue reduction of $13.5 billion over three years.

[85] John F. Kennedy, "Remarks at the National Conference of the Business Committee for Tax Reduction," September 10, 1963. Available at http://www.presidency.ucsb.edu/ws/index.php?pid=9400&st=&st1=#axzz2fXtYw3Gq.

[86] Zelizer 1998, 257–278.

[87] Reginald Maulding, "Budget Statement," April 3, 1963, *Hansard*, Vol. 675: c490–494.

evaluating Canada's tax code. It urged the decrease of the highest marginal rate from 80 percent to 50 percent (it was lowered to 60 percent in 1972) and called for the end of inheritance taxation (which was repealed in 1971). Again, the commission's logic focused on growth and the tax system's effect on it:

> The narrow tax base and some extremely expensive incentive or con-cessionary provisions built into the present system mean that, to raise the required revenue, tax rates have to be higher than would otherwise be necessary . . . . [T]his has the effect of driving labor and capital away from activities that are heavily taxed and drawing them into tax-favored activities . . . . [U]nless these pressures nicely compensate for non-tax distortions in the market, labor and capital are less productively employed than they should be.[88]

The tax system, here as elsewhere, was not represented as a tool of redistribution or equity, or merely the means of paying for government spending. Rather, the tax system was an instrument that could depress growth rates by leading to the misallocation of labor and capital, or it could be designed to encourage efficient allocation. This is very different from a "conscription of wealth" or a class-based argument, as columnist Walter Lippmann acknowledged with some wonder:

> A generation ago it would have been taken for granted that a war on poverty meant taxing money away from the haves and turning it over to the havenots . . . . But in this generation . . . a revolutionary idea has taken hold . . . . [T]he size of the pie can be increased by invention, orga-nization, capital investment, and fiscal policy, and then a whole society, not just one part of it, will grow richer.[89]

Lippman here articulates what I have called a parametric shift in the exchange between central authority and population (predicated on a new way of repre-senting economic activity, which I discuss below).

Using taxation to manipulate consumption and investment decisions was relatively new because prior to the world wars the tax base—at least those pay-ing taxes to the central government—was limited to a small section of society. Now, with a broadened base, policymakers would not have to rely on confisca-tory rates on a small part of the society. Rather, they could lower taxes on this fraction to encourage economic growth and compensate with increased taxes

[88] Carter Commission 1966, 24.
[89] Quoted in Zelizer 1998, 210.

on labor and consumption, affecting the economic decisions of a far greater proportion of the population. Sweden, for example, has a high tax burden and generous social spending. The Social Democrats introduced a consumption tax in 1959, at a rate of 4.2 percent, which has been raised incrementally (it is currently 25 percent for most goods and services). Taxes on labor in Sweden are comparatively high: in 1981, a family of four with an average income in the United States paid 14.3 percent of its income in taxes, while a similar Swedish family paid 34.1 percent.[90] Sweden provides an instructive example of the general concern with growth: a generous welfare state is paid for through growth-maximizing policies, ideally, and when growth is insufficient, increased taxes on a broad base. Paradoxically, tax systems in states with high social transfers turn out to be more regressive than those in less generous states like the United States because the former rely more on labor and consumption taxes to raise revenue.[91] In the absence of costly war, it is only in a few places that the population has consistently proven willing to supply the state, but even in these (mostly Scandinavian) locales, that willingness can wither if state polices can be shown to hinder growth.

This historical discussion leads to the question of whether economic growth is indeed a priority for the population. Has the population come to deemphasize war-making and prioritize economic issues, as my argument would predict? To examine the veracity of this proposition cross-nationally, I turn to the World Values Survey, the broadest cross-national panel data of public opinion.[92] The temporal scope of the survey is limited, with broad coverage only beginning in 1990, and there are no comparable surveys from between 1800 and 1950, the high point of war-making. It would appear that we are unable to contrast contemporary popular expectations of the state with popular expectations of the state as it developed through costly war and empire. However, we can infer shifts in popular expectations indirectly. There are aspects of contemporary life that would appear befuddling to nineteenth-century observers, most obviously technology like the Internet, but more subtly concepts that did not exist at the time and so could not have formed the basis for state intervention. By looking at contemporary responses to questions that would have been unthinkable in the nineteenth century, we can gauge how popular expectations of the state have shifted to take in new, in the sense of previously undefined, areas of life. I will look at two such questions: about the environment, and, more tellingly, about economic growth.

[90] Steinmo 1993, 39.

[91] Lindert 2004.

[92] World Values Survey Waves 2-6. Available at http://www.worldvaluessurvey.org/WVSContents.jsp.

The question about the environment has a straightforward logic: until the 1960s, the environment and related concerns like pollution or climate change were barely acknowledged, much less an area for state intervention. Since then, however, popular concern about environmental issues has risen, raising the question of whether individuals see tackling environmental issues to be the responsibility of the state. Figure 5.3 shows the extent to which respondents to the survey believe the state should do something about the environment. (The coverage, however, is limited to three survey waves.)

The survey responses suggest that pluralities or majorities do see a role for the state in dealing with environmental issues. Even in poorer societies like China and India where policymakers represent environmental concerns as subordinate to economic ones, a sizable minority expects the state to reduce pollution. My point is simply that for the nineteenth century "strong" state, such an expectation would have been unthinkable.

The second, more important, area is the importance of the economy in popular expectations. The specific question posed to survey respondents is to list the primary "aims of the country." There are four options—"a high level of economic growth"; "making sure this country has strong defense forces"; "seeing that people have more say about how things are done at their jobs and in their communities"; "trying to make our cities and countryside more beautiful." I provide two visualizations to convey the primacy of economic growth as a concern over having strong defense forces, the closest proxy for concerns about war (note there is no question about actually engaging in war or conquest). Figure 5.4 presents the percentage of respondents who identify "a high level of economic growth" as the No.1 aim.

Figure 5.4 suggests that individuals prioritize economic growth, but it does not give us a sense of how much they prioritize economic growth relative to

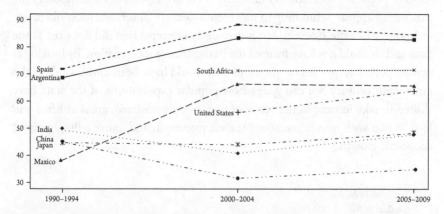

Figure 5.3 Percentage of respondents who "agree" or "strongly agree" that "government should reduce environmental pollution"

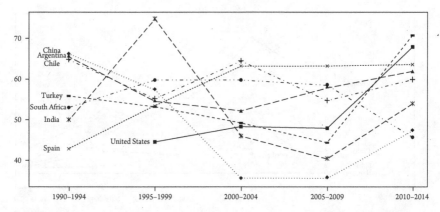

Figure 5.4 Percentage of respondents identifying "economic growth" as "No.1 priority of country"

national defense. To convey the relative priorities of economic growth and having strong defense forces, I computed the ratio of respondents saying the former was No. 1 to those saying the latter was No. 1. The results are shown in Figure 5.5.

As Figure 5.5. shows, even though the popular concern about defense has increased since 2000, *in no state at no time* did more respondents say that having strong defense forces was the No.1 priority than those who said economic growth was the No.1 priority. The flat solid line indicates that respondents are equally concerned; only 1 of 39 data points—namely, China in the 2000–2004 round—shows respondents even equally concerned about the two issues, much less prioritizing defense over the economy.

That economic growth is so central to popular expectations and so much more central than maintaining national defense has twofold significance for my argument. First, as seen in the last chapter and this one, there is a tension between the state's ensuring economic growth and its ability to extract and intervene in the economy. While there is disagreement about whether governments should raise taxes somewhat higher than their current levels, very few policymakers advocate a return to the rates of marginal taxation implemented during the world wars. As Piketty puts it, "There is no significant support for continuing to expand the social state at its 1930–1980 growth rate (which would mean that by 2050–2060, 70–80 percent of national income would go to taxes)."[93] Given current understandings of the effects of taxation, popular expectations that the state must ensure economic growth also restrict the state's ability to extract to pay for the other services it is expected to provide.

[93] Piketty 2014, 481.

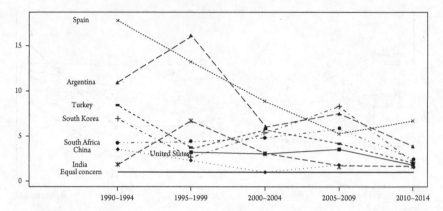

Figure 5.5 Ratio of respondents saying "economic growth" is No. 1 priority compared to respondents saying "strong defense forces" is No. 1 priority

The prior point is a practical one, namely, that the extractive capacity of the state is limited by the priority of economic growth. The second point is epistemological. The very notion of economic growth, as increase of GDP, could not have been a national priority in the nineteenth century because the concept of GDP did not exist until the 1930s. GDP developed out of efforts to measure the extent of unemployment and deprivation during the Great Depression, in contrast to prior efforts, such as William Petty's in the seventeenth century, to measure wealth for purposes of taxation.[94] (The term "economy" referring to an object or aggregate is also an artifact of the early twentieth century; its previous use was to describe calculated action akin to what we would now call utility-maximization.[95] That economy was a mode of analysis rather than an object of analysis can be seen in Adam Smith's claim that political economy "proposes to enrich both the people and the sovereign.")[96] The development of GDP transformed the ability to represent economic activity, an activity that until then, Keynes had lamented, was akin to "grop(ing) in barbaric darkness."[97] Transforming how economic activity was seen was necessary for intervention in the economy, first to deal with unemployment and then to guide the war effort in the Second World War. Put another way, the discussion of tax reform as boosting economic growth would have been unthinkable in the nineteenth century because the concept of GDP and high rates of taxation were absent in that period. These interventions, in turn, transformed popular expectations of what

[94] Poovey 1998, 125–128.
[95] Mitchell 2002, 80–84.
[96] Quoted in Poovey 1998, 237.
[97] Quoted in Philipsen 2015, 64.

the state could and should do. To be sure, subjects have always expected rulers to intervene when economic conditions have worsened. But this expectation was different, as suggested by the case of food riots, a form of popular protest common between the seventeenth and early nineteenth centuries.[98] A food riot is episodic and, in the absence of broader measures of economic activity, unconnected to aggregate phenomena such as agricultural productivity or climate change. Consequently, even if the ruler was expected to respond to a food riot, he could do so on a piecemeal basis, by disbursing relief, without having to intervene in the broader causes of food shortages. Beyond responding to extreme events, rulers were not expected to calibrate economic activity on a regular basis because they did not have the analytical tools to do so, *and neither did the population*. The concepts of GDP and economic growth provided those tools, and their proliferation is evident in the survey data presented above. Now that economic indicators, from growth to unemployment to inflation, are consistently tracked, individual experiences of deprivation can be placed in broader context, and with it, the performance of the state measured.

Finally, it is worth noting that the development of GDP was not independent of the state. Prior estimates of national income were compiled by individuals like Petty who sought to influence the king (with little success), and Vauban in 1707 who faced censure for revealing unflattering conclusions about state finances.[99] By contrast, the definition and measurement of GDP was the outcome of a US government initiative to understand the economic activity of the population. It was then adopted in the 1953 United Nations System of National Accounts. States were not compelled to adopt GDP, but effectively, they had to because UN membership dues were assessed based on this figure.[100] Until the 1930s then, economic growth could not have been the criterion by which the population evaluated the performance of the state; insofar as it has become such a critierion, it is largely due to the state itself. GDP and economic growth are concepts that are endogenous to state formation; they facilitate state intervention but also constitute expectations of order that can be wielded against the state.

The surveys provide suggestive evidence that the state is now expected to intervene in a wider range of activities than could be imagined in the nineteenth century. The three trends—the state's promise to provide welfare as it moved away from waging absolute war; the sudden war-motivated spurt in the supply of the state that made it possible; the postwar expectation of economic growth rather than progressive taxation to finance services—leads us to reinterpret the

---

[98] Tilly 1986, 173–178.

[99] Piketty 2014, 55–58; Poovey 1998, 126–138.

[100] Philipsen 2015, 130, 135.

linear story of Euro-American state formation. Russell and others featured in the last chapter had argued that the state after 1945 had lost the ability to protect its people in the event of war, and so an alternative to the war-making state was necessary. Instead, the state was restaged to prevent war, for which it took on an expanded and permanent role. But its ability to play this role, initially possible because of a war-motivated revenue spurt, had become a gamble on economic growth. What would happen when growth slowed?

Sympathy for the Neoliberal

An economic slowdown could spark several responses to bring the demand for services into equilibrium with the supply of the state. If growth was the primary concern, one could reduce spending. If redistribution was the primary concern, one could raise taxes on the wealthy and maintain social spending. But these are incremental rather than existential questions; none implies that the state is self-undermining. Yet, in the 1980s, the rhetoric of a "crisis of the state" was common, and political reformers ascended to power under slogans like Reagan's "nine most terrifying words in the English language: I'm from the government, and I'm here to help." Why this "state-phobia"?

The war-preventing state had taken an expanded and permanent role in everyday life because of prior wars. But the willingness to sacrifice for the state, in the absence of war, could be expected to wane if alternatives to the state articulated a way to provide services with less sacrifice. Neoliberal intellectuals and reformers identified the new and expanded role of the state as undermining the very goals—managing economic growth and delivering services—the state had set for itself. Put another way, the state's new role endogenously distorted the economy and everyday life. That is, as the state took on more functions, it altered individual behavior in ways that reduced aggregate welfare. This was not the result of capricious and unpredictable state action but the result of the state doing what it promised to. For example, if individuals expect interest rates to rise as output increases—and central banks are expected to raise interest rates when this happens—they will scale back investment, bringing the boom to an end.[101] Consequently, neoliberals argued that markets could do a better job at ensuring growth and providing social services. That is, neoliberals offered markets as an alternative to the state, whose policies were lowering growth and undermining the ability to deliver services. This was a "crisis" of the state because the state after 1945 had come to be responsible for a variety of functions rather than

[101] Hence, the economist Rudiger Dornbusch suggested that postwar economic expansions did not die of natural (or exogenous) causes but were murdered by the Federal Reserve.

war-making, to the degree that it shaped individual decisions on work and family. By throwing into question these functions, especially welfare, neoliberalism went beyond a technical debate on "right-sizing" the state to a political movement that questioned the state itself—the "state-phobia" that Foucault observed at the end of the 1970s. Its lasting effect has been to create a gap between the demand for services and popular willingness to supply the state because it has posited an alternative means of providing services that the population can prefer to supplying the state.

A contrast will illustrate how novel the neoliberal formulation of the market as a viable alternative to the state was. Neoliberal critiques of state intervention, especially in welfare policy, are sometimes compared to Victorian concerns about how public provision would make the poor lazy and erode other values like thrift and self-reliance.[102] The efforts to reduce welfare, it follows, are designed to turn the clock back to a prior age when the poor went unfed and unschooled. But this misses two salient features of neoliberalism and how it differs from the classical liberal and Social Darwinist arguments that are seen as its predecessors. First, in neoliberal arguments, unlike nineteenth-century ones, there is the expectation that the poor will be fed and schooled. Nineteenth-century arguments, as we saw, conceded that the poor would go unschooled and unfed if there was no state intervention, hence the establishment of various ad hoc programs from the 1880s onward. In neoliberal arguments, markets, if left alone, would boost incomes or lower the cost of services so that the demand for services could be satisfied; markets are a superior alternative to state provision of goods. Markets would deliver efficiencies through competition that would enable the population to purchase services of a higher quality than the state could provide. Markets did not internalize the entire cost of services, but they promised to make up the difference between the demand for services and the population's ability to pay for them, whether by lowering the costs of services or raising incomes. This would have made no sense in the nineteenth century, when the market was acknowledged, even by its supporters like Ricardo and Mill, to be an inadequate supplier of services for the poor. Even those who opposed state provision of social services, like Spencer, acknowledged that the market would not supply them.

Second, in the nineteenth century, it was not the role of the state to intervene in daily life. Contesting then-meager state efforts to provide income support or education was not a challenge to the role of the nineteenth-century state: the latter was a war-making entity, and debates over welfare provision were marginally relevant to that function. By contrast, to target the post-1945 state as provider of welfare was to challenge the state in how it related to the majority of its citizens,

---

[102] E.g., Goodin 1988.

through quotidian processes like how one's children were schooled, which doctor one saw, and so on. To challenge the state's ability to manage these processes, as neoliberalism did, was to challenge the rationale of the state as it had come to be articulated in the 1940s and beyond.

Consider Milton Friedman's invocation of his self-professed "master," Adam Smith, on public provision of education. In a newspaper article, Friedman noted Smith's argument in *Wealth of Nations* that paying the schoolmaster from public funds would lead him to neglect his duties. By contrast, Smith wrote "those parts of education, it is to be observed, for the teaching of which there are no public institutions, are generally the best taught."[103] The schoolmaster's incentives were distorted by the lack of competition, and this worsened outcomes for students. But Smith went on to note that if education was only provided by private sources "the common people" would go unschooled because "they have little time to spare for education .... [T]heir parents can scarce afford to maintain them even in infancy" much less provide basic schooling.[104] While competition supplied high-quality schooling to those who could afford it, the same logic undersupplied it on an aggregate basis. Thus, Smith advocated the building of a "little school" using public funds to top up the teacher's salary (the rest through fees low enough that even the poor could pay) in every parish so that the basics, however mediocre, would be provided.[105] Friedman, in his invocation of his "great master," did not mention that Smith was advocating public funding to make up for the "common laborer's" inability to afford education! Smith, like the other nineteenth-century voices we saw in Chapter 3, *was advocating a role for the state that was greater than existed in his day*. The state and the market were not alternatives. Rather, the state supplemented markets where the latter (frequently) failed to provide services. As John Stuart Mill reiterated in 1848, "in England, and most European countries, elementary instruction cannot be paid for, at its full cost, from the common wages of unskilled labor .... [T]he alternative, therefore, is not between government and private speculation, but between a government provision and voluntary charity."[106]

The point is not that Friedman misread Adam Smith. The point is that Smith acknowledged that markets were not providing education to the poor and even mediocre state provision would be an improvement. By contrast, Friedman argued that state provision *worsened* education, and turning education over to markets would improve outcomes at individual and aggregate level.[107] For

---

[103] Quoted in Friedman 1973, 72.

[104] Smith 2000, 842.

[105] Smith 2000, 843.

[106] Mill 1994, 340.

[107] Friedman 1982, 85–107.

Smith (and Mill), the state was a meager, but necessary, supplement to markets, which provided the best instruction, but not enough of it. The poor would go unschooled if the costs of education were externalized onto them. For Friedman, the market was an alternative to the state, in that it would reduce the cost of education so that the poor could afford it: "The absence of alternatives where there is no market does not mean that none would arise when there is one."[108] If the state got out of the education business, the market would supply education; this was not what Smith and other nineteenth-century liberals argued.

Education was important in itself but also for its effects on the economic growth that was to pay for services.[109] If education improved the quality or "human capital" of individual workers, mediocre state provision of education would crowd out private provision of schooling and reduce the need for individuals to invest in their children's education.[110] Lower-quality education reduced individual productivity and growth over time, compromising the state's ability to pay for education at the same time that private provision was stifled. The state's role in providing services would undermine its long-run ability to provide those very services. The state's very policies diminished the economic growth that was necessary to pay for the services it promised, rendering it self-undermining.

The privatization of education is an example not just of how the market is an alternative to the state in providing a service for individuals, but also how the market, by achieving efficiency gains that enable the population to satisfy their demand for services, can achieve the broader aims of society while state intervention compromises those goals. Public education may have been established to provide opportunity, but it was actually a driver of inequality, Friedman argued, because the wealthy could move to districts with better schools.[111] The resultant rise in property prices in districts with good schools kept the poor out, increasing inequality on two levels: the rich child would be in a better school, and his parents' house would appreciate in value as more people wanted to move into that school district. Meanwhile, poor children could not leave inadequate, even violent, schools without a family relocation, ironically made costlier by the policy to assign students to schools based on their place of residence, that is, because of the state.[112] This is a consequential inversion: if state programs designed to reduce inequality actually perpetuate it—undermining the exchange—then market solutions do not just benefit the wealthy and hurt the poor. The reader will recall that nineteenth-century thinkers either accepted, like Ricardo, these

[108] Friedman 1973.
[109] E.g., Becker 1962.
[110] Becker and Tomes 1986, S17.
[111] Friedman 1982, 92–93.
[112] Friedman 1973.

negative effects, or like Spencer, welcomed them. Keynes had summed up this commonality in his quip that "the principle of the survival of the fittest could be regarded as a vast generalization of the Ricardian economics."[113] And so did nineteenth-century radicals: Marx was so convinced that evolutionary competition typified economic activity that he wanted to dedicate the first volume of *Das Kapital* to Darwin.[114] Friedman posed the opposite: even the poor would benefit *directly* from market provision, not just indirectly from economic growth (as Smith's "universal opulence which extends itself to the lowest ranks of the people").[115] The promise of better schools for the poor was crucial for the popular and electoral appeal of neoliberalism; it tapped into the "disillusionment" Stuart Hall sensed of ordinary Britons who "experienced (the state) in negative and oppressive ways" and supported Margaret Thatcher.[116] Neoliberalism did not just blame the state and promise to pare it back; it gave the population an alternative to the state.

Smith wrote at a time when the centralized state was not responsible for welfare. The costs of education and health provision were externalized onto the population, and the majority could not afford them. Thus, even as life expectancy for the English aristocracy was beginning to rise after 1750 as the result of medical innovations only they could afford, life expectancy for the general population remained unchanged between 1550 and 1850.[117] The state in 1776 was barely a supplement to market provision, much less an alternative. Smith was arguing for the former, and the latter was improbable. Friedman wrote at a time when the state had suddenly become responsible for welfare instead of protection in war, and the relationship between state and market could be proposed as either mutual supplements or competitive alternatives. By posing markets as an alternative (because the state distorted market incentives) rather than a supplement (markets adding to state provision where it fell short) Friedman identified the state as the problem. The problem with the state was that it did not function like the market.[118] By throttling competition, it distorted the market functioning that would satisfy the demand for services. At a time when popular willingness to sacrifice was waning in the absence of costly war, markets offered an outside option through which the supply of the state could be reduced without lowering the demand for services.

---

[113] John Maynard Keynes, *The End of Laissez-Faire* (1926). Available at www.panarchy.org/keynes/laisszefaire.1926.html.

[114] Darwin demurred; Gay 1994, 39.

[115] Smith 2000, 12.

[116] Hall 1980, 27.

[117] Deaton 2013, 81–87.

[118] Foucault 2008, 116–118.

The formulation of state and market as alternatives was a development of the 1940s and beyond because the nineteenth-century state had not played such a significant positive role in boosting economic growth and certainly not in everyday life. Hayek had formulated this opposition as follows:

> Resources and needs exist for practical purposes only through somebody knowing about them and there will be always be infinitely more known to all the people together than can be known to the most competent authority. A successful solution can therefore not be based on the authority dealing directly with the objective facts, but must be based on a method of utilizing the knowledge dispersed among all members of society, knowledge of which in any particular instance *the central authority* will know neither who possesses nor whether it exists at all .... [T]his is precisely the function which the various "markets" perform.[119]

Hayek was making an epistemological as well as political intervention, a parametric shift in how the role of the state was understood. It was not the criticism of the state per se that was new: classical liberals had lambasted mercantilism. But classical liberals had argued that the state stifled *exchange*, which Smith had called a "certain propensity in human nature."[120] Mercantilism stifled exchange by reducing the size of the market and hindering the division of labor, for Smith the source of wealth, for Ricardo the basis of comparative advantage.[121] Neoliberals, by contrast, argued that the state stifled *competition* by distorting the price mechanism (this argument was also made by the Ordoliberals discussed in Chapter 4).[122]

The price mechanism was, and here Hayek followed a line of thought that stretched back to Condillac, what revealed individual preferences and showed individuals where to invest, increasing aggregate well-being.[123] Information unencumbered by the state created incentives, while incentives provided by the state distorted the price mechanism and obscured information.[124] Rather, competition would be stifled because individuals would not know where to invest, and the *expectation* of state intervention would alter individual decision making. In terms of the post-1945 exchange between the central authority and the population

---

[119] Hayek 1944, 37, emphasis mine.
[120] Smith 2000, 14.
[121] Smith 2000, 19–23.
[122] Foucault 2008, 118–119.
[123] Foucault 2008, 48, footnote 6.
[124] Gilder 2012, xiv.

around ensuring economic growth and securing against the business cycle, Hayek rethought the parameters within which that exchange is conducted. That is, the new role of the state distorted individual behavior by its very operation, *reducing the economic growth that the state promised to provide and the increased services that were predicated on growth.* The exchange wherein the central authority had come to be responsible for intervening in the economy and protecting the population from downturns in the business cycle was undermining economic growth and hurting the population. This meant that the market should not be supplemented by the state, as Smith had argued. Rather, the market should replace the state. Friedman applied this analysis to argue for the privatization of education, but this logic—I should emphasize, novel logic—could be wielded not just against particular programs but also to mobilize popular dissatisfaction against the state by highlighting the claim that the state distorted everyday life.

Consider the vexed issue of the family. The dislocations of the nineteenth century had raised the issue of women working for wages. John Stuart Mill had argued that this should be facilitated by legislation so that women need not be dependent on their husbands.[125] But by the turn of the century, reformers were making the point that the labor market did not provide even working women and families with either livelihood or independence.[126] Therefore, in arguments for the "family wage," the state was expected to supplement labor income. In some of the more radical arguments, like that of H. G. Wells, state provision would reduce the need for women to stay in patriarchal family structures. For Wells— who wrote that "a woman with healthy and successful offspring will draw a wage for each one of them from the State, as long as they go well . . . . [U]nder the State she will control her child's upbringing"[127]—the state was explicitly an alternative to the family. But for the most part, reformers represented state provision of welfare as a supplement, not an alternative, to family provision.

In neoliberal arguments, state support was not represented as a supplement for families. Rather, state support (or the expectation thereof) distorted decision making about marriage and employment. Again, this understanding marked a shift between classical liberalism and neoliberalism. Adam Smith, Friedman's colleague Gary Becker wrote, had understood the incentives for child-rearing as driven by non-economic motives like altruism.[128] The family and the economy were separate realms for Smith because they were governed by different logics. Smith saw the family governed by altruism—"benevolence" in his term—but

---

[125] Mill 1994, 138, 344–345.
[126] Pedersen 1993, 40.
[127] Wells 1906, 58–59.
[128] Becker 1981, 1.

suggested that altruism could not underpin cooperation between strangers, hence the need for market mechanisms.[129]

Becker did not disagree that people could show altruism toward family members, but he argued that altruism should be understood in economic terms. Becker's most famous example is the "rotten kid theorem."[130] A benevolent parent who gives gifts to all her children can induce even a "rotten kid" not to harm his sibling. The mechanism is simple: if the rotten kid harms his sibling, say by breaking the gift the latter received from the parent, the parent can deter the rotten kid from doing so in future by either redistributing from the remaining children or taking money out of investment, which reduces future gifts to all. Either action reduces the rotten kid's allocation. If his current or future income depended on such gifts, even the rotten kid has an interest in not harming his siblings. Altruism could be induced, even in "rotten" or selfish kids, and therefore altruism would be the dominant behavior in families because altruists would behave altruistically anyway, and selfish individuals could be induced to behave altruistically. Here, altruism is an economic choice (or a particular form of selfishness: the kid is still rotten!), and decisions within the family do not follow a logic separate from that of market transactions. This argument has been criticized—for example, the rotten kid need not harm the sibling, but can just loaf around rather than work, eventually forcing the parent to give larger gifts to equalize utility among children—but the criticism just confirms the parametric shift that "household mysteries" can be understood under economic logic.[131] As George Stigler would put this (new) idea, "most ethical values do not conflict with individual utility-maximizing behavior."[132]

If family dynamics were, at core, economic dynamics, the distortions state intervention introduced into economic behavior detrimentally affected the most intimate parts of everyday life. In a famous critique of welfare policy, the American commentator Charles Murray described the decisions of a hypothetical working-class couple, Phyllis and Harold.[133] If they had conceived a child in 1960, before welfare benefits programs were extended, Harold would have had "no choice" but to marry Phyllis and work to support the family. After 1970, however, Phyllis would receive greater benefits if she remained unmarried, so the couple had no incentive to marry. By linking changes in long-established social institutions like marriage to recent changes in state policy, Murray suggested that the state was undermining long-running social mores of concern to groups

[129] Coase 1976, 544.
[130] Becker 1981, 7–9.
[131] Bergstrom 1989.
[132] Stigler 1981, 177.
[133] Murray 1984, 156–164.

who had never heard of Friedman and Becker. But their logic was echoed by those who explained the problem of out-of-wedlock births as one of economic incentives. The problem for Murray was not moral or cultural pathologies, as the Victorians saw the working classes and as the 1960's Moynihan Report had represented the plight of black families.[134] This logic would have been unthinkable to classical liberals, who, first, saw family life as distinct from economic decisions, and second, lived in a period when the state could not distort family life. But economic concerns about welfare could be articulated to a moral concern about a "crisis of the family" as Reagan did in a radio address:

> I'm talking about the crisis of family breakdowns, especially among the welfare poor, both black and white. In inner cities today, families, as we've always thought of them, are not even being formed. Since 1960 the percentage of babies born out of wedlock has more than doubled. And too often their mothers are only teenagers. They're children—many of them 15, 16, and 17 years old with all the responsibilities of grownups thrust upon them. The fathers of these children are often nowhere to be found. In some instances you have to go back three generations before you can find an intact family. It seems even the memory of families is in danger of becoming extinct.[135]

Welfare gave mothers incentives not to marry, and state support diminished the need for the father to be a provider, detracting from his sense of self. As the commentator George Gilder put it in 1981, "Welfare, by far the largest economic influence in the ghetto, exerts a constant, seductive, erosive pressure on the marriages and work habits of the poor. . . . [W]elfare continuously mutes and misrepresents the necessities of life that prompted previous generations of poor people to escape poverty through the invariable routes of work, family, and faith."[136] The state, in this view, had internalized costs that were previously provided by the individuals, families, and the private sector, and rendered these sources of social order and meaning marginal.[137] In other words, H. G. Wells's dream had come true: the state was functioning as an alternative to the family and private charity! But, contra Wells, this was not a good thing; it had brought on a "crisis" of the family. State provision had not just undermined the economic growth that had

---

[134] Murray 1984, 162.

[135] Ronald Reagan, "Radio Address to the Nation on Welfare Reform," February 15, 1986. Available at http://www.presidency.ucsb.edu/ws/?pid=36875.

[136] Gilder 2012, 171.

[137] Gilder 2012, 158.

to provide the increased demand for services; it had compromised family values and public safety, motivating popular support for neoliberalism. For example, Murray would argue a few years later that welfare increased illegitimacy, creating large numbers of young men, who, bereft of fathers, would act out, to the extent, Murray feared, that "the current levels of illegitimacy already threaten the institutions needed to sustain a free society."[138]

Overwrought? Of course, but the exaggeration was central to neoliberalism's political achievement. Neoliberalism did not articulate a crisis of the state because economic growth fell. Neoliberalism articulated a crisis of the state because the post-1945 state's rationale was to ensure economic growth and provide functions that had historically been the responsibility of the family and community, and neoliberalism showed how the state failed to do so. These unfulfilled "expectations of order" were wielded against the state by the promise that markets could fulfill them. Neoliberalism identified this inability through its epistemological innovations; it did not create it. By proposing, however, that markets and families could do a better job at fulfilling these functions than the state—in Murray's words to "leave the working-age person with no recourse whatsoever except the job market, family members, friends, and public or private locally funded services"[139]—neoliberal reformers ignored a history where these institutions had, in fact, failed to fulfill these functions. If markets in future failed to supply these services, there could presumably be calls for the state to step back in.

In conclusion, we can reinterpret Habermas's sense that "the program of the social welfare state . . . is losing its capacity to project future possibilities for a collectively better and less endangered way of life" and Hall noting a "a deep and profound disillusionment among ordinary people" with the state. Habermas and Hall were observing the end of a brief interlude when, under very specific conditions, the supply of the state and the demand for services had increased together. But those conditions—costly but winnable war—were not replicable, and in the absence of costly war, the population could prefer alternatives to the state that promised a higher level of services for a lower level of sacrifice. Neoliberalism was that alternative, and with its emergence, popular willingness to supply the state waned relative to the demand for services. The post-1945 state is self-undermining just as its war-making predecessor had been.

---

[138] Murray 1994, 18.
[139] Quoted in Goodin 1988, 17.

6

Origins of Anarchy

> The task of reconstruction can thus be simply stated: to allow the West
> Indian people . . . to become true men instead of what one critic has
> savagely called us, mimics.
>
> Eric Williams[1]

> REPORTER: What do you think of Western civilization?
> GANDHI: It would be a good idea.
>
> M. K. Gandhi[2]

While Western observers were preoccupied with averting nuclear war, anti-colonial movements were beginning to score successes. Between 1945 and 1970, the imperial system within which modern European states developed came to be replaced by the international or anarchical system as 75 new states emerged. The emergence of these states begs two questions. Did their leaders and publics expect to copy the European experience of war-making and state-making, which would have led to more wars as the number of potential conflict dyads increased? Or did they expect to do something different, akin to the parametric shift described in Chapter 4 where the costs of war appeared too high, and observers called for alternatives to the state to avoid war? (For ease of reference, the table in note 12 summarizes information about the anti-colonial leaders described below.)

The nineteenth century offers an intriguing precedent. In 1804, the new Haitian polity declared itself, in its inaugural constitution, the Empire of Haiti, and its ruler, Dessalines, "emperor."[3] The term was no misnomer, for Haiti took over its neighbor, now the Dominican Republic in 1822, fought a resistance movement from 1838, and occupied it until 1844. (In the Dominican Republic,

---

[1] Williams 1993, 276. This critic was probably V. S. Naipaul, also of Trinidad, who wrote *The Mimic Men* in 1967.

[2] Quoted in Duara 2001, 99.

[3] Quoted in Fischer 2004, 275.

Independence Day commemorates a victory against Haitian forces.) Given its historically weak position, it seems surprising that Haiti would seek to control a foreign society. Similar to Italian leaders like Mazzini, Haitian leaders like Dessalines and Henry Christophe saw becoming an empire and fighting wars as a necessary condition for recognition as an equal among the world's nations.[4] They organized their society on a war footing, so to speak, delaying land redistribution to freed slaves and pouring money into national defense.[5] By contrast, the colonized were condemned to a subordinate position formalized in international law. In this nineteenth-century context, Imperial Japan's defeat of Russia in 1906 was greeted by a chorus of praise and feelings of vindication from leaders in colonized societies.[6] Gandhi, of all people, interpreted the Japanese victory as a sign that "the peoples of the East will never, never again submit to insult from the insolent whites."[7]

The idea that decolonized states should engage in war and empire echoes a central premise in contemporary international relations theory and theories of state formation: that states seeking to survive in the international system should emulate stronger states, who prior to decolonization were imperial powers engaged in large-scale conflicts.[8] Similarly, observers in the early twentieth century had understood war, even interstate war, in racialized terms and predicted a coming "war of races."[9] Even advocates of racial amity like the Indian philosopher Brajendranath Seal and German sociologist Ferdinand Tönnies were moved to note, respectively, that "races, empires, nationalities, are in perpetual collision today," and non-Western societies "were admiring our civilization just at the time when it was being most criticized in Europe."[10] As decolonization began in 1949, the British secretary for the Commonwealth, Phillip Noel Baker, told Parliament that the future conflict would be "between the peoples of Asia and Africa on the one hand and the peoples of European origin and culture on the other."[11] Such expectations that the future would look like the past implied not only that the European state was self-enforcing, a view I have

---

[4] In the 1870s, the rulers of Germany, Austria, Russia, Turkey, Britain, China, Japan, and Persia were nominally emperors; Hobsbawm 1987, 56–57.

[5] Du Bois 2011, 52–55.

[6] In the West, the rise of Japan was seen as a case of emulation. For example, the American naval strategist Alfred Mahan had in 1900 suggested that "in Japan, and as yet in Japan alone, we find the Asiatic welcoming European culture"; Mahan 1970, 150.

[7] Quoted in Lake and Reynolds 2008, 168.

[8] Waltz 1979, 97, 128; Mearsheimer 2001, 166–167; Wimmer 2013.

[9] Lake and Reynolds 2008; Füredi 1998.

[10] Record of the Proceedings of the First Universal Races Congress 1911, 24, 46.

[11] Quoted in Baum 2006, 172–173.

shown was breaking down in Europe, but would be reproduced by the work of non-Europeans.

To those in the anti-colonial movements, such a view represented, first, an overly optimistic view of European development (which they saw as violent and self-undermining); second, the continuation of a colonial mentality wherein colonial subjects could not author their own history and hence make their own future. Insofar as they featured in history, they did so, to paraphrase James Mill's statement from Chapter 3, as "an interesting part" of various European histories. But in that history, they were unequal, and undeserving of inclusion in the exchange that had developed in Europe. At issue therefore was the ability of the colonized, the Calibans of Asia and Africa, to author their *own* histories.

In what follows, I will show that anti-colonial movements represented the development of centralized European states, predicated on a lack of exchange, or non-exchange, with the colonial population, as a self-undermining process that could not be repeated. This required postcolonial polities be organized to deliver economic development rather than organized for war and conquest. Anti-colonial leaders[12] did not expect their populations to be able to supply the state as they were impoverished and backward, hence the need for alternatives to the state like federations and cooperative relationships with former colonizers. But these alternatives were not expected to compel popular sacrifice. In the absence of popular sacrifice, anti-colonial leaders conceptualized development as a top-down process involving planning, foreign aid, and coercion, for which a centralized state was necessary. The postcolonial state was not quite an exchange like the one that developed in Europe; nor was it entirely the repetition of the non-exchange that characterized the colonial state. Rather, the postcolonial state should be understood as a gamble that the population could be developed using colonial-style coercion and foreign assistance. In the absence of war, the

[12]   *Table 6.Footnote* **Anti-Colonial Leaders**

Region	Leader (state, year of independence)
Africa	Nnamdi Azikiwe (Nigeria, 1960), Amilcar Cabral (Guinea-Bissau, 1974), Jomo Kenyatta (Kenya, 1963), Seretse Khama (Botswana, 1966), Kwame Nkrumah (Ghana, 1957), Julius Nyerere (Tanzania, 1961), Leopold Senghor (Senegal, 1960)
Caribbean	Chhedi Jagan (Guyana, 1966), Norman Manley (Jamaica, 1962), Eric Williams (Trinidad, 1962)
Middle East	G. A. Nasser (Egypt, 1952)
South Asia	M. K. Gandhi (India, 1947), Jawaharlal Nehru (India, 1947)
Southeast Asia	Sukarno (Indonesia, 1949)

postcolonial state did not need to be self-enforcing; hence, postcolonial leaders could gamble without establishing an exchange with the population. But
equally, the population did not have to supply the state and could always prefer
alternatives to it, which I will describe in Chapter 7, if the state failed to deliver
development. The gap between the demand for services and the supply of the
state in the postcolonial world emerged at independence; and alternatives to the
state preceded and constituted the postcolonial state.

The Colonial Non-Exchange

The impact of colonialism on the exchange between the central authority and
the population in the postcolonial world has been undertheorized in analyses
of state formation and international relations. This is partly because little attention has been paid to how anti-colonial movements reacted to colonial rule,
both being constrained by its effects but also breaking from it; partly because
scholars have been too quick to conflate anti-colonialism with nationalism and a
demand for a sovereign state;[13] and partly because the constitutive importance
of race and empire in pre-1945 international relations and state formation has
been neglected.[14] To properly theorize this requires examining the *lack* of an
exchange, or non-exchange, with the population in the colonial context.[15] The
population never preferred the colonial state to alternatives; it was imposed by
force, in a process Ranajit Guha has termed "dominance without hegemony."[16]
This non-exchange created novel challenges, first for individual natives seeking
to become political subjects, discussed in this section, and then for collective
movements, described in the next section. At its simplest, the experience of
colonial rule reduced the appeal of emulating the colonizer.

Nineteenth-century European states had developed through limiting wars in
Europe but relaxing those limits in the colonies. This drew on an understanding
of colonial populations as unequal to Europeans because they did not possess
a state. These, I have argued, were the parameters within which the costs of war
appeared manageable and facilitated state formation in Europe. The native was
hardly unaware of these parameters. Fanon stated the problem thus: "At the
risk of arousing the resentment of my colored brothers, I will say that the black
is not a man."[17] On the one hand, the native was a non-entity in the colonial

[13] Lawrence 2013.
[14] Vitalis 2010.
[15] Mbembe 2001, 186–189.
[16] Guha 1997, 24–30.
[17] Fanon 1967, 8.

order of things; as shown in Chapter 3, even when he fought, he was not a combatant due the rights of protection under the laws of war. There was no subject-position that simultaneously recognized the native's humanity and his specificity as a native: the native qua native was defined by what he was not and could not be.[18] On the other hand, to become a subject like the European, to prefer European customs to one's own, was to affirm and reproduce the very order that enslaved the native.[19] In the colony, there was no exchange as developed in Europe: the colonial power may have (occasionally) bestowed goods on the native, but the native could never claim those goods as a matter of right. The colonizer always retained the right to *not* recognize the native, no matter how much he tried to emulate the colonizer. C. L. R. James positioned his hero, Toussaint L'Ouverture, the leader of the Haitian Revolution, and his successor Dessalines, the first emperor of Haiti, on the two sides of this dilemma. For Toussaint, France and the Rights of Man were the model for building Haiti. But France would ultimately attack Haiti again and imprison Toussaint. Dessalines, on the other hand, rejected the French model and called all black Haitians to do the same.[20] As Shilliam nicely puts James's own view, "Toussaint was right . . . but Dessalines was not wrong."[21]

Over time, the native came to realize that this recognition would never be bestowed: Dessalines was mostly right, but his commitment to violence was too costly. Because of the racial categories that developed in the nineteenth century, even the native who committed to emulation was not recognized as European, meaning he could not make claims as a matter of right. The best the native could aspire to, and the goal of colonial policy, was to be a mimic.[22] Macaulay's infamous "Minute" on Indian education, for example, was designed to train "a class of interpreters between us and the millions whom we govern—a class of persons Indian in blood and color, but English in taste, in opinions, in morals and in intellect."[23] The subject of this class was split or alienated.[24] Biological markers like blood and color separated him irrevocably from the Europeans.[25] However, he had to separate himself from the other natives in order to serve his interpretive function. Fanon cuttingly described this denial of one's own customs: "The colonized is elevated above his jungle status in proportion to his adoption of the

---

[18] Fanon 1967, 110, 220; Said 1978.

[19] Mudimbe 1988, 183–186.

[20] James 1989, 286–288.

[21] Shilliam 2006, 400.

[22] Bhabha 1994, 89.

[23] Bhabha 1994, 87; Metcalf 1990, 22–23.

[24] Fanon 1967, 69, 112; Bhabha 1994, 43–45.

[25] Although, as discussed in Chapter 3, race and nation were frequently conflated in the nineteenth century; Bell 2007, 113–119.

mother country's cultural standards . . . . [H]e becomes whiter as he renounces his blackness, his jungle."[26]

To give another example, V. S. Naipaul's Caribbean narrator in *The Mimic Men* was schooled to believe that "to be born on an Isabella, an obscure New World transplantation, second-hand and barbarous, was to be born to disorder."[27] The native was unable to become a subject in any full sense. He could be a native, defined solely as the opposite of reason, civilization, and power.[28] Or he could be a mimic, "pretend[ing] to be real, to be learning, to be preparing [himself] for life" in the "true, pure world" that would always be denied him.[29] (The language of "purity" indicates the rigidity of the boundaries between races that developed in the nineteenth century.) The impossibility of being something other than native or mimic was testified to by the Indian nationalist Bipin Chandra Pal. Pal had become an Indian magistrate who

> had not only passed a very rigid test on the same terms as British members of the service, but had spent the very best years of the formative period of their youth in Europe. Upon their return to the homeland, they practically lived in the same style as their brother Civilians [i.e., British members of the service], and almost religiously followed the social conventions and the ethical standards of the latter. In those days the India-born Civilian practically cut himself off from his parent society, and lived and moved and had his being in the atmosphere so beloved of his British colleagues. In mind and manners he was as much an Englishman as any Englishman. It was no small sacrifice for him, because in this way he completely estranged himself from the society of his own people and became socially and morally a pariah among them . . . . [H]e was as much a stranger in his own native land as the European residents in the country.[30]

Here, as Macaulay intended, "to be Anglicized is *emphatically* not to be English."[31] And the effort also brought mockery, for "all that the colonized has done to emulate the colonizer has met with disdain from the colonial masters . . . . [T]hey explain to the colonized that all those efforts are in vain, that he only acquires an additional trait, *that of being ridiculous*."[32]

[26] Fanon 1967, 18.
[27] Naipaul 1967, 141–142; Memmi 1967, 120–121.
[28] Said 1978; Fanon 1967, 14, 93, 97.
[29] Naipaul 1967, 175.
[30] Quoted in Anderson 1991, 92–93.
[31] Bhabha 1994, 87, emphasis in original.
[32] Memmi 1967, 124, emphasis mine.

Nineteenth-century colonialism was represented as bringing a state to those who lacked one. Prior reliance on treaties and working through colonial inter-mediaries like commercial companies was overridden by force. Local interme-diaries were deemed unequal, and as far as possible, usurped.[33] By contrast, the European state emerged as an exchange: protection for extraction. The colonial state, in its existence and in its practices, therefore symbolized the native's inabil-ity to govern himself.[34] Never having possessed a state, the native required alien rule—what John Stuart Mill called "a vigorous despotism"—to educate him as to the requirements of governing oneself.[35] In 1839, former British Member of Parliament (MP) Edward Cust described the "fundamental principle" of "colo-nial dependence" as follows: "To give to a colony the forms of independence is a mockery; she would not be a colony for a single hour if she could maintain an independent station."[36] For the individual native chafing under the disdain of the European was the analogue, at a collective level, that to be recognized as an equal was entirely at the discretion of the colonizer.

Therefore, the parameters within which the exchange developed in Europe were predicated on two correlates in the colonies, essential for limiting the costs of war, and with it, state formation. The native who behaved like a native could not be part of the exchange developing in Europe; as I will detail in the next chapter, he was under the "despotism of Custom" and hence had "no history."[37] Nor could the native who picked up European habits. Neither behavior could guarantee recognition. The lack of exchange in the colonies lowered the costs of European state-building because natives could not make costly claims for rights and representation, despite serving in colonial militaries, and force could be used against them without limit (shifting these parameters to assert equal-ity would raise the costs of war, whether to grant the conquered more rights or limit the use of force against them, or to reward natives who had fought in colo-nial conquests). Thus Pal's individual frustration had an analogue at a societal level. Gandhi had initially pushed for a semi-autonomous India being included in an expanded British polity, but by the 1920s he pushed for independence as he came to understand that the British would never treat Indians as equals.[38] Similarly, West African leaders initially imagined being part of a communauté including France, but as they realized that individual Africans would not receive equal rights, they pushed for independence.

---

[33] The process of replacing local systems of rule was partial, and divided sovereignty lasted long into the nineteenth century; e.g., Mamdani 1996; Lewis 2013.

[34] Guha 1997, 65.

[35] Quoted in Bhabha 1994, 137.

[36] Quoted in Bhabha 1994, 85.

[37] Mill 1975, 66.

[38] Gandhi 1938, 15.

How could the native become a man? One option was to compel the European to recognize him through force. This was what Haiti did in the early nineteenth century, and non-European monarchs in Egypt and China had sought to do so by importing European military techniques in the eighteenth and nineteenth centuries.[39] Right into the twentieth century, some Islamic anti-colonial activists sought to form alliances with the Japanese to violently challenge European rule.[40] But, as we will see below, the costs of such an approach were understood to be formidably high. The second option was to rely neither on force, which was too costly, nor recognition from the European, which would not be forthcoming anyway. The point missed in theories of international relations and state formation is that emulation was *not* an obvious choice in the postcolonial world. To emulate was to affirm the colonial logic that natives had neither state nor history, and they could not ever have these things without becoming European. But even the latter effort depended, in the last instance, on recognition from Europeans, a recognition that historical experience suggested was not likely to be forthcoming. Given this, Fanon cautioned against trying to emulate:

> In no way should my color be regarded as a flaw. From the moment the Negro accepts the separation imposed by the European he has no further respite, and "is it not understandable that thenceforward he will try to elevate himself to the white man's level? To elevate himself in the range of colors to which he attributes a kind of hierarchy?" We shall see that another solution is possible. *It implies a restructuring of the world.*[41]

Fanon's statement had two implications: first, it was necessary to rethink the racialized parameters within which the European exchange had developed; second, evaluating the costs of war in view of these altered parameters might have led to different decisions from those that nineteenth-century figures like Dessalines and Mazzini had made. Did anti-colonial leaders do either or both?

Parametric Shift (or Why War No Longer Makes States, Part 2)

The quest to rethink the parameters within which European states developed began with confronting the question of emulation. As Gandhi explained, responding to the question, "why ape the West?"

[39] Ralston 1996.
[40] Esenbel 2004.
[41] Fanon 1967, 81–82, emphasis mine.

To make India like England and America is to find some other races and places of the earth for exploitation. So far, it appears that the Western nations have divided all the known races outside Europe for exploitation, and that there are no new worlds to discover. Among the exploited, India is the greatest victim. . . . But if India and China refuse to be exploited, what will happen to the exploiters? And if the Western nations plus Japan are likely to come to grief, in the event of India and China refusing to be exploited, what can be the fate of India trying to ape the West? Indeed, the West has had a surfeit of industrialism and exploitation. If they who are suffering from the disease are unable to find a remedy to correct the evils, how shall we, mere novices, be able to avoid them?[42]

Here, not only were the costs of war high for the colonized, but they were high for the colonizer too. Reproducing the European process of state formation, with its associated racial hierarchies, would only increase these costs further.

The exchange between central authority and population in Europe had developed through colonial conflicts and competition, predicated on a non-exchange in the colonies. Recognizing natives as equals due rights, and eventually services, would have increased the costs of the exchange and potentially reduced popular willingness in Europe to prefer it to alternatives and supply the state. In Gandhi's view and those of other anti-colonial leaders, these conflicts had proven hard to control and had ultimately undermined the exchange *in Europe*. To reproduce that process would be a mistake, and in any case, it required subscribing to racial hierarchies that the anti-colonial movements had contested. War and conquest were understood to be too costly to form the rationale for the institution that would succeed the colonial state.[43] Certainly, this choice was constrained, in that conquest more generally was seen to be excessively costly, and the great powers were moving to prevent large-scale war. But acknowledging that the conditions of choice were constrained does not mean that anti-colonial leaders had no agency at all in choosing what postcolonial polities would look like. If they were mere mimics, we should have seen them uncritically reproduce the racialized thinking associated with European state formation, even if they lacked the material capacity to wage war.

Here I contrast my explanation with two others that stress the material weakness of postcolonial states and great power interference. In the first explanation,

---

[42] Gandhi 1965, 51, 84, 9, 51, 161; Gandhi, 1938, 30; Gandhi 1962, 11, 16.

[43] Marcus Garvey had made a similar point in 1922: "If white men continue to exploit yellow men, if white men continue to exploit black and brown men, if yellow men continue to exploit brown and black men, then all we can look forward to is a reign of wars and rumors of wars"; Garvey 1989, 31.

the lack of conquest in the postcolonial world resulted from postcolonial societies being materially weak or socially divided and not cohesive. This argument is theoretically flawed: material weakness should lower the costs of conquest and make it more likely.[44] As the number of states doubled between 1950 and 1975, and most of these states were materially weak, we should have seen a rise in the rate of conflicts breaking out. This did not occur; instead that period saw eleven wars—both balance of power wars and wars of conquest—less than half the average number of wars per twenty-five-year period in the nineteenth century (the average was twenty-eight).[45] Between 1945 and 1995, the number of interstate wars and armed interventions per state was a third of the level in the nineteenth-century European state system.[46] State weakness does not offer much explanatory purchase as a cause of war or the lack thereof.

The second explanation is that the great powers prevented postcolonial polities from engaging in war and determined the institutional choice of statehood. While there was certainly great power involvement, this argument exaggerates their influence. At a theoretical level, great power involvement could increase as much as prevent war, by supporting proxy wars, for example. Empirically speaking, if great powers prevented war, there would be more wars initiated in areas peripheral to great power competition, like Africa, and less where they were heavily involved, like the Middle East.[47] Again, this was not the empirical pattern. Rather than attribute the lack of war to absences—of material capacity and agency—in the postcolonial world, we have to take seriously the possibility that anti-colonial movements shifted the parameters within which the costs of war were calculated. The effect was to make the expected costs of war appear higher than in the nineteenth century, because war imposed costs on the colonizer as well as the colonized.

The view that centuries of war and empire had impoverished the colonized society and brutalized the colonizer as well was articulated by most anti-colonial leaders.[48] Azikiwe likened imperialism to "a boomerang . . . which ultimately destroys him who wields it."[49] Cabral encouraged Portuguese soldiers to leave

[44] If low material capacity is seen as lowering the costs of rebellion and making intrastate war more likely, surely the same mechanism means interstate conquest is also less costly.

[45] Wimmer and Min 2009.

[46] Holsti 1996, 23.

[47] There is no consistent relationship between bipolarity and the initiation of conflict in the postcolonial world; Miller 2007, 16.

[48] Similar views were articulated in Europe as well. During the Boer War, Herbert Spencer wrote that "the exercise of mastery inevitably entails on the master himself some form of slavery, more or less pronounced"; quoted in Gay 1993, 44. Later, George Orwell wrote of how playing the role of a colonial official in Burma revealed to him that "when the white man turns tyrant it is his own freedom that he destroys"; Orwell 2009, 8.

[49] Azikiwe 1937, 68.

Guinea-Bissau and overthrow the fascist dictatorship in Lisbon instead of serving "the interests of some rich families in Portugal, which have nothing to do with the true interests of your families or your people."[50] Nehru noted the similarities between imperialism and Nazism, which stemmed from deeper problems of Europe itself,[51] going on to say that "imperialism and the domination of one people over another is bad and so is racialism . . . but imperialism plus racialism can only lead to horror and *ultimately to the degradation of all*."[52] In almost identical terms, Nkrumah wrote, "Racialism not only injures those against whom it is used but warps and perverts the very people who preach and protect it; and when it becomes a guiding principle in the life of any nation . . . then that nation digs its own grave."[53] Norman Manley echoed Gandhi's argument that one could not solve the problem of "racialism" through emulating the colonial powers:

> The greatest danger that confronts the human race is race itself, and the patterns of thought that set race against race, and we despise South Africa and we despise Rhodesia. We should be proud to think that we can and must avoid copying them or the United States or England; the only difference being that we are on top and the whites underneath.[54]

Anti-colonial leaders identified the centrality of racial thinking and conflict in European development. To them, race and colonialism were not incidental to nineteenth-century European state formation and international relations.[55] Most of them concurred with W. E. B. Du Bois's sense that "it is this competition for the labor of yellow, brown, and black folk that is the cause of the present war."[56]

The colonial state embodied the lack of an exchange with the population, predicated on racial hierarchies, that led, inevitably, to conflict. In rejecting this, anti-colonial leaders had to shift the parameters within which the European exchange had developed. To gain popular support, they had to promise a different service than protection in war, for colonial populations had never received that protection anyway. This service could not require a high level of sacrifice from the population, already chafing under colonial rule. Finally, the institutional form within which this good was to be delivered had to differentiate itself from the colonial state in important ways.

---

[50] Cabral 1979, 164, 216.
[51] Nehru, 2004, 534, 603; Gandhi 1942, 15, 33, 40.
[52] Nehru 2004, 356, emphasis mine.
[53] Nkrumah 1961, 127; Fanon 1967, 36–38, 106–112; Azikiwe 1937, 199, 254.
[54] N. Manley 1971, 381.
[55] Nor was it to European and American observers of the time; Bell 2007; Vitalis 2010, 911.
[56] Du Bois 1917, 441.

To this end, anti-colonial leaders emphasized that war was not an ineluctable aspect of human nature, class struggle, or an inevitable effect of competition under anarchy, positions they associated with European thought. This was not self-serving: nineteenth-century thinkers from Hegel through Marx had posited conflict as being both the driver of history and as more or less unavoidable.[57] Around the turn of the century, this view of inevitable conflict was extended to racial and civilizational categories.[58] Anti-colonial leaders, however, rejected the inevitability of "race war." For them, the war-proneness of colonial powers stemmed from outmoded cultural and racial notions of superiority.[59] Where they persisted, as in South Africa and Rhodesia, these hierarchies posed the "threat of a racial explosion of unprecedented proportions."[60] Other leaders echoed Lenin's thesis of imperial war in their justification for rejecting capitalism and adopting socialism, or they suggested that Fascism was a natural outgrowth of European ideas of racial superiority that had long been in operation in the colonies.[61] But whatever the intellectual parallels, the idea that war was a European pathology implied that non-Europeans did not have to repeat the process of war and empire that had driven European state formation.

If war and empire were too costly and not worthy of emulation, so too was the state that had emerged through it. It might not be surprising that Gandhi proclaimed that "the state represents violence in a concentrated and organic form."[62] But even Nehru, now remembered as a statist, wrote that "the national state is too small a unit today and small states can have no independent existence . . . . [T]he national state is thus giving place to the multi-national state or to large federations."[63] Nkrumah argued that "it is now an indisputable historical fact that the creation of the small independent states in Europe provided the fertile soil out of which developed the national jealousies, dissensions and disputes which culminated in the First and Second World Wars."[64] Nkrumah's dismissal of the creation of new states in eastern Europe is puzzling; surely these were the results of movements contesting the Austro-Hungarian and Ottoman empires.[65] We might have expected Nkrumah to *support* this previous process of "decolonization." That he did not is not a historical misreading but consistent with his and other's diagnosis that the European state that developed through

---

[57] Gay 1993, 529.
[58] Lake and Reynolds 2008, 49–113.
[59] E.g., Azikiwe 1937, 274–277.
[60] Khama 1980, 162–163.
[61] Nkrumah 1963, xiii; Nehru 2004, 534, 603.
[62] Gandhi 1962, 64–65.
[63] Nehru 2004, 591.
[64] Nkrumah 1961, 201.
[65] Neuberger 1976.

war was self-undermining.[66] The replacement of empires by national states on the European model was not always the goal of the anti-colonial movements; popular support for anti-colonialism was not the same as popular willingness to supply the state. In fact, the national state was anticipated by anti-colonial leaders *as likely to be incapable of fulfilling the challenges of independence even if war could be avoided.*

This concern about the viability of actually existing political units and communities promoted a wide range of institutional visions. Consider the disagreement between Gandhi and Nehru. Gandhi's vision for independent India was a society of self-sufficient "village republics" organized around local or "cottage" industries and agriculture.[67] He contrasted this to Nehru's focus on "industrialism" and inveighed "God forbid that India should ever take to industrialism after the manner of the West."[68] Nehru vociferously disagreed with Gandhi's economics, fuming that "for a country to do away with industrialization would lead to that country falling prey, economically and otherwise to other more industrialized countries."[69] As a preference for industrialization was shared by most postcolonial leaders, this necessitated larger polities to maximize economies of scale and bargaining leverage in international politics. These "larger polities" might have led to shared jurisdictions and policy coordination, as industrialization was understood to be hard to achieve on one's own. Norman Manley explained the need for the Caribbean Federation, which included a customs union and some common services like shipping, as "we must create a large enough area, small although it will be in the face of the colossi who bestride the world today, but a large enough area to give us a voice."[70]

The challenge of independence was not political survival or territorial aggrandizement. War had come to be understood as too costly and conferring no benefits on the colonized. This shift from nineteenth-century understandings elevated a different good as the basis of an exchange with the colonized population. Writing in *Foreign Affairs* nine years before Indian independence, Nehru signaled this: "The vital and most important problem that faces us in India is the appalling poverty of the people.... [W]ill political independence help us diminish this, as well as the numerous ills that flow from it?"[71]

This elevation of the economic as the promise of anti-colonialism was repeated often. Nehru wrote in a private letter that the anti-colonial movement,

---

[66] And, relatedly, should caution against conflating anti-colonialism and nationalism, as Lawrence points out; Lawrence 2013.

[67] Gandhi 1962, 54.

[68] Gandhi 1962, 29.

[69] Quoted in Gidwani 2008, 86.

[70] N. Manley 1971, 166, 163–170.

[71] Nehru 1938, 231.

far from "moving the masses in a revolutionary sense," had merely aroused the "sympathy but no more" of many and would lose even this if it did not develop into an economic program.[72] Others articulated some version of the view that "national liberation, the struggle against colonialism, working for peace and progress—independence—all these are empty words without meaning for the people, unless they are translated into a real improvement in standards of living."[73] Nyerere went as far as to say that "we must have economic development or we have no political stability."[74] This alternative vision of international order and its purpose endured, for example, in Jamaican Prime Minister (and son of Norman) Michael Manley's statements a decade apart that "the fundamental rationale of third-world politics is economic," and "the rationale of the Third World is the search for economic answers."[75] Development, at inception, implied a gap between the demand for services and the population's ability to support the institution that would deliver development.

Independent postcolonial states, especially small ones, would not be viable in the world economy: they could not deliver the services the population demanded. Leaders saw decolonized states as too small, facing disadvantageous terms of trade and with populations lacking the necessary capital and skills. The population, in other words, could not supply the state or any other institution capable of delivering development. Thus postcolonial leaders needed to reach outside for assistance, and articulate common interests in regional and transnational forums or face "neocolonialism."[76] Michael Manley, recalling the failure of the Caribbean Federation of the 1940s and 1950s, noted a continuing need for a regional grouping of Caribbean states to articulate jointly a policy for trade and foreign capital. He called for a "common economic diplomacy in which, to put it at its simplest, the Caribbean must be as concerned about the fate of Ghana's cocoa as Ghana should be concerned about the fate of Caribbean sugar."[77] This extended his father Norman's argument from a little more than a decade previously:

> Even Europe has been compelled to unite for industrial, trade and commercial reasons and to form a thing called the European Common Market . . . [Y]ou go down to Central America and those little republics there—they have been forming a customs union and a common market among themselves. That is the pattern of development for the future.[78]

---

[72] Quoted in Gopal 1976, 148.
[73] Cabral 1979, 241; Nkrumah 1962, xv, 43, 45; Kenyatta 1968, 213; Khama 1980, 82.
[74] Nyerere 1974, 73.
[75] M. Manley 1970, 109; M. Manley 1982, 65.
[76] Jagan 1966, 402; Williams 1993, 287.
[77] M. Manley 1970, 109.
[78] N. Manley 1971, 172.

These alternatives foundered for contingent and structural reasons. When asked to support these alternatives explicitly, like the vote on the Caribbean Federation in 1961 that Jamaicans rejected, the population showed itself unwilling to pay the costs. At a structural level, this revealed that popular support for anti-colonialism was limited to supporting an outside option that reduced extraction and repression, not a commitment to supply the state or another institution that would compel sacrifice. Put another way, the population had supported the anti-colonial movement to reduce extraction and repression and receive services they had previously had to provide for themselves. They had not rallied in support of a new institution that would extract and repress. The failure of the Caribbean Federation did not mean that the population would supply the Jamaican state, a small, poor state in unfavorable market conditions.

Independent statehood needs to be seen as one of several possible institutional arrangements, none of which could compel the population to sacrifice more than the colonial state already had. From the second quarter of the twentieth century, the colonial powers had an alternative to independent statehood—namely, various forms of dependency in which the colonial power would continue to offer tutelage to the colonized.[79] The effort to deny equality to non-white polities, often neglected in international relations scholarship, was a persistent theme until the middle of the twentieth century. At Versailles, the "Anglo-Saxon nations" led by Great Britain opposed a Japanese preamble to the convention asserting "racial equality."[80] After the Second World War, Soviet efforts to amend the Declaration of Human Rights to allow "self-determination" for colonial peoples were defeated in 1948 and 1950, and a narrowly phrased resolution passed in 1952, against the opposition of Western states, who with the exception of Greece, voted against it.[81] This resistance persisted into the 1960 Declaration on the Granting of Independence to Colonial Countries, for which the United States, supporting its allies with colonies, abstained from voting.[82] British officials envisioned a hierarchical system in which the Indian government remained within an expanded Commonwealth, following from the Home Rule negotiations in the 1930s that promised Indians some representation.[83] Maintaining the empire after 1945, specifically imperial trade preferences, was crucial for Britain's plans to repay its war debt.[84] As I noted above,

---

[79] E.g., the French scholar Paul Mus, who advocated independence for Vietnam but a continuing role for France in reconstruction; Said 1993, 208–209.

[80] Lake and Reynolds 2008, 299–302.

[81] Voeten 2011, 265–266.

[82] The vote was 89 for, 0 against, and 9 abstentions (United States, United Kingdom, France, Spain, Portugal, Australia, Belgium, South Africa, and the Dominican Republic).

[83] Gopal 1976; Spruyt 2005.

[84] Steil 2013, 190–192.

right until the 1920s, Gandhi was sympathetic to some type of dependency.[85] Similarly, Senghor was keen on the option of a layering of sovereignty that left West Africa within the French Union.[86] Within a hierarchical system, functions such as security could be contracted out to the colonial power, as in Egypt, where formal independence had been granted in 1922 but British troops remained on Egyptian soil.[87] For a brief period, the United Nations was mandated to supervise territories under the "trusteeship system," the successor to the League of Nations' mandate system.[88]

In the long run, such arrangements foundered as neither anti-colonial leaders nor their populations trusted the colonial powers to treat them as equals. But this did not mean the postcolonial state had done away with alternatives to the state, especially alternatives that could serve as outside options to challenge the state. In the absence of costly war, brought about by the anti-colonial movements, alternatives to the state that commanded loyalty among a section of the population could not be stamped out of existence without provoking resistance. This was consistent with the origin of anti-colonial movements that were transnational *before* the articulation of nationalist goals or the adoption of the national state.[89] Anti-colonial leaders were influenced by metropolitan ideas but also drew on the ideas of their peers. Intellectuals like Rabindranath Tagore had sought to found a pan-Asian movement since the late nineteenth century.[90] African-American luminaries like Du Bois, who organized the 1919 Pan-African Congress,[91] and Marcus Garvey were prime movers in pan-African movements; Garvey's United Negro Improvement Association (UNIA), with its nearly million members, called for Africa for the Africans and petitioned the League of Nations to govern Germany's African colonies (as did the 1919 Pan-African Congress in a resolution).[92] For the UNIA, it was not territorially determined citizenship, but holding shares in the UNIA shipping company, the Black Star Line, that constituted the pan-African political community.[93] Many African leaders had interacted in Europe with American and West Indian intellectuals such as C. L. R. James, George Padmore—Nkrumah was hosted by Padmore

[85] Gandhi 1938, 15.

[86] Burbank and Cooper 2010, 422–423; Lawrence 2013, 2, 231.

[87] They left only after Nasser, who led a coup against the monarchy in 1952, began negotiating their withdrawal in 1954; Nasser 1955, 199–200; Young 2001, 188–190.

[88] Kay 1967, 787–788.

[89] Young 2001.

[90] Duara 2001; Esenbel 2004; Mishra 2012.

[91] Du Bois actually revived the Pan-African Congress, which was initially established in 1900 by Sylvester Williams, a West Indian lawyer, and an African American minister, Alexander Walters, again revealing the transatlantic nature of African anti-colonialism; Shepperson 1960, 306.

[92] Mazower 2012, 165; Shepperson 1960, 308.

[93] Shilliam 2006, 397–399.

on James's introduction in London, and Padmore later served as an advisor to Nkrumah—and Aime Cesaire, and they had participated at the various pan-African congresses, in a community Gilroy has termed "the black Atlantic."[94] In West Africa and South Asia, several decolonized states emerged from the same anti-colonial movement.[95] Cabral had collaborated in the establishment of the Angolan People's Movement for the Liberation of Angola (MPLA), which informed his own organization of the African Party of Independence of Guinea and Cape Verde (PAIGC) in Guinea-Bissau.[96] The connections went beyond alliances of convenience to mark a collective sense of self from which individual subjectivity could emerge. As James emphasized, "The road to West Indian national identity lay through Africa."[97] Leaders identified national goals with broader communities. In his speech declaring the nationalization of the Suez Canal, for example, Nasser declared that as a consequence of his actions, "the Egyptian people are fully conscious of their sovereign rights and Arab nationalism is fully awakened to its new destiny."[98] The post-independence order was never just a statist order because, in the absence of costly war, the population could always prefer an alternative to the state.

Analyzing fifty years of state weakness after decolonization, scholars have come to argue that postcolonial states are artificial creations, meaning that their borders were arbitrarily drawn by colonial powers with little regard for preexisting group boundaries and therefore fundamentally weak at inception.[99] It is common knowledge now to talk of, as a recent *New York Times* feature on unrest in the Middle East put it, "the inherent instability of the Middle East's artificial states."[100] A more sympathetic view identifies the inability of the postcolonial state to forge enduring ties with its public.[101] I am arguing that insofar as postcolonial states are "artificial," it is because popular support is tenuous, and anti-colonial leaders were fully aware of this.[102] This fear drove them to articulate alternatives to the state as necessary for meaningful independence.

Anti-colonial leaders anticipated that the postcolonial state, in the language of this book, would not be self-enforcing. The Senegalese intellectual Cheikh

---

[94] Gilroy 1992, 1–40.

[95] Cooper 2005, 225–230.

[96] Young 2001, 283; Davidson 1969, 31.

[97] James 1989, 402.

[98] G. A. Nasser, "Speech on September 15, 1956," available at http://www.fordham.edu/halsall/mod/1956Nasser-suez1.html.

[99] Clapham 1996; Holsti 1996; Herbst 2000; Wimmer 2013.

[100] Scott Anderson, "Fractured Lands: How the Arab World Came Apart," *New York Times Magazine*, August 10, 2016.

[101] Davidson 1992, 291.

[102] This implies that presumably "natural" states—the opposite of "artificial" states—in Europe and North America can also experience a waning of popular support.

Anta Diop's verdict that "the days of the nineteenth-century dwarf states are gone . . . . [O]ur main security and development problems can be solved only on a continental structure and preferably within a federal framework,"[103] was echoed by many leaders. We have seen Nehru, for example, cast doubt on the prospects for survival of European-style states and the European state-system.[104] African and Caribbean leaders frequently voiced skepticism as to whether their independent states could remain sovereign in anything other than the juridical sense.[105] Nkrumah and Kenyatta opined that for African states to achieve sovereignty in the meaningful, that is to say, economic, sense, and avoid "neocolonialism," they had to work in concert and ideally as a collective.[106] Equally, because of anti-communist leaders like Houphouet-Boigny of Cote d'Ivoire who maintained strong ties with the ex-colonial power, or domestic groups receiving support from the great powers, like Forbes Burnham in Guyana, a lack of unity created the possibility that postcolonial states would be co-opted by "neo-colonialists" in a repetition of divide and rule.[107] As late as 1946, Mohammed Ali Jinnah rejected the offer of what would become Pakistan *a year later* as "a mutilated and moth-eaten state," preferring a federated South Asian structure including Hindu- and Muslim-majority states, with some functions like defense and communications being centralized.[108] Larger polities and transnational groupings were more than the idle speculations of intellectuals and dreamers; they foreshadowed future difficulties for postcolonial states to align the demand for services with popular willingness to sacrifice—what we now call state weakness.

Disagreements on institutional arrangements reflect the difficulty in compelling popular support after independence that anti-colonial leaders expected. When the French instituted a referendum in 1958 in individual territories, offering a choice between independence and the withdrawal of aid or maintaining a dependent relationship with France, Senghor opposed independence and criticized Guineans, led by Sekou Toure, for voting for it.[109] Senghor's logic was that retaining a federal West African polity linked to France would allow this larger grouping to claim independence from France later, while establishing independent states would prevent a West African federation from emerging and lead to "the division of Africa into units too small to challenge European states."[110]

---

[103] Diop 1978, iii.

[104] Nehru 2004, 591–592.

[105] E.g., Nkrumah 1962, 33; Nkrumah 1963, 173–193; Nyerere 1968, 378; Diop 1978, 15; N. Manley 1971, 165, 167, 172.

[106] E.g., Nkrumah 1961, x–xi, 217–218; Nkrumah 1963, 132–149; Kenyatta 1968, 215.

[107] Fanon 1967, 192; Jagan 1966, 404, 403–424.

[108] Jalal 1990, 21–22.

[109] Walraven 2009, 271.

[110] Neuberger 1976, 524; Cooper 2005, 228.

Others wanted the federal West African polity to stay in a reformulated relationship with France.[111] On the one hand, the largest possible polity would give the average inhabitant of Dakar the best chance of development.

On the other hand, the inability to deliver development might motivate the average Dakar resident to demand secession into even smaller polities. As Immanuel Wallerstein characterized the latter possibility "Every African nation ... has its Katanga."[112] Of course, as East Timor or Bangladesh or Kashmir indicated, the problem was not just an African one nor limited to small states. The danger was that Senegal (or Indonesia or India) was neither big nor effective enough to deliver the "meaningful" economic independence the anti-colonial movements had promised, nor small enough to satisfy ethnic or linguistic particularity. Anti-colonial leaders did not just conflate political independence with the promise of economic development; they understood that the latter was necessary for continued public support, given that they had eschewed war-making. Nkrumah was not alone in arguing that independence and sovereignty were "milestone(s) on our march to progress .... [I]ndependence by itself would be useless if it did not lead to great material and cultural advances by our people."[113] Camus, arguing against an independent Algeria that did not include French settlers, had said more or less the same thing: "A purely Arab Algeria would not be able to achieve economic independence, without which political independence is not real."[114]

The choice to pursue economic development instead of war and conquest was the product of learning that the costs of colonialism were unacceptably high and could not be repeated. This choice was endogenous to European state formation, the experience of which had reduced the likelihood of its own replication. It did not mean that interstate war was impossible in the postcolonial world, merely that postcolonial polities would not be organized to engage in the types of costly but winnable war that had yielded centralized states in Europe. This implied, from the start, an expectation of a lower level of extraction and sacrifice from the population. At the same time, making sacrifices in war would not be the means by which the population made claims for services. Because they were foregoing the process through which an exchange, even if a self-undermining one, had developed between central authority and population in Europe, anti-colonial movements entertained the possibility of various institutional arrangements

---

[111] Lawrence 2013, 160–164.

[112] Quoted in Neuberger 1976, 525.

[113] Nkrumah 1961, 109.

[114] Camus 2014, 177. For this reason, Camus supported the Lauriol Plan, a federal scheme in which the French colonies would receive expanded representation in Paris, creating "two categories of equal but distinct citizens"; Camus 2014, 182, 181–184.

other than a state. These alternatives to the state, however, could not compel popular sacrifice either, and in the face of this, postcolonial leaders faced a challenge: how to deliver development when the population was unwilling or unable to contribute to it?

Discipline and Develop

For Kenyans, an early indication that the institutions of the colonial state were not going away came in Jomo Kenyatta's speech on Independence Day. After asseverating in English for the benefit of the attending duke of Edinburgh, Kenyatta switched to Swahili:

> Another point, my brothers, is this: do not think that, because there is no longer a Colonial Government, there will no longer be need to respect the country's laws. The laws of the country will remain; the Police and Prisons will remain.[115]

This statement encapsulated a salient fact: despite all the talk of federations and village republics, postcolonial polities became states and saw an increase in the size and scope of the state after decolonization. Ranajit Guha, one of the most perceptive observers of colonialism, saw the postcolonial state and its practices as materially the same as the colonial state, only differentiating itself through nationalist narratives that valorized the role of elites.[116] I will suggest that despite the continuities—namely, that neither state was self-enforcing—there was an important difference between the colonial and postcolonial state in what it promised the population. If the colonial state was a non-exchange where the population had no rights,[117] the postcolonial state was a gamble that the population could be developed by top-down action.

Anti-colonial leaders had promised to deliver economic development to their populations rather than war and conquest. The need for development, however, stemmed from a colonial understanding of that population as unable to contribute meaningfully to development, even if they expected it. Guha has described the contempt Indian leaders, including Gandhi, articulated for their publics.[118] This contempt was not unique to Indian anti-colonialists. For

---

[115] Kenyatta 1968, 216.
[116] Guha 1997, 101–102. On the African case, see Young 1994.
[117] This is not to say that the colonial state was never developmental but that any developmental initiative was discretionary, not because it was owed to the population.
[118] Guha 1997, 139.

anti-colonial leaders, European rule had not just impoverished the colonized in material terms, but it had also robbed them of their ability to organize their own society through divide-and-rule policies and racial doctrines that emphasized the inferiority of the natives.[119] Colonialism had "sapped the strength and moral energies" of Egyptians according to Nasser; Nkrumah said it had made Ghanaians "lethargic."[120] Kenyatta in 1948 had urged Africans to "eschew idleness" and "get rid of our reputation for robbery and theft."[121] Even more damning, for Nehru, than reputations ascribed by foreigners was the very *fact* of colonial rule, which revealed the degeneration of Indians: "It seems clear that India became a prey to foreign conquest because of the inadequacy of her own people and because the British represented a higher and advancing social order."[122] Azikiwe termed the inability of 150 million black persons to rule themselves evidence of "racial devolution."[123] Gandhi summed up anti-colonial leaders' diagnosis of native failure when he said that Britain had not taken India, "we have given it to them."[124] (That the colonized had "given" up power to the colonizer also indicated the inadequacy of precolonial traditions and institutions—the caste system in the Indian case, "superstition" in the African—and precluded a return to them.) Anti-colonial leaders castigated the colonial powers for the distressing material condition of the colonized, with good reason—life expectancy had not improved in the colonies even as it had increased in Europe between 1850 and 1950—but also blamed the colonized for letting this happen.[125]

Given this "devolution" and "inadequacy," postcolonial leaders declared that "economic answers" could not come from the formerly colonized in their traditional economic activities or as they engaged in private enterprise.[126] Rather, the population—their economic choices and everyday habits—would have to be transformed, by force if necessary. Postcolonial leaders generally represented their populations as passive objects to be acted on, not subjects acting for themselves. Nasser offered a representative example: "The standard of living of the masses must *be* raised, education *expanded* and social consciousness *developed* throughout the land so that the people will understand the duties and privileges

---

[119] E.g., Jagan 1966, 71–72, 329, 334.

[120] Respectively, Nasser 1955, 200; Nkrumah 1963, 50.

[121] Kenyatta 1968, 44, 53.

[122] Nehru 2004, 305.

[123] Azikiwe 1937, 172.

[124] Gandhi 1938, 31.

[125] Bourguignon and Morrisson 2002, 742; Deaton 2013.

[126] Therefore, these were not liberal, or individual-rights based movements, as has been argued in the international relations literature; Philpott 2001; Reus-Smit 2013. For a detailed argument to this end, see Moyn 2010.

of citizenship."[127] The "people" did not understand "the duties and privileges of citizenship": they had to be *made* into citizens. The notion that people required leadership after independence was a repetition of the pre-independence idea that "before we can make real headway, we must train these masses of men who have a heart of gold, who feel for the country, who want to be taught and led," as Gandhi had said in 1920.[128] For anti-colonial leaders, the colonized were *behind the present,* "backward" in that they did not occupy the same time as either Europeans or anti-colonial leaders.[129] The fact of colonial rule revealed the colonized to have been backward in the past; the impact of colonial rule had made them backward in the present. It was left to leaders like Nasser and Nehru to bring them into the present *sometime in the future.* Until that future, however, the colonized were not capable of being participants in an exchange with the likes of Nasser and Nehru.

Postcolonial leaders saw their challenge as delivering economic development to an impoverished population incapable of contributing to the process until some undefined point in the future.[130] On the one hand, this was self-serving: the population had clearly participated in the anti-colonial movements so it could hardly be said to be incapable.[131] On the other hand, in the absence of war, the population was likely unwilling to sacrifice more than they already had for the colonial state, even as development meant a higher demand for services. As popular willingness to supply the state would be limited, postcolonial leaders implemented a series of decisions in which the population was unable to participate and which required a centralized power structure to implement. Hence, I liken the developmental state to a gamble that did not require popular cooperation, not an exchange. The push for alternatives to the state was countered by the immediate imperative of economic development.[132] Anti-colonial leaders expected to take and enforce unilateral decisions on behalf of their population once independence was achieved, as the following exchange between the American novelist Richard Wright and Nkrumah suggests. In visiting the then–Gold Coast in 1953, Wright was struck less by the visible material impoverishment and more by the "chronic lack of self-confidence" and the "cryptic

---

[127] Nasser 1955, 209, emphasis mine.

[128] Quoted in Amin 1995, 13; Guha 1997, 100–151.

[129] Fabian 1982.

[130] Development, from the point of view of postcolonial leaders as much as Western aid agencies, as Ferguson pointed out, was "depoliticized"; J. Ferguson 1994.

[131] Fanon 1963, 188.

[132] A more critical view is that anti-colonial leaders preserved the colonial state to hold on to power, much like the Communist Party did in the USSR. This was true in many cases, but even those leaders who accepted democratic institutions, like Nehru and Norman Manley, espoused similar centralizing tendencies.

servility" that colonial rule had inflicted on Africans.[133] When he shared his concern with Nkrumah, the latter did not really disagree:

NKRUMAH: The level of ideological development here is not very high.
WRIGHT: Uh hunh.
NKRUMAH: There are but two or three of us who know what we are doing.[134]

Wright spent the rest of his trip traveling Ghana and becoming even more convinced that his friend Kwame was correct in his diagnosis of the abilities of his compatriots. So, on leaving Ghana, he wrote Nkrumah a letter in which he urged the Ghanaian leader to "MILITARIZE" African life, not for war, but "to free minds from mumbo-jumbo."[135] And in this quest, Wright urged, the "*temporary discipline* that will unite the nation" could only be imposed by Africans, not through foreign assistance or aid.[136]

I have introduced Wright's argument at length because he offers a useful schematic for what postcolonial leaders actually did, namely, the gamble that characterized the postcolonial state. Nkrumah (and others) adopted one side of Wright's approach but not the other. Nkrumah, and other leaders, would implement top-down "discipline." The population was not able to participate as equals, and their inability to contribute would be compensated for through foreign assistance. Nkrumah summarized this logic by saying that "colonial rule precluded the accumulation of capital among our citizens which would have assisted thorough-going private investment in industrial construction . . . . [I]t has, therefore, been left to government, as holder of the means, to play the role of main entrepreneur in laying the basis of the national social and economic advancement."[137] Centralization of power—the postcolonial state—was needed to deliver development to a backward population. To this end, the postcolonial state would lead in economic planning and development programs (and restricting trade).[138] But it would also reach out to foreign powers and multilateral agencies for material and epistemic resources.

Two examples of planning reveal the process through which the role for the state was articulated around development rather than conquest.[139] Nasser described his regime's "clear-cut policy for rebuilding the country around new foundations": the High Dam at Aswan to increase agricultural yields; expanding

---

[133] Wright 2008, 134, 220.
[134] Wright 2008, 86.
[135] Wright 2008, 415, caps in original.
[136] Wright 2008, 415, emphasis mine.
[137] Nkrumah 1963, 119; Nkrumah 1958, 53; Nasser 1955, 204–208.
[138] Senghor 1964, 160; Nyerere 1968, 142, 358; Williams 1993, 267; Nehru 2004, 435–444.
[139] On planning as the rationale for the state in India, see Chatterjee 1993, 200–205.

industrial production; and addressing the trade deficit.[140] Each project involved an elevated role for the postcolonial state. The High Dam project involved resettling large numbers of individuals (often coercively); boosting industry required centralizing and coordinating the allocation of capital through a "national Board of Production" and an Industrial Bank; to address the trade deficit, the regime would engage in the "elimination of illicit practices," which in practice involved some expropriation of wealthy landowners and monopolies, and limited redistribution of land.[141] Similarly, when Nehru broached the range of issues in independent India that need to be "jointly and centrally directed," he included defense, defense industries, transport, communication, economic planning, customs, currency, exchange, even air services.[142] A wag might note that after *this* list, Nehru may as well have stated something like "and if we need all that, we may as well come out and say we need a state." Irony would be superfluous:

> Thus we arrive at the *inevitable and ineluctable* conclusion that . . . *a number of important and basic functions of the state must be exercised on an all-India basis* if India is to survive as a free state and progress . . . . [T]he alternative is stagnation, decay, and disintegration, leading to loss of political and economic freedom, both for India as a whole and its various separated parts.[143]

In Egypt and India, the establishment or restaging of the state began indirectly: there were many functions that could not be provided by the population, impoverished as they were, and it was impossible to coordinate these functions without centralization.[144] The anti-colonial movements promised development rather than conquest. But for this, they needed an *expanded* state, not a minimal one to provide policing and limited defense. Market forces were seen as attenuated; hence, costs like education were to be internalized by the state rather than externalized on individuals. This was consistent with the logic that to gain popular support, the anti-colonial movements had to promise a higher level of services but not a higher level of extraction (if they did, the population could prefer alternatives).

The state envisioned by postcolonial leaders was exactly what Gandhi had feared and inveighed against, writing that "centralization cannot be sustained and defended without adequate force."[145] Indeed, sometimes colonial-era

---

[140] Nasser 1955, 204, 204–207.
[141] Nasser 1955, 207; Mitchell 2002, 43–44.
[142] Nehru 2004, 593.
[143] Nehru 2004, 593–594, emphasis mine.
[144] Gidwani 2008, 93–94.
[145] Gandhi 1962, 52.

institutions and practices were necessary to implement development, even at the risk of provoking popular anger. Postcolonial leaders acknowledged the irony when they, for example, retained the bureaucrats from the colonial civil service. The reader will recall that these bureaucrats, in Macaulay's design of Indian education and Bipin Chandra Pal's anguish about his situation as such a functionary, were educated to be removed from and disdainful of their native societies. So how could they continue to implement policy, and govern at a remove from their compatriots even after independence? Nehru explained that the increasing role of these functionaries was largely unavoidable because of "the fact that our other human material, with a few exceptions, [is] very poor."[146] Similarly, Nkrumah retained the bureaucrats because he feared the "possibility of a situation of instability which would enable Britain and other colonial powers to point at us the finger of scorn and gloat over the disastrous effects of handing over self-government 'prematurely' to Africans."[147] The retention of colonial institutions within the postcolonial state essentially flipped the narrative of the anticolonial movements: once stagnant and therefore deserving of their subjection by the colonial state, the now-independent population needed the state to avoid stagnating and losing its freedom all over again. This role for the state stemmed from the anti-colonial leadership's sense that the population could not supply the state at independence. So who would do so?

Contra Wright's admonitions to eschew help from the West, Nkrumah would write in *Foreign Affairs* that "the leaders of the new Africa have no alternative but to look for outside assistance."[148] In the same journal three years prior, Nasser had noted receiving assistance from the United Nations and the United States for agricultural schemes.[149] It is more than a metaphor that Nkrumah and Nasser asked for aid in a journal that in 1910 had been founded as the *Journal of Race Development*.[150] My point is that anarchy and the interstate system emerged from a transnational context where empire, hierarchy, and race predominated. These hierarchies facilitated popular willingness to supply the state in Europe and North America, and diminished it elsewhere. From inception, postcolonial polities relied for their development—the basis for satisfying popular demand for services—on a collaborative relationship with the outside world. The imperial

[146] Quoted in Gopal 1980, 36.

[147] Nkrumah 1963, 89.

[148] Nkrumah 1958, 53.

[149] Nasser 1955, 205.

[150] Vitalis 2010; Mazower 2012, 165. Like *Foreign Affairs* today, the journal was not a hotbed of racist or discriminatory writings. Among the contributors while it was titled the *Journal of Race Development* was W. E. B. Du Bois (1917). The title merely shows the centrality of racial and civilizational themes in international politics at the time.

system within which European states developed was war-prone because imperial competition intensified commitment problems. The transition away from
that system endogenously reduced the risk of conflict because the role of the
state and its relationship with other states was transformed. The parameters
within which the costs of war were calculated for anti-colonial leaders were very
different from those for nineteenth-century Europeans. The racial categories
that had contained the costs of war were unacceptable; consequently, the costs
of war were seen to be far higher. In appealing for help in *Foreign Affairs*, anti-
colonial leaders were articulating a new role for the postcolonial polity, one that
required collaborative rather than antagonistic relations with the outside world.
By eschewing costly war, anti-colonial movements abjured precisely the conditions in which the exchange could be self-enforcing and the population would
supply the state at a high level. As this was a reaction to how Europe had developed, the lack of a self-enforcing exchange in the postcolonial world, or the prevalence of weak states, is endogenous to European state formation.

This shift coincided with new ideas and policies in Europe and North
America. The idea that "development" was a distinct object of analysis emerged
in the 1950s.[151] John Kenneth Galbraith recalled that when he was beginning
his doctoral work in 1949, "as a different field of study, the special economics
of the developing countries were held not to exist . . . . [I]n the next fifteen years
in the United States these attitudes were decisively reversed."[152] The economist
Wolfgang Stolper would write of his work with the Nigerian government in 1963:

> Economic development of underdeveloped countries, as this is under-
> stood today, is a concept of relatively recent origin. Of course, there was
> no deliberate policy of development in Nigeria around 1900 or 1910;
> but then it was not considered the proper role of government to pro-
> vide economic development at home either.[153]

Similarly, the policy of foreign aid for economic development, as Hans
Morgenthau observed in 1962, was a novelty in the West.[154] "Development
economics" and foreign aid were absent from the parameters conditioning the
exchange that developed in Europe.

Consequently, what happened in the postcolonial world was the opposite
of European state formation. In Europe, state organization was initially military
organization. Leaders extracted domestically, establishing an exchange with the

---

[151] Cullather 2010, 6–7.
[152] Quoted in Escobar 1995, 57.
[153] Stolper 1963, 398.
[154] Morgenthau 1962, 302.

population, to engage in interstate conflict. In the postcolonial world, leaders signaled they would not wage interstate war and would instead pursue development to extract from foreign sources, which reduced the need to tax the population and bargain with them.[155] This was noted by development economists at the time: W. Arthur Lewis estimated that 20 percent of GDP was required to pay for the services that "underdeveloped countries now demand for themselves," but tax collections lagged this number.[156] The composition of the tax take also indicated lower reliance on the postcolonial population: the primary revenue sources were rarely income and sales taxes, but excise taxes, especially in Africa.[157] Income taxes were on a narrow base, and taxation at a local level was neglected. This was understandable—for the center, the cost of collecting taxes on poorer people at a local level probably exceeded the benefit and would provoke discontent—but also revealed an unwillingness to decentralize taxation and service provision to local levels.[158] The tax ratio in postcolonial countries was thus similar to or slightly higher than that in Europe and North America prior to the world wars, but taxation was more centralized. However, as I showed in Chapter 5, European states prior to 1914 provided very marginal public services outside of defense. Anti-colonial movements were therefore promising economic development that exceeded what those nineteenth-century polities delivered to their populations and which would require a higher level of extraction than most postcolonial states actually instituted.

How Things Could Fall Apart

While the restaging of the state in the postcolonial world mirrored aspects of the restaging in the West, such as the understanding that war was too costly and the focus on economic issues, there was a key difference. The war-making/state-making process in the West, even if had proved self-undermining, had created an exchange between the central authority and the population in which latter could make claims, and had led to a massive increase in taxation. The population, for a time, preferred

---

[155] Note here that whether foreign support was motivated by realpolitik or altruism, it ignored and often obscured the preferences of the population, so it could not substitute politically or informationally for a process of bargaining; J. Ferguson 1994, 254–267; Mitchell 2002, 209–234.

[156] Lewis 1966, 106. In 1963, the economist Nicholas Kaldor estimated that "underdeveloped" countries collected 8 to 15 percent of their GDP in taxes, compared with 25 to 30 percent in developed countries; Kaldor 1963. Between 1975 and 1998, the tax to GDP ratios for low-income and lower-middle-income countries were 13.9 percent and 17.5 percent, respectively; Teera and Hudson 2004, 796.

[157] Bates 2008, 99.

[158] Lewis advocated broadening the tax base, and believed that rural individuals needed to be taxed at a local level, with the money spent locally so they would be willing to pay; Lewis 1966, 116–118, 120–121.

the exchange to alternatives and was willing to supply the state in the face of costly war. By contrast, the postcolonial state, by eschewing costly war and focusing on development, was not compelled to establish an exchange with the population. Its promise of economic development, supported by foreign aid (and later debt), was something to be *given* by the state: it was a one-sided gamble that the state could deliver services before the population would prefer alternatives.

This created a self-undermining dynamic. The decision to pursue development without relying on a backward population occurred through promising the population a level of economic development that postcolonial leaders knew would be difficult to achieve in the best of conditions. They were not promising a return to pre-colonial polities or the nineteenth-century war-making European state, which had delivered very few public services. This difficulty would be compounded, almost to the point of impossibility, in small, independent states. On the one hand, the postcolonial state had to force a population "enveloped in darkness,"[159] into the modern world. On the other hand, to gain popular support to evict the colonizer, the anti-colonial movements had expanded the demand for services while reducing the ability of the postcolonial state to use force and demand sacrifices from the population. In the absence of costly war, the population could always prefer alternatives to the state if the postcolonial state failed to deliver services or engaged in excessive repression and extraction.

In the musician Frank Zappa's view, a "real country" needed at least "a beer and an airline." Postcolonial leaders may have held some variant of this belief because they created national airlines at the same time that they doubted whether their citizens could fly planes or afford tickets: in 1958, the Nkrumah government established Ghana Airways through a joint venture with BOAC, the precursor to British Airways, which would provide staff until Ghanaians could do those tasks. More generally, postcolonial leaders promised to develop a population they saw as backward. This was different from the colonial state, where natives were never expected to fly planes (quite literally in the case of the Allied militaries where South Asians and Africans performed menial roles); or the European state, where Europeans were expected to be pilots and passengers. Postcolonial leaders were promising to transform their populations into pilots and passengers through a top-down coercive process. This process drew on colonial institutions and help from the former colonial powers who possessed the capital and knowledge the population lacked. Postcolonial state-building was thus a one-sided gamble rather than a self-enforcing exchange. I now turn to why the gamble was self-undermining, namely, how state formation in the postcolonial world threw up alternatives to the postcolonial state that the population could prefer to widen the gap between the demand for services and the supply of the state.

[159] Azikiwe 1937.

7

Suffering Spectators of Development

Africa's postcolonial disposition is the result of a people who have lost
the habit of ruling themselves.

Chinua Achebe[1]

In the last chapter, I suggested that the postcolonial state should be understood
as a one-sided gamble to deliver development made on behalf of the population.
In delivering development, the postcolonial state would take on costs that had
previously been externalized on the population, sometimes sharing these costs
with foreign powers, further reducing the need to bargain with the population.
Thus, rights and development were to be given to the population, not claimed.
By contrast, the Euro-American state involved an exchange wherein rights and
entitlements could be claimed by the population due to their sacrifice in war.
The colonial state was one-sided as well, involving no mechanism for the colonized to claim rights, but none were promised either, so the colonial state could
be characterized as lacking an exchange at all.

The postcolonial gamble and the colonial non-exchange shared a common
understanding of the colonized as a creature, or a captive, of "custom."[2] For
nineteenth-century Europeans, custom was the "property" of the colonized, in
the dual sense that it was the possession of and was "proper" to the colonized.
Custom was the opposite of a legal order that allowed individuals to claim rights
and become subjects capable of governing themselves, that is, the opposite
of a state.[3] Custom varied by location. In India, it was caste that condemned
individuals to perpetual subjection; in Africa, tribe had the same effect; in the
Middle East, adherence to Islam imposed servility on the population.[4] The
colonized could not transcend their outmoded customs; they were inhabitants

---

[1] Achebe 2012, 2.

[2] I could have used the term "tradition" but for consistency with nineteenth-century usage, I use
"custom."

[3] Hegel 1967, 220.

[4] Respectively, Dirks 2001; Mamdani 1996, 51; Said 1978, 208.

of an "anachronistic space."[5] As anachronisms, they were to be conquered and brought into the future by truly historical subjects. John Stuart Mill epitomized this view:

> The greater part of the world has, properly speaking, no history, because the despotism of Custom is complete. This is the case over the whole East. Custom is there, in all things, the final appeal; justice and right mean conformity to custom; the argument of custom no one, unless some tyrant intoxicated with power, thinks of resisting. And we see the result. Those nations must once have had originality; they did not start out of the ground populous, lettered, and versed in many of the arts of life; they made themselves all this, and were then the greatest and most powerful nations of the world. What are they now? The subjects or dependents of tribes whose forefathers wandered in the forests when theirs had magnificent palaces and gorgeous temples, but over whom custom exercised only a divided rule with liberty and progress.[6]

On this, colonial and anti-colonial forces agreed: as we saw in Chapter 6, anti-colonial leaders were rarely complimentary of the customs that their compatriots were so beholden to, and that had made them vulnerable to conquest. Nehru, for one, approached India "almost as an alien critic, full of dislike for the present as well as many relics of the past that I saw . . . . [D]id I know India? I who presumed to scrap most of her past heritage?"[7]

Yet, for anti-colonial leaders, custom did not disqualify their compatriots from governing themselves in future because, in the name of these very "relics," the population had rebelled against the colonial power. Feeling their customs threatened by a foreign invader, illiterate peasants had mobilized, and in these multiple revolts lay the basis for self-rule. Indeed, Gandhi described the Congress as "essentially a peasant organization" despite the party's leadership coming from the upper and middle classes.[8]

Custom simultaneously justified the gamble—without development, the colonized would never be able to rule themselves—but could redound against the postcolonial state. Specifically, I will argue that custom was transformed, first, in the colonial period into a technology of governance, using new techniques

---

[5] McClintock 1995, 66. The view that Asia was "stagnant" developed from the 1760s onward, at the same time that a linear-progressive model of history came to be dominant in Europe; Koselleck 2004, 12; Osterhammel 2014, 68.

[6] Mill 1975, 66.

[7] Nehru 2004, 41.

[8] Hardiman 1981, 1.

like censuses that drew rigid boundaries around particular groups.[9] Then, in the postcolonial context, custom became a technology of rebellion, to articulate previously disaggregated local struggles to challenge the writ of the state. The categories of collective backwardness—custom, for short—necessitating the gamble can be used as outside options for the population, or sections thereof, to reject it. In the absence of costly war, the population in the postcolonial world periodically prefers these outside options, or alternatives to the state, to challenge coercion and extraction, and demand development. The effect is to reduce the supply of the state relative to the demand for services. More fundamentally, as the outside option—customary identities as rigid, exclusive categories—is a product of state formation, its exercise renders the postcolonial state self-undermining.

The Problem of Local Cretinism

When Gandhi called the Congress essentially a peasant organization, he acknowledged that it was the rural masses who had rebelled most frequently. Ranajit Guha noted 110 peasant uprisings in a 117-year span in India alone.[10] However, despite their frequency, peasant revolts, whether in India or elsewhere, had not amounted to a full-scale challenge to the colonial state (hence the official response to them considered them non-political—"those periodic outbursts of crime and lawlessness to which all wild tribes are subject"[11]—consistent with the analysis in Chapter 3). In the Zambezi Valley in what is now Mozambique, for example, between 1878 and 1904, only four years did not have some sort of rebellion or peasant revolt against Portuguese rule.[12] But not until 1917 did a united front rise that aimed to evict the Portuguese, a relatively weak colonial power, altogether.[13] This pattern held more broadly. Many of these colonial revolts are not included in datasets of insurgency. This is partly because of data limitations, but partly because the threshold for insurgency—1,000 battle deaths—was higher as a proportion of population in the nineteenth century (world population was 0.9 billion in 1800, 1.6 billion in 1900, and 6 billion in 2000).[14] Extant datasets and analyses underreport the frequency of colonial insurgencies. But despite their regularity, Guha noted, these revolts were "not

---

[9] Said 1978, 72; Appadurai 1996, 117, 114–135.

[10] R. Guha 1999, 1–2.

[11] This was a description of the Chuar rebellion in India in 1798; quoted in Guha 1994, 337.

[12] Isaacman 1976, 104.

[13] Isaacman 1976, 156.

[14] Esteban Ortiz-Ospina and Max Roser, "World Population Growth," 2016. Available at https://ourworldindata.org/world-population-growth/.

yet equipped with a mature and positive concept of power, hence of an alternative state and a set of laws and codes of punishment to go with it."[15]

Forms of peasant protest seemed to manifest this lack. Take, for example, collective opposition to land appropriation. One option was simply exit or maroonage, to move to another territory.[16] Another was to represent the appropriation as the decision of a mid-level official and revolt as a protest to the ruler.[17] Or there could be a revolt targeting and destroying symbols of rule, like land records. These were often conducted in the name of a deity, as when participants in the Santhal hool or rebellion insisted that they were not fighting, rather, the "Thacoor (god) himself will fight."[18] Of course, there were a variety of micro-level acts of resistance, from sabotage to shirking, but my concern is these three forms of collective protest and whether any aspired to found a new order. The first option, exit, neither challenged the existing order nor founded a new order. The second, customary rebellion, confirmed the existing order by investing greater responsibility in the ruler. The third, rebellion, was frequent and disruptive but short-lived; it did not challenge the existing order beyond imposing costs on it.

The peasants may have rebelled frequently, but they did not have "a mature and positive concept of power" that could sustain and aggregate their rebellion through alliances with a "supralocal" actor.[19] Rather, their rebellions foundered on what Trotsky had bemoaned as "local cretinism," "history's curse on all peasant riots."[20] Gramsci had made a similar point of Italy: "The southern peasants are in perpetual ferment, but as a mass they are incapable of giving a unified expression to their needs."[21] A Kwame Nkrumah, by contrast, did have a positive concept of power. He was a "supralocal" actor who could potentially forge alliances between local struggles. But Nkrumah was all alone—an "alien critic"—isolated among the colonial functionaries who did not see him as equal, and disdaining the "local cretinism" of his compatriots. Richard Wright saw in the contrast between backward peasants and the forward-looking Nkrumah the only alliance that could evict the colonizer:

> The only people who are solidly against the imperialists are precisely those whose words and manner of living had evoked in [a Nkrumah]

[15] R. Guha 1999, 166.
[16] Isaacman 1976, 98; Herbst 2000; Scott 2009.
[17] Guha 2000, 89–96.
[18] Quoted in R. Guha 1999, 28.
[19] Kalyvas 2006, 383, 381–386. Also see Christia 2012.
[20] Quoted in R. Guha 1999, 278.
[21] Gramsci 1957, 42.

that sense of shame that made him want to disown his native customs. They want national freedom, but, unlike him they do not want to "prove" anything. Moreover, they don't know how to organize. They are willing to join him in attempting to drive out the invaders; they are willing, nay, anxious, on the oaths of their ancestors, to die and liberate their homeland. But they don't want to hear any talk of ideas beyond that....[22]

Nkrumah had to provide a positive concept of power that could articulate localized acts of protest into a cohesive alliance against the colonizer. But this, after decolonization, would lapse back into a patchwork of disconnected and backward collectivities unless Nkrumah moved swiftly to free minds from "mumbo-jumbo."[23]

Wright's apprehension that what motivated popular support of the anti-colonial movements would fade quickly was echoed more broadly. Fanon wrote, "Nationalism, that magnificent song that made the people rise against their oppressors, stops short, falters, and dies away on the day that independence is proclaimed."[24] Nkrumah echoed him: "Independence by itself would be useless if it did not lead to great material and cultural advances by our people."[25] For "real" independence, the postcolonial state had to act on its public to develop them, as Nkrumah's counterpart Nyerere moved swiftly to do. During "villagization" in Tanzania, the Tanzanian government, confronted by "the traditional outlook and unwillingness to change"[26] of the peasants, collaborated with the World Bank to "persuade"[27] the peasants to move to "streamlined" villages. An official explained the imperative for this "persuasion" as follows: "Tanzania could not sit back seeing the majority of its people leading a "life of death." ... [T]he State had, therefore, to take the role of the 'father' in ensuring that its people *chose* a better and more prosperous life for themselves."[28] The people did not really *choose*, as they did not have the option to reject development; in this sense development was given to them. Hence I call the basis of the postcolonial state a one-sided gamble taken by the state on behalf of the population, not a two-sided exchange where both bargained and reached agreement on what development meant and how to pursue it. If Wright had told Nkrumah to "MILITARIZE"

[22] Wright 2008, 287–288.

[23] Wright 2008, 415.

[24] Fanon 1963, 203.

[25] Nkrumah 1961, 109.

[26] A Tanzanian civil servant, quoted in Scott 1998, 241, emphasis mine.

[27] The term is Nyerere's; Nyerere 1968, 357.

[28] Quoted in Scott 1998, 234, emphasis mine.

African life "for development, not war," Nyerere actually did so in 1973, mobilizing militia and regular troops in "Operation Planned Villages." The consequence, he announced proudly in 1976, was that "something like 70 percent of our people have moved homes in the space of about three years."[29] The force of the postcolonial state repeated a colonial understanding of the public—that their customs marked them as backward—but differentiated itself from the colonial use of force and the colonial regime's assumption that the backwardness was irrevocable, by gambling that it could bring the public into the present. The precedent of peasant protest, however, marked a warning that the postcolonial state's use of force could not last forever.

Wright, unlike some fellow travelers of the anti-colonial movements like Jean-Paul Sartre, had anticipated this possibility. He understood Nkrumah's task as a gamble with a significant downside. But he did not precisely explicate the nature, the enormity, or the persistence, of that downside. In his memoir, Chinua Achebe provides a better metaphor in his description of his father, a missionary, trying to convert Achebe's great-uncle, a chief in his own community. After the proselytizer's exhortations, the great-uncle pointed to his chief's insignia and asked what he was to do with it. The question of the insignia, in itself, was not important. But it stood in for the "awesome question" the great uncle "had essentially asked: what do I do to who I am? What do I do to history?"[30] Fifty-odd years prior, in *Things Fall Apart*, Achebe had fictionalized the same paradox, an African asking a missionary, "If we leave our gods and follow your god, . . . who will protect us from the anger of our neglected gods and ancestors?"[31]

The postcolonial state promised something different from either the African or Christian god. On the one hand, there was the promise of uplift, because the postcolonial state promised to develop its population, particularly those historically excluded, and bring them into history. The promise of uplift, however, required them to give up their customs—their history, their gods—for it was their customs that had marked them as subordinate. The customs of tribal forest-dwellers, who did not have written histories or scripts, had rendered them incapable of establishing states, for example.[32] A tribal was not capable of governing either himself or others. Hence, development meant transcending tribal customs.

Yet the very idea of the tribal in colonial and postcolonial ethnography was one of if not invented traditions, at least invented *boundaries*.[33] That is, while the

---

[29] Quoted in Scott 1998, 245.
[30] Achebe 2012, 13.
[31] Achebe 1958, 126.
[32] Clastres 1989.
[33] Oberoi 1994.

traditions or customs certainly existed—I am not claiming that tribe or caste did not predate colonial rule—and their practice enabled communities to differentiate themselves from each other, the boundaries between those communities in precolonial times were not as discrete or immutable as indicated in the ethnography of the time and as applied in technologies of governance.[34] Take the seemingly autochthonic tribal. First, tribal populations were not necessarily isolated; rather, they were enmeshed in trade networks and other forms of exchange.[35] Second, tribal populations moved, and therefore they were not autochthonous inhabitants of specific areas. In this sense, they were not indigenous.[36] Third, tribal populations intermixed to some degree, so treating them as entirely separate groups was misleading. Edmund Leach began his ethnography of highland Burma by describing a witness in a court case in 1930 who understood himself and his family as simultaneously belonging to two presumptively separate "racial" categories, Shan, who are Buddhist, and Kachin, who are not.[37] In Chapter 3, I suggested that nineteenth-century racial categories had very shaky biological foundations; if anything, the categories were even shakier in the colonies, where practices were conflated with race. Leach noted that these practices were fluid, which made efforts to identify fixed "racial" groups quixotic at best:

> It has usually been accepted as dogma that those who speak a separate language form a unique definable unit, and that this unit group of people has always had a particular culture or history . . . . [I]t is groups of this sort which are meant when we find reference to the "races" and "tribes" of Burma. This convenient academic doctrine does not relate to the facts on the ground. It can easily be established that most of these supposedly distinct "races" and "tribes" intermarry with one another. Moreover it is evident that substantial bodies of population have transferred themselves from one language group to another even within the last century.[38]

Similarly, the basic categories of caste and religion governing the census in India occasioned consternation for those administering it. In 1871, the author of the census report from the Northwest Provinces wrote that "the whole question of caste is so confused, and the difficulty of securing correct returns on this subject is so

[34] Bayly 2004, 223–227; Osterhammel 2014, 464, 608.

[35] S. Guha 1999, 40, 43–46; Comaroff and Comaroff 1991.

[36] And conversely, the groups they traded or fought with were not alien, as Tutsis were understood to be in Rwanda; Mamdani 2001a, 75.

[37] Leach 1964, 2–3, 229.

[38] Leach 1964, 48–49.

great, that I hope on another occasion no attempt will be made to obtain information as to the castes and tribes of the population."[39] The commissioner of the 1881 census in Punjab similarly would write of the difficulties in counting Hindus, Sikhs, and Muslims as distinct categories, saying that "the various observances and beliefs which distinguish the followers of the several faiths in their purity are so strangely blended and intermingled, that it is often impossible to say that one prevails rather than another, or to decide in what category the people shall be classed."[40]

The boundaries between groups in precolonial Asia and Africa had been "fuzzy," in Sudipta Kaviraj's term.[41] An individual could be a member of multiple communities at once—a linguistic community, part of a (often mobile) village, a religious group—and the boundaries between them were permeable.[42] This individual could be a subject of several sovereigns with overlapping jurisdictions. Or the individual and her community could escape the rule of any sovereign. But for the centralizing purposes of colonial governance, that individual had to belong to a community marked by exclusive characteristics that did not change over time. This was a parametric shift in the understanding of custom from a set of local adaptations with bewildering diversity to discrete characteristics that could be standardized and tabulated across local conditions. The move from fluid, and thus malleable, identities to fixed and unchanging ones mirrored a shift away from eighteenth-century understandings of physiology as malleable. Count Buffon, who attributed the backwardness of New World natives to the wet climate of North America, also maintained that an African child raised in Paris with French food and customs would see the color of his skin change to white.[43] While Buffon's was an extreme case, aspects of physiology like skin color were seen as alterable until the rise of racial categories in the nineteenth century.[44] (From the mid-nineteenth century onward, such race-mixing was seen to bring about civilizational decline.)[45] As colonial possessions came under the direct control of the metropole around the middle and end of the nineteenth century, "fuzzy" communities were transformed into rigid categories through colonial governing modalities like censuses, cadastral surveys, and separate electorates.[46] These communities, whose boundaries and permanence were constituted by

[39] Quoted in Dirks 2001, 202, 200–212.

[40] Quoted in Oberoi 1994, 9.

[41] Kaviraj 2010, 56–57.

[42] Indeed, as Owen Lattimore had noted of the Mongols, the permeability and lack of fixed characteristics was a means to escape state power; quoted in Scott 2009, 210–211. On similar phenomena among native American groups generally called the Plains Cree, see Asch 2014, 136–138.

[43] Seth 2010, 207–208; Osterhammel 2014, 858–860.

[44] Wahrman 2004, 83–117.

[45] Young 1995, 99–109.

[46] On how colonial rule fixed the category of caste in India, and Hutu and Tutsi in Rwanda, see, respectively, Dirks 2001, 3; Mamdani 2001a.

these new "enumerative strategies," should be understood less as a representation of reality and more as an effort to construct a governable, controllable, reality. But we must not forget that this effort was pervaded by error and an illusion of control.[47] I recall here Said's description of Orientalism less as an effort to represent the reality of India or Egypt, and more an effort to construct an object called India or Egypt that could be captured: "We need not look for correspondence between the language used to depict the Orient and the Orient itself, not so much because the language is inaccurate but because it is not even trying to be accurate."[48]

An example of a map from colonial India illustrates this attempt to construct an object that could be captured, and how it was frustrated. The Dangis, inhabitants of forests in Western India, took the names of their villages with them when they changed location, so in 1899, almost half of the village names in a British map from 1882 were in the wrong place![49] The broader point is that the tribal as a distinct community with a fixed address ("the indigenous") was a construction of the state, an attempt to fix a heterogeneous, mobile, (and often ungoverned) group within homogeneous, territorial categories.[50] This effort caused problems for colonial ethnographers, one of whom noted the difficulty of using language categories in the Burmese census:

> Some of the races or "tribes" in Burma change their language almost as often as they change their clothes. Languages are changed by conquest, by absorption, by isolation, and by the general tendency to adopt the language of a neighbor who is considered to belong to a more powerful, more numerous, or more advanced tribe or race . . . . Races are becoming more and more mixed, and the threads are more and more difficult to untangle.[51]

The slippage between tribe and race, both deriving from a third category, language, gives a sense of the miscoding at work here, and how now taken-to-be settled categories like ethnicity had much more fluid boundaries a little more than a hundred years ago.[52] In India, "caste" and "tribe" would be conflated

[47] Appadurai 1996, 116–117; Dirks 2001, 198–227.
[48] Said 1978, 71; Mitchell 1988.
[49] Skaria 1999, 56.
[50] Scott 2009, 238–261.
[51] Quoted in Scott 2009, 239.
[52] On how South Asian tribes were similarly (mis)coded in racial terms, with distinctions between upper-caste Aryans and lower castes or tribals with "Negroid" features, see S. Guha 1999, 10–29; Bhukya 2008, 105–106. One of the problems with contemporary analyses of ethnicity as it affects conflict and state formation and their starting point in the mid-twentieth century is that they

by nineteenth-century ethnographers.[53] This is similar to the "racial" categories in nineteenth-century Europe, where Irish and Jews, among others, were
not entirely white, and "race" and "nation" were often conflated, as we saw in
Chapter 3.[54] Language was not the only shared characteristic that could mark an
entire "tribe"; groups like the Meos in India were classified as a tribe based on a
common propensity to engage in crime (the so-called "criminal tribes").[55] The
category of the tribal was a colonial construction created in order to govern these
groups even though it effaced the complexity and fluidity of how they actually
lived. Despite the tenuous basis of these categories, they were adopted as marking distinct groups, knowable by their "customs"—language, ritual, profession.

Captives of custom, with their lack of writing and shifting cultivation, were
stateless and incapable of establishing states. From the mid-nineteenth century
onward, they were increasingly denied political and legal recognition as enemies
or allies, even when they had previously been recognized as such and had signed
treaties. This denial ignored the political aspects of custom, especially its anti-
statist potential. Shifting cultivation, for example, is a political as much as an
economic choice: it enables its practitioners to flee a polity where the basis of
extraction is sedentary agriculturists who can be located and taxed.[56] Exit from
the state, and statelessness more generally, need not mean the lack of political
community. Rather, statelessness can be an alternative to the state or "outside
option" as discussed in Chapter 2.[57] But statelessness was not interpreted as a
political act or consciousness in the colonial view of the noble savage and less
romantic notions like that of the criminal tribe.[58] Alternatively, anti-colonial
leaders would acknowledge that these were political communities, but only
incipient ones, precursors to modern, aggregated societies. They did have rights,
in contrast to the lack of rights under colonial rule, but these rights were to be
given on a collective basis rather than claimed by individuals. Both colonial and
postcolonial rulers ignored, or deemed irrelevant, the anti-statist aspects of custom and how it could enable exit and rebellion. Neither was self-enforcing, but,
given the understanding of the population as backward and unable to establish
an alternative order, colonial and postcolonial rulers did not expect to need a self-
enforcing exchange. They expected the non-exchange to persist unchallenged by

posit as exogenous categories whose emergence and consolidation are endogenous to conflict and
state formation.

[53] Beteille 1998, 187; Xaxa 1999.
[54] McClintock 1995, 52.
[55] Mayaram 2003, 130–142.
[56] Scott 2009, 190–196.
[57] Clastres 1989.
[58] Clastres 1989; Mayaram 2003.

Table 7.1 **Contrasting Exchange in West, Postcolonial Gamble, Colonial Non-Exchange**

	Rights	*Basis of mobilization*
Exchange (Europe)	Rights, to be claimed	Individual
Gamble (postcolonial)	Rights, to be given	Collective
Non-exchange (colonial)	No rights	None

a population used to despotism, or unable to coordinate large-scale rebellions, like the tyrannies theorized in Chapter 2 (Table 2.1). Table 7.1 summarizes the differences between the gamble in the postcolonial world from its European and colonial counterparts.

The colonial non-exchange was "under no obligation to the colonized and this latter is owed nothing by the state but that which the state, in its infinite goodness, has deigned to grant and reserves the right to revoke at any moment."[59] The exchange in Europe recognized the individual as a member of the population that could claim rights as a result of taxation and military service. The postcolonial gamble was a combination: it did not see individuals as capable of claiming rights, but it did promise to give rights to the population, understood in collective categories like the tribal. The colonial and postcolonial non-exchange, not being self-enforcing, could persist only until the population could organize to challenge it.

The postcolonial gamble sought to elevate the tribal above tribal status. The tribal, who may not have consented to the gamble conducted in her name, faced the risk of losing whatever community she possessed, backward though it may have been, and getting nothing in return. The Indian novelist Mahasweta Devi's historical fiction offers a series of suggestive metaphors for this dilemma. The journalist Puran Sahay travels to Pirtha, a famine-struck area predominantly populated by tribals. In Pirtha, he finds a tribal boy had painted a picture of a pterodactyl on a cave wall. Sahay is puzzled: how would an uneducated tribal know what a pterodactyl was? It turned out that an actual pterodactyl, a metaphor for the prehistoric condition of tribal India, visited the boy at night. When the pterodactyl died the boy buried him in a cave. Because of this tie to their past, and despite the desolation of the area, the tribals would not leave Pirtha. Sahay, in terms that recall Achebe, acknowledged their logic: "How can one rob a people of the supernatural, of myth, what is in their understanding an unwritten history, when the present time has given them *nothing*?"[60] But clinging to this unwritten history also had a strategic logic.

[59] Mbembe 2001, 35.
[60] Devi 1995, 178, emphasis mine.

As the postcolonial state promised development instead of war-making, the population was not expected to claim their right to govern, whether collectively or individually, but was to be *given* rights. Postcolonial leaders disdained both the content and form in which their population would make claims. To a degree now forgotten, anti-colonial and postcolonial leaders expressed concern about customary identities,[61] even (or especially) the customary identities like that of the tribal that could constitute a community that could contest the power of the postcolonial state. At its starkest, anti-colonial leaders were skeptical of nationalism itself for its divisive tendencies; Nkrumah, as seen in the last chapter, had been critical of the creation of new states in Europe for letting loose these tendencies.[62] It was therefore necessary to limit nationalism for, as Nehru put it,

> The nationalist ideal is deep and strong; it is not a thing of the past with no future significance. But other ideals, more based on the ineluctable facts of today, have arisen, the international ideal and the proletarian ideal, and there must be some kind of fusion between these various ideals if we are to have a world equilibrium and a lessening of conflict. The abiding appeal of nationalism to the spirit of man has to be recognized and provided for, but its sway limited to a narrower sphere.[63]

Nationalism, in this argument, was to be limited to a secondary sphere of public life (eventually to become irrelevant or transcended). If it was not, it would be a problem in the postcolonial era—what Fanon called the risk that anti-colonial unity "crumbles into regionalism inside the hollow shell of nationality itself."[64] There was the obvious fear of secessionism, which leaders like Azikiwe inveighed against, and against which violence was readily deployed.[65] More subtly, the forms of collective mobilization common in anti-colonial movements, from exit to rebellion to non-violent demonstrations, would be a hindrance after independence had been achieved. After independence, Nehru wrote in a letter, "I have almost come to the conclusion that it would be a good thing if we stopped all other work and concentrated on our economic and food policy and how to implement it with the greatest rapidity."[66] The reader will recall the elevation of

---

[61] This had precursors in Europe, where groups like the Bretons, who were seen as backward, were made into Frenchmen in a process akin to internal colonization; Weber 1976.

[62] Nkrumah 1961, 201.

[63] Nehru 2004, 45.

[64] Fanon 1963, 159.

[65] Azikiwe 1961, 102, 20, 114–115.

[66] Quoted in Gopal 1980, 97. In 1965, a US Agency for International Development (AID) report about food shortages in India would conclude, "The real threat to India is not invasion through the Himalayas [but] disintegration of the as yet fragile Indian state .... [E]conomic growth has become

"economic" concerns for other leaders discussed in Chapter 6. The irony of this was that political practices common to anti-colonial protest were castigated after independence by anti-colonial leaders. For example, Nehru criticized protests by Sikh activists using Gandhian methods of non-violent agitation as "absolutely wrong," and the strike as a practice whose "time is gone."[67]

Rather than make claims of their own through political processes, like the bargaining that had occurred in Europe or the anti-colonial movements themselves, the postcolonial population would be given development. The act of giving marked their present inability to supply the state, and the assumption that, barring occasional disruptions under the grip of custom, the population would cooperate with development programs. Development presumed backwardness—marked by custom—and posited that it could be overcome by the postcolonial state. As emphasized in the last chapter, this made the postcolonial state the active agent (and made development a costly proposition). But development was not guaranteed; despite the technocratic faith of postcolonial leaders in industry and planning, there was no certainty that their schemes would work (and indeed, they often did not). Development, as postcolonial leaders saw it, was an unavoidable gamble. But for the tribal, development was a gamble in which she had an existential stake—where she could lose her history and get nothing in return—taken by another. The tribal was not consulted on either the gamble itself or the form it would take—namely, industrial development with its associated environmental costs and neglect of rural affairs.

The gamble was predicated on colonial understandings of the population as backward and incapable of founding a state. In one sense, this was correct: the many insurgencies of the colonial period lacked a positive concept of power.[68] But in another, the very "customary" categories used for governance could be mobilized against the state because they could articulate a variety of previously short-lived uprisings into persistent insurgencies. The impoverished individuals in Pirtha could challenge the failures of development if they could link their struggles with other tribals. But they could only do so because of the categories developed during colonialism and then continued by the postcolonial state. The parametric shift transforming custom into a technology of governance— discrete boundaries between groups, unchanging group identities—also transformed custom into potentially a technology of rebellion that could ally previously unconnected groups waging local struggles. Custom raised the costs of state formation—as the state was now responsible for bearing the costs of

the test of political success" by which standard the postcolonial state "hasn't done well enough"; quoted in Cullather 2010, 217.

[67] Quoted in Chakrabarty 2007, 37.

[68] Scott 1977, 218.

developing the backward—and lowered the supply of the state, first, necessarily, because the population were seen as unable to contribute to development; second, contingently, when sections of the population mobilized under customary identities to challenge state power. The gamble underpinning the postcolonial state meant that the postcolonial state emerged as a polity where the demand for services exceeded the supply of the state right from the start, along with outside options that the population could prefer if the gamble failed.

The Weaponization of Custom

Postcolonial leaders understood the risks of organizing their societies for development. Nyerere, for one, had made the stakes quite clear: "We must have economic development or we have no political stability."[69] Mahasweta Devi put it more eloquently: "India makes progress, produces steel, the tribals give up their land and receive nothing . . . . . [T]hey are suffering spectators of the India that is traveling towards the twenty-first century . . . . [T]hat is why they protest."[70] Devi highlights three necessary conditions for tribal protest. First, the self-consciousness of being "tribal," an identity creating alliances between hundreds of geographically dispersed and linguistically diverse groups, in opposition to India; second, a sense of progressive historical time where they are stagnant spectators, and India is accelerating into a developed future; third, a claim to the land on the basis of being the "original inhabitant" that precedes India's possession of the land. All three—the self-contained "tribal"; the idea of progressive historical time; and the status of "original inhabitant"—are colonial constructions (or more precisely, categories of governance developed by the colonial state).[71] The tribal-India relationship potentially shares the same structure as the Indian-British relationship: a foreign occupier that has impoverished the colonized.

The window between independence and the accusation that the postcolonial state was a colonial occupier could be brief indeed. The Biafran insurgency began just seven years after Nigeria became independent. Achebe would later explain the rationale as "Nigeria needed to liberate itself anew, this time not from a foreign power but from our own corrupt, inept brothers and sisters!"[72] While noting the invocation of colonization, I will offer a slightly different interpretation of postcolonial insurgencies. On the one hand, I want to flag the concern of

---

[69] Nyerere 1974, 73.

[70] Devi 1995, xi.

[71] Scott calls this process "ethnogenesis"; Scott 2009, 255–259. As before, I emphasize that what is important about these categories is the exclusivity of the boundaries.

[72] Achebe 2012, 244.

anti-colonial leaders that small polities could not achieve meaningful independence. Nehru reiterated this point, saying of Naga secessionism, "I consider it fantastic for that little corner between China and Burma and India—a part of it is in Burma—to be called an independent State" and "to think in terms of Pakistan when the modern trend is towards the establishment of a world federation is like thinking in terms of bows and arrows as weapons in the age of the atom bomb."[73] Even successful insurgencies that establish a state will find it difficult to deliver services, and given that difficulty and the low probability that an insurgent movement will indeed be able to found a new state, it makes more sense to understand popular support for, and participation in, an insurgency as the exercise of an outside option against the state. The outside option, as theorized in Chapter 2, is useful for the population even if they do not share the insurgent leadership's goals because it reduces the state's ability to extract and repress.[74] So popular support for an insurgent movement need neither share the political goals of the leadership nor have the goal of establishing a new state, as Wimmer suggests.[75]

On the other hand, I want to avoid two tendencies dominant in political science: first, the tendency to see insurgencies as stemming purely from absences in the postcolonial world, such as the absence of state capacity or the lack of economic growth; and second, to see forms of customary identity as more or less invariant. These variables—low economic growth, state capacity, customary identity—appear exogenous to insurgencies. By contrast, I will suggest that low economic growth and state capacity were also true of the colonial state, where insurgency was common but short-lived, whereas customary identities were a product of efforts to manage colonial populations that have been reinvented in the process of insurgency and other contentious politics. These identities, after decolonization, simultaneously necessitated the gamble on development but also enabled the formation of alliances to challenge the postcolonial state. Insurgencies emerge as a consequence of state formation in the postcolonial world in contrast to how interstate war and empire drove state formation in Europe.

Most research on civil war and insurgency focuses on the period after 1946, so until recently, important changes in these conflicts between the nineteenth century, when colonial rule was expanding and becoming more centralized and less privatized, and the contemporary era have been missed.[76] The crucial change

[73] Respectively, quoted in Guha 2007a, 281; quoted in Pandey 1990, 242.

[74] I assume, in fact, that individual insurgents have diverse motivations for fighting, and often are driven more by local issues than the broader political cleavages underpinning the conflict; Kalyvas 2001, 102–109; Kalyvas 2006, 4–5, 91–104.

[75] Wimmer 2013.

[76] Exceptions are Lyall and Wilson 2009; MacDonald 2013.

between colonial and postcolonial insurgencies is that the latter are almost twice as long on average, and victories by postcolonial states over insurgents are less frequent than victories in the colonial period.[77] Scholars have noted that insurgencies after 1945 have lasted six to seven years on average,[78] but they have not contrasted this with the shorter insurgencies of the nineteenth century; hence, some of the generalizations about insurgencies are more conditional on the era in which they happen than currently appreciated. The contrast between the two periods is not purely the effect of a few extremely long insurgencies after 1945, for the median insurgency in the nineteenth century lasted less than two years, while since 1950, the median insurgency has lasted six years. Table 7.2 presents data for 143 insurgencies involving the primary European colonial powers in Asia and Africa, and insurgencies involving the decolonized states that followed.

Table 7.3 adds insurgencies involving the Austrian Empire, Russia, Japan, and the United States, including the Indian wars, to the insurgencies in the prior table, for a total of 178 insurgencies.

In both datasets, the mean and median insurgency length was lowest during the height of colonial expansion in the late nineteenth century.[79] By the second half of the twentieth century, insurgency length more than doubled (and the success rate for the incumbent diminished).[80] The length of an insurgency affects state capacity in at least two ways: extended insurgencies degrade infrastructure and make it harder to deliver public goods; they also increase tensions between communities and individuals who may not have been enemies prior to the fighting.[81] Further, the existence of insurgencies is indicative that the state is not self-enforcing, as insurgencies are to be expected in polycentric orders like empires, where there is no monopoly on violence. Understanding contemporary state weakness requires understanding why contemporary insurgencies are so enduring.

The extant explanations for the incidence of insurgencies since 1945—low opportunity costs for fighting because of poverty, the exclusion of sections of the population from political power, weak state capacity, a permissive international environment for weak states—cannot explain these changes.[82] Colonial

---

[77] A victory means that the incumbent, whether an imperial power or a state, eliminates the insurgent group. By this classification, stalemates where the group neither wins a military victory nor is eliminated are classified as defeats for the incumbent; Lyall and Wilson 2009.

[78] E.g,. Fearon 2004; Hironaka 2005; Balcells and Kalyvas 2014.

[79] Said 1993, 8.

[80] Balcells and Kalyvas argue that the success rate of post-1945 states is higher than the Lyall and Wilson dataset suggests, but these states still win at a slightly lower rate than during the colonial period; Balcells and Kalyvas 2014.

[81] Respectively, Ghobarah, Huth, and Russett 2003; Kalyvas 2006.

[82] Respectively, Collier and Hoeffler 1998; Wimmer 2013; Fearon and Laitin 2003; Hironaka 2005.

Table 7.2 **Insurgencies in Areas Colonized by Major European Powers, then Decolonized, 1800–2000**

Years of initiation	Number of insurgencies	Average duration (in years)	Median duration (in years)	Victory rate for state (%)
1800–1825	7	3.7	3	86
1826–1850	8	2.5	2	88
1851–1875	12	5.8	1	92
1876–1900	30	2.5	1	70
1901–1925	14	2.8	2	71
1926–1950	12	7.7	4	54
1951–1975	34	8.6	6	39
1976–2000	26	8.4	6	19

Source: Lyall and Wilson 2009

Table 7.3 **Insurgencies in Areas Colonized by Major European Powers, plus Insurgencies in Areas Occupied by Austrian Empire, Japan, Russia, and Indian Wars in North America**

Years of initiation	Number of insurgencies	Average duration (in years)	Median duration (in years)	Victory rate for state (%)
1800–1825	8	4.4	4	78
1826–1850	16	4.4	2	88
1851–1875	21	4.4	2	91
1876–1900	36	2.6	1	72
1901–1925	17	2.8	2	71
1926–1950	14	7.5	4	57
1951–1975	35	8.8	7	40
1976–2000	31	7.7	5.5	19

Source: Lyall and Wilson 2009

populations were impoverished and excluded from political power by definition. Colonial states were not strong states, relying on a range of intermediaries even as they sought to assert direct rule. Yet colonial states were able to swiftly subdue what we now know were frequent peasant revolts (put differently, these revolts in colonial states did not grow into long-running insurgencies). This was true even for a weak colonial state like Mozambique under the

Portuguese.[83] Why the difference? Why are insurgencies longer and more successful (or at least, less unsuccessful) after decolonization?

The shift between the colonial and postcolonial periods lies in the emergence of categories of governance, emerging in the late colonial period and continuing in the postcolonial era, which can be used to organize and sustain rebellions. Ranajit Guha wrote that colonial insurgents lacked a positive concept of power because their rebellion did not pose an alternative to the colonial state. They either defended their customs against encroachment from outsiders or appealed for redress to the customs themselves.[84] The fuzzy nature of custom in the precolonial and early colonial periods meant that while a range of violent local disputes continued, these disputes mostly did not metastasize into large-scale rebellion or inter-communal violence.[85] Put another way, participants in local disputes lacked the ability to form alliances with those outside their immediate vicinity and maintain their struggle. Custom, however, should be understood as operating at a local level and pertaining to a small community. So, while Hindu and Sikh peasants rose against Muslim landlords in nineteenth-century India, the lack of a pan-Indian Hindu or Sikh identity meant that the struggles stayed localized and were not part of a religious civil war across South Asia.[86] Communities were crosscut by a range of affiliations and consequently were not rigid and exclusive.[87] But when "customary" identities were wielded as exclusive and exclusionary, they could be used to articulate local struggles into a broader front. Consequently, the scale and persistence—not the incidence—of violence in the postcolonial period is largely an effect of colonial classifications of communities as mutually exclusive identities within a centralized state, which are then wielded against the state.[88] It is these "customary" identities, recent in origin, with their associated "positive conception of power" that account for the difference between colonial and postcolonial insurgencies. The move from "local cretinism" to enduring and trans-local rebellion is a parametric shift, beginning in the late nineteenth century, in the use of "customary identities" for purposes of governance. This shift enables local struggles to create alliances through newly exclusive categories.[89] To reiterate, it is the exclusivity of the categories

---

[83] Isaacman 1976, 35–39.

[84] Scott 1977.

[85] Kaviraj 2010, 57.

[86] Pandey 1990, 235–236, 241.

[87] For examples of religious syncretism, see Oberoi 1994; Mayaram 2003; Bayly 2004, 34, 43.

[88] For example, the first case of large-scale violence between Hutu and Tutsi occurred in 1959; Mamdani 2001a, 105.

[89] To be sure, the availability of foreign support for governments and insurgents also prolongs civil wars and reduces incentives for the combatants to bargain with the population; Kalyvas and

that is new, not the categories themselves: tribe and caste certainly predated colonial rule.

I will illustrate these claims through the example of forest-dwellers or Adivasis in central India and insurgencies occurring in this territory over the colonial and postcolonial periods. Adivasi means "original inhabitant." These groups account for around 8 percent of India's population (84 million people in the 2001 census), of whom approximately 70 million are in central India. "Development" statistics for Adivasis are dreadful: 50 percent live below the poverty line, 76 percent are illiterate, and 57 percent do not have access to safe drinking water.[90] They have been disproportionately affected by development projects like large dams: despite comprising only 8 percent of the population, Adivasis account for 40 percent of displaced persons in India between 1951 and 1990.[91] Finally, the Indian state has sold off forest land—land declared state property by colonial legislations like the Land Acquisition Act of 1894—for logging and mining, and most development projects intended for the Adivasis have not reached their intended beneficiaries.[92] The contemporary situation reflects persistent neglect: in the anti-colonial movement, Adivasis (then referred to as "tribals") were barely mentioned until the late 1930s.[93]

In the past two decades, large parts of central India have seen the rise of an insurgency by a group called the Naxalites. The Naxalites had first come to prominence in 1967 as a group of student radicals who moved from fomenting an uprising in rural West Bengal to engaging in urban terrorism. But that group had mostly been snuffed out by the 1970s. The contemporary manifestation of the Naxalites has fought a low-intensity but territorially widespread conflict currently in its second decade. In 2011, the Indian government estimated that Naxalites were active in 182 districts (28 percent of the total districts in India), of which 83 (13 percent) were "severely affected," meaning either under the control of the Naxalites or experiencing high levels of violence.[94] Between 2004 and 2011, the conflict accounted for 6,000 casualties.[95] The prime minister at that time repeatedly named the Naxalites the biggest threat to India's internal

---

Balcells 2010. However, foreign support is predicated on the prior existence of organized groups that can mobilize and forge alliances.

[90] Guha 2007b, 3306.

[91] Sainath 1996, 73.

[92] Sundar 2007, 251–257; Sainath 1996, 69–132.

[93] Guha 1996, 2376.

[94] Ministry of Home Affairs, November 22, 2011. Available at http://www.satp.org/satporgtp/countries/india/maoist/documents/papers/DATA_%20Extent_Naxal_Violence.pdf.

[95] These figures are from the Ministry of Home Affairs, available at http://www.satp.org/satporgtp/countries/india/maoist/data_sheets/fatalitiesnaxalmha.htm.

security. The duration and perception of threat are quite different from those of insurgencies in colonial South Asia, where the longest campaign lasted four years (the first Anglo-Afghan War) and rarely threatened the colonial state (with the exception of the 1857 Mutiny, and that too was a disaggregated struggle). The peculiarity is that Naxalites are active in areas and among tribal populations that had seen short-lived uprisings against the British as well, such as the uprisings now recalled as the Santhal hool (1855) and the Birsa Munda ulgulan (1900). In sum, in the areas in which the Naxalites operate, there has always been poverty, the population has always been politically marginalized, and rebellions have occasionally irrupted, but only recently has there been a long-lived insurgency. Why is the contemporary conflict so enduring and threatening?

The consensus explanation for why insurgencies break out—that the Indian state is too weak to police remote areas—is insufficient.[96] Material weakness is virtually a constant. Consider the Telengana uprising led by communists in then-Hyderabad state in 1948. The princely ruler, the Nizam, was unable to quell the revolt and asked for the Indian Army's protection, in return for which Hyderabad would join the Indian Union.[97] Using strong-arm tactics, the army repressed the rebellion in less than three years, so it is puzzling that a significantly more powerful Indian military has failed to achieve a similar result six decades later. Poverty and/or inequality as a predictor of insurgency is, again, relatively constant over this time period: tribal populations have consistently been poorer than other Indians.[98] The argument that the Adivasis rebel because they are excluded from political power is insufficient because tribals have always been marginalized: this would predict revolts in both colonial and postcolonial India but tells us little about why the contemporary revolts endure.[99] Finally, the international environment has had little constraining impact on the behavior of the Indian government, which has deployed significant force against the Naxalites, including mobilizing village militias, with little international sanction.[100]

The standard exogenous factors do not provide an adequate explanation for why this insurgency, and postcolonial insurgencies in general, are so much longer than colonial ones. Instead, we must look at the insurgents and their

---

[96] Fearon and Laitin 2003.

[97] Dhanagare 1974, 126.

[98] Income statistics during the colonial period are unreliable, but on at least one measure—famines—the colonial period was much worse, with several large famines in the Central Provinces between 1896 and 1900; Davis 2001, 141–175. By contrast, since independence there have been no large-scale famines in India.

[99] E.g., Wimmer 2013, 150–154.

[100] MacDonald 2013. Unlike the proponents of other insurgencies, which are often prolonged by foreign support, the Naxalites have not had such aid, suggesting that foreign support is not a necessary condition for prolonged rebellions, even if it is usually associated with them.

"positive concept of power." When we do so, it becomes clear that insurgencies are the tip of the iceberg of state weakness in the postcolonial world. The
organization of customary identities for governance has created enduring interest groups that operate as "outside options." Through these outside options, the
population can occasionally challenge the state violently, but more frequently
can make demands for private benefits and club goods, goods that can be
shared within a particular group but withheld from other groups. The exercise
of the outside option reduces the supply of the state and increases the demand
for services. Paradoxically, the outside option is a product of the state's efforts
to organize the population so they can be governed: the state has, in effect,
produced an alternative to it. For this reason, the postcolonial state is a self-
undermining institution.

The Indian Constitution commits to "safeguarding" the interests of
Adivasis.[101] As the term "safeguard" suggests, the state is to "give" rights and
goods to the Adivasis, whose backwardness makes them unable to "claim"
these for themselves. Consistent with the insights of colonial anthropology,
the Adivasis are understood as original inhabitants with their own distinct customs, centered on an unmediated relationship with the forests. The anthropol-
ogist and government advisor Verrier Elwin noted that contact with outside
groups had impoverished the Adivasis, and so the postcolonial state took on the
responsibility to protect the Adivasi from "expropriation from his agricultural
land and virtual serfdom under the moneylender."[102] To a greater degree than
the colonial state, which perceived these groups purely as encroachers on public forest land, the postcolonial state conceded them some rights to the land,
based on the idea that Adivasis were the original, pre-political inhabitants of the
forests.[103] The category of Adivasi has come to be written into practices of governance in India, including the census, affirmative action policies, and a recently
established Ministry of Tribal Affairs. This is an example of how the postcolonial
state has internalized the costs of protecting and developing Adivasis that the
colonial state did not incur. These constitutional protections notwithstanding,
Adivasi rights have often been violated as the state has sold off forest land to private interests or enclosed it as wildlife sanctuaries.[104] And while sizable resources
have been devoted to development programs for Adivasis, these have, for reasons of discrimination, poor design, and corruption, rarely reached the intended
beneficiaries.

[101] Guha 2007b, 3305.
[102] Elwin 1963, 14.
[103] Skaria 1999, 278.
[104] Damodaran 2006, 190–192; Guha 2007b, 3306.

These failures are highlighted by the Naxalites—for example, in a document titled "Party Programme":

> Vast majority of the adivasis have long been deprived of their land and other traditional means of livelihood without providing any alternative. The forest produce and mineral resources, which were traditionally in their possession, are being forcibly taken away by the imperialists, the CBB [comprador big bourgeoisie], the feudal classes, contractors, money lenders and usurers, unscrupulous traders, bureaucrats, and other exploiters mainly from outside, resulting in the disintegration of their traditional economy. The mining, quarrying, other industrial activity and building up of big dams devastated lives and livelihoods of the adivasis. Moreover, they have been neglected socially, culturally and politically.[105]

The Adivasis "traditionally" possessed forest resources, they have been exploited by "outside" forces, and they have been "neglected" by the powers that be. Such references to the backward condition of Adivasis are frequent in Naxalite documents. Two in particular bear emphasis. First, "the adivasis are still in the pre feudal production relationships."[106] Adivasis collect forest produce and engage in shifting cultivation, which could quite easily be interpreted by the Naxalites as an effort to flee state power and marking a political consciousness,[107] but they are represented as backward and pre-political. Just as the anti-colonial leadership saw peasant revolts as the inchoate desire for independence requiring leadership, so—the second reference—goes the Naxalite justification for the failure of colonial revolts, as explained by the Naxalite leader, Ganapathy, in his "theory of low-intensity conflict":

> In peasant revolts, in armed adivasi revolts and in 1857 first war of Indian independence, farmers, adivasis and artisans had not developed to provide a conscious leadership on their own. They didn't develop into a nation wide shape and character. These revolts had fought only for re-establishing the feudal system. Peasantry which is engaged in small scale production in backward economic system can't visualize a new society.[108]

---

[105] Party Programme n.d. Available at http://www.satp.org/satporgtp/countries/india/maoist/documents/papers/partyprogram.htm.

[106] Policy Programme of Janathana Sarkar 2004. Available at http://www.satp.org/satporgtp/countries/india/maoist/documents/papers/JANATHANA%20SARKARS.htm.

[107] Scott 2009.

[108] Ganapathy n.d., 23, emphasis mine.

Here, peasant and Adivasi revolts over history are local struggles against out-side encroachments on custom: customary rebellions that reaffirm the existing "feudal" order and are insufficient to reverse centuries of oppression. Ganapathy repeats the persistent idea that revolts, while important, lacked a "positive concept of power" as the basis of a "new society." In other words, Ganapathy's rhetoric echoes that noted big bourgeoisie Gandhi who had said popular dem-onstrations could not "procure swaraj [self-rule] for India unless regulated and harnessed for national good."[109]

Just like Gandhi and the Congress, it falls to the Naxalites to impose some vision of a new society rather than allow the Adivasis to exist as before. Essentially, Naxalites posit that they can achieve the development that the Indian state has conspicuously failed to deliver. For example, male and female Adivasis distill and consume alcohol, in contrast to upper-caste Hindus who prohibit alcohol consumption among women.[110] Under the logic that Adivasis spend too much money on alcohol, leaving them open to exploitation, the Naxalites have imple-mented anti-alcohol campaigns, including breaking pots of liquor in public (on a less repressive note, they have also introduced fish farming techniques).[111] Anti-alcohol campaigns have a historical lineage as a disciplinary tool in Indian anti-colonialism. Gandhi had urged the Congress to implement them, and during the Telengana insurrection in then-Hyderabad state, workers of the Communist Party of India initially collaborated with the Congress to cut down toddy (a palm from which alcohol is distilled) trees before realizing that this destroyed the livelihood of their own supporters.[112] Consistent with how the Indian state approaches the issue, the Naxalites cannot allow the Adivasis to remain Adivasi. So, for those Adivasi groups like the Gondis who do not have a written language, the Naxalites have sought to develop a script and even introduce textbooks in the language.[113] As the jailed Naxalite leader Kobad Ghandy points out, the fact that the Naxalites challenge the Indian state through violence should not obscure "the key question ... [of] how to develop the country and its people."[114]

As we saw in Chapter 5, the idea that poverty was not a natural phenomenon or a moral issue but a political problem to be solved by the state developed in the second half of the nineteenth century. These ideas were not extended to the col-onies until the anti-colonial movements highlighted the poverty of the natives as a failure of the colonial state, requiring independence. In 1880, the Indian Famine

---

[109] Quoted in Guha 1997, 139.
[110] Shah 2011, 1105–1106.
[111] Pandita 2011, 100–103.
[112] Dhanagare 1974, 122.
[113] Pandita 2011, 66.
[114] Ghandy, in Pandita 2011, 186.

Commission essentially rejected any idea that the parlous condition of the poor was the problem of the colonial state: "the doctrine that in time of famine the poor are entitled to demand relief . . . would probably lead to the doctrine that they are entitled to such relief at all times, and thus the foundation would be laid of a system of general poor relief, which we cannot contemplate without serious apprehension."[115] Nehru had castigated British rule in 1938, noting India's "grinding poverty, widespread illiteracy, a general absence of sanitation and medical relief" to conclude that "the very backwardness of a people is a condemnation of its government."[116] Seven decades later, Nehru's condemnation was wielded against the postcolonial state. Ghandy, for example, noted that 55 percent of India's population is poor by the UN's Multidimensional Poverty Index (Nehru's "grinding poverty"), 100,000 die of waterborne diseases annually, and only 34 percent of India's population has access to government hospitals (Nehru's "general lack of sanitation and medical relief").[117] Ghandy concluded his condemnation of the postcolonial state just as Nehru did his "condemnation" of the colonial state: "such then is the horrific condition of the people of our country—that too after six decades of independence . . . . [I]s it not time to discuss various alternate models to better the policies of governance?"[118] These three statements over thirteen decades—the first where the state takes no responsibility to prevent starvation, the second implicitly accepting that responsibility and extending it to education and medical relief, and the third extending that responsibility even further—show the extent to which costs previously externalized onto the population have come to be borne (or at least promised) by the state or alternatives to the state.

The postcolonial state and the Naxalites seek to give Adivasis, understood as a collective, rights they cannot claim for themselves. Both internalize costs that were previously borne by the Adivasis; indeed, they compete to offer the Adivasis more even as they do not expect the Adivasis to be able to contribute to their own development. The Adivasis remain an object to be developed, not a subject that can mobilize themselves, or individuals claiming their own rights. But is this accurate? While it would be incorrect to represent Adivasis as a monolithic group, it is worth highlighting two themes around contemporary Adivasi mobilization that suggest, at the very least, that Adivasi self-representation is consistent with how the state and Naxalites represent Adivasis. This self-representation is increasingly being used by Adivasis to

---

[115] Quoted in Davis 2001, 33.

[116] Nehru 1938, 232.

[117] Ghandy, in Pandita 2011, 187–189. Similarly, Ganapathy highlights that 77 percent of Indians live on less than 20 rupees (US $0.50) a day; e.g., Ganapathy, "No one can kill the ideas of Azad!" 2010. Available at http://www.bannedthought.net/India/CPI-Maoist-Docs/Interviews/Ganapathy-101108-Full-Final.pdf.

[118] Ghandy, in Pandita 2011, 189.

create alliances with other Adivasis waging local struggles. The consequence is that Adivasis are trying to preserve the category Adivasi as an outside option, unlike the postcolonial state and the Naxalites who are trying to eliminate Adivasis as Adivasis.

The first theme is the relatively new identity "Adivasi" as uniting a quite bewildering diversity of tribes under a common "indigenous" label.[119] In the 1980s, Adivasi activists began to participate in the UN Working Group on Indigenous Populations with the goal of being classified as indigenous people under emerging international norms.[120] Activists protesting the dam on the Narmada River in the early 1990s, for example, mobilized groups divided on caste lines under the slogan "Adivasi ekta zindabad" (long live Adivasi unity).[121] In early nationalist histories, Adivasi struggles were either downplayed or excised entirely.[122] To combat this, nineteenth-century uprisings like the Santhal hool are highlighted to create a consciousness of resistance over time.[123] The second theme is the concept of "diku" or outsider, which can be and has been wielded against Indian plains-dwellers as well as Europeans: in the 1930s, the first assertion of Adivasi identity in Chotanagpur coalesced against the anti-colonial Congress as diku![124] Historical evidence suggests that Adivasis were relatively mobile; they were not settled autochthons as colonial ethnography had it.[125] But representations of Adivasis attribute their impoverishment to wily outsiders—colonial intermediaries, plains traders—who have swindled them over time.[126] This is a parametric shift in how formerly mobile and disconnected tribal populations represent themselves within a pan-Indian collective as Adivasi, and part of a transnational community as indigenous. On this basis, Adivasis can claim land as "indigenous" against the Indian state, which claims that Adivasis are no more indigenous than other Indians.[127] Ultimately, the World Bank would cite this argument in withdrawing support for the Sardar Sarovar dam project in 1994.[128] The category "Adivasi" is a technology of protest, and potentially rebellion. It

[119] Skaria 1999, 277.

[120] Karlsson 2003, 415.

[121] Baviskar 1995, 180.

[122] Devi 1995, xi.

[123] Sarkar and Sarkar 2009, 14.

[124] Damodaran 2006, 184–185; Xaxa 1999, 3595.

[125] A similar process of colonial classification occurred in Africa, with the distinction between race and tribe; Mamdani 2012, 46–47.

[126] Hardiman 1987.

[127] Karlsson 2003, 407; also see Beteille 1998. Initially, nationalist scholars like G. S. Ghurye contested the claim that Adivasis were animists, arguing instead that they were "backward Hindus"; Guha 1996, 2383–2384; Bhukya 2008, 108.

[128] The Bank policy on projects that affect indigenous peoples—Operational Directive (OD) 4.20—was articulated in 1991.

articulates, through alliances, what would otherwise be local struggles against more powerful landowners and investors who have state support. This has several consequences for the Indian state, and postcolonial states in general: first, collective violence is more enduring than in the colonial period; second, the possibility of alliances from outside a locality may create incentives for local violence. More fundamentally, Adivasi mobilization suggests that the population, in the absence of costly war, will try to keep alive the outside option or alternative to the state. By remaining Adivasi, with its connotation of backwardness, Adivasis can demand services while not having to supply the state. Rather than a case of Adivasi customs surviving, Adivasis are surviving through custom.[129] The postcolonial state is always vulnerable to the exercise of these outside options, which reduce the supply of the state, from the customary group itself and from other groups who refuse to subsidize the former group, even as the demand for services increases.

Contemporary Adivasi mobilization, or Naxalite violence on behalf of Adivasis, is not customary rebellion, an appeal to the sovereign that stabilizes the existing order. In Bastar, an area where the Naxalites are currently active, there were several short-lived rebellions appealing to the king—indeed, the most recent one, in 1966 (i.e., after Indian independence), sought to bring the king back to power[130]—but the Naxalite presence in Bastar has lasted significantly longer and makes no appeal to customary authority. Such insurgencies mark an ongoing failure of the existing order by highlighting the inability to deliver development. They weaken the postcolonial state in ways that their predecessors did not weaken the colonial state. However, the marker of this failure—namely, the persistence of Adivasi backwardness—reinscribes the categories of the state even as it challenges them. Naxalites and Adivasis themselves use the term Adivasi within the connotations of custom, backwardness, and autochthony that the postcolonial state continued from the colonial period. Custom is preserved to be "weaponized" against the state, even though it is an artifact of the state.[131] This is the self-undermining basis of the postcolonial state, that on the basis of its own governing categories, its population can exercise their outside option and reject the gamble.

The weaponization of custom can be understood through a contrast with a historical moment discussed in Chapter 3. In 1813, Prussia first passed, then immediately rescinded, a decree requiring every citizen to resist invading armies with all available weapons.[132] The initial decree intended to channel the power

[129] Comaroff and Comaroff 2009, 19.
[130] Sundar 2007, 218–225.
[131] Xaxa 1999, 3589.
[132] Schmitt 2004, 29–30.

of the people armed, protecting their own homes and villages, against foreign invaders. The rescinding of the decree was an indication that the people armed were difficult to control because they could exercise their outside option in the service of local concerns and become, as Clausewitz feared, "something 'dangerous' which—so to speak—falls outside the sphere of the judicial state."[133] Instead of relying on militias, European rulers moved to constitute standing armies.[134] The Euro-American state, in mobilizing for costly war, could compel the population to give up their outside option. The postcolonial state has never been able to do so. In the absence of costly war, the population benefits from the ability to exercise an outside option. But, as I have argued, the outside option is a product of the postcolonial state and its promise of development. Challenges to the postcolonial state such as insurgencies are endogenous to state formation, not aberrations.

Anti-colonial leaders had anticipated this. Given the poverty of their people, they knew development would be difficult. Nkrumah expressed the difficulty and risk of failure:

> The leaders are now expected, simply as a result of having acquired independence, to work miracles. The people look for new schools, new towns, new factories. They *expect* political equality to bring economic equality. They do not realize what it may cost. In this situation, however poor the country, the new government cannot sit and do nothing. Construction must begin. There must be something to show for independence. And if there is nothing to show, popular discontent may split the country apart.[135]

"Expectations of order": Nkrumah promised development because anything less would destabilize the state. Development was elevated above the state—or more precisely, the continued existence of the state was predicated on winning the gamble on development. Development was expected to be costly because the postcolonial state had to take on costs the colonial state had not and the population could not. If it failed, the inability to deliver development would be laid against the state and the population would exercise their outside option. The outside option would only disappear if the population were no longer bound by custom—if Adivasis, for example, became industrial workers. If custom persisted, the postcolonial state could be castigated just as the colonial state was. It did not need disgruntled Biafrans or Naxalites to make the theoretical argument

---

[133] Quoted in Schmitt 2004, 31.

[134] Tilly 1992, 46.

[135] Nkrumah 1958, 51, emphasis mine.

that colonialism had not ended with independence; the term "neo-colonialism" was coined by none other than Kwame Nkrumah. Nkrumah used it to castigate his enemies, but could be turned against him, or any postcolonial leader, as the Naxalites have done.

The postcolonial state is thus self-undermining in a way that the colonial state, which made no claim to develop its population and saw frequent insurgencies as non-political, was not. The self-undermining basis of the postcolonial state lies in, first, the categories of governance, based on customary identities it inherited from the colonial state, and second, the gamble that it had to develop these collectivities bound by custom into modern subjects, which imposed costs that the colonial state did not bear. This created the incentive for mobilization on the basis of these customary identities. These mobilizations preserve the customary identity, if in reinvented form, and articulate a range of local struggles into, at worst, enduring challenges to the state, and at the very least, constant demands for services that exceed the willingness to supply the state.

The Postcolonial Gamble

The Euro-American state emerged as an alternative to monarchical regimes through a process of bargaining, what I have called an exchange between the central authority and the population. But what drove the exchange in Europe and America—interstate war and colonial conquest—was to be eschewed in the postcolonial context and replaced by development. This can be seen in two previously discussed statements (in Chapters 3 and 6 respectively). Cecil Rhodes urged the British government to resettle poor Britons in southern Africa to avoid civil war in Britain; Julius Nyerere advocated economic development if "we are to have political stability." Rhodes's statement punctuated a process of war and bargaining that led to the sudden expansion of public services in Britain after 1900. By contrast, Nyerere promised to deliver at least a simulacrum of the public services only recently introduced in the West, without the process of bargaining (and the sudden rise in taxation after 1900) that war and empire had necessitated. As Nyerere anticipated, the lack of development would undermine the postcolonial state. But, and this Nyerere did not anticipate, the gamble, rather than the exchange, that development was predicated on would itself prove a point of contention. It could be represented as a repetition of colonialism, a failure to realize an alternative to the colonial state. Across the postcolonial world, welfare indicators have improved since colonialism— to give just one example, disparities in life expectancy between European and non-European states increased between 1820 and 1950, and have subsequently diminished[136]—but insurgencies have been lengthier than under colonialism and, more important, have represented the postcolonial state as similar to a colonial power. This paradox illustrates expectations, not the reality, of order. Insofar as insurgency is linked to state weakness, "weakness" should be understood less as a material condition, because "weak" postcolonial states wield more coercive power and deliver more to their citizens than colonial states ever did, and more as a structural feature of the postcolonial state, namely, that it emerged by promising more services than it could compel the population to supply. Contemporary state weakness is function of "expectations of order" rather than material shortcomings.

Equally, the continued salience of "customary" identities is an artifact of the modern state. These identities enable collective action, whether to access goods from the state or to fight against it. They enable the articulation of local struggles through alliances into an enduring challenge to the state, in contrast to colonial-era revolts that stayed localized or appealed to customary authority. Put another way, local struggles are a constant over history; the variable is the emergence in the late nineteenth century of fixed customary identities that enable alliances that can sustain enduring civil wars or make continuous demands on the state. The "weakness" of the postcolonial state stems from two historical developments that portend future struggles: five decades-plus of minimal bargaining (often facilitated by foreign support); and the strengthening of outside options that challenge the state or make demands on it. This history should lead us to reject theoretical models in which the population should prefer the central authority to secure property rights or protect against predators.[137] The postcolonial state fifty years after decolonization is not a benign entity in popular memory or experience! The postcolonial population's "priors" are, first, that centralization is a gamble that has more often than not failed;[138] second, there exist outside options that can be used to insure against the gamble. These priors militate against giving up the outside option and paying a high level of tax to the central authority. I will argue in Chapter 8 that ignoring this logic has led to the failures of state-building ventures in the last two decades.

In conclusion, we can revisit the historical relationship of the stateless and the state. Pierre Clastres wrote that "the history of peoples without history is the history of their struggle against the State."[139] Stateless peoples only entered into history when they challenged the state. Even then, as we saw in Chapter 3,

---

[136] Bourguignon and Morrisson 2002, 742; Deaton 2013.

[137] E.g., Bates 2008; North, Wallis, and Weingast 2009.

[138] At an individual level, as Gupta points out, postcolonial subjects encounter the state not as a unified entity but as a bureaucrat or office that is often arbitrary and seldom accountable; Gupta 2012.

[139] Clastres 1989, 218.

their resistance was understood as crime and madness, and they were denied recognition as combatants.[140] This is no longer possible. Rather, the previously stateless draw on the categories of the state—custom and development—as an outside option that can articulate a range of local struggles into alliances against the state. Contra James Scott, I would argue that the modern state has not overcome the resistance of the stateless.[141] What we now see is not a history of the stateless against the state but a proliferation of claims against the state on the state's terms. A year before his death, Chinua Achebe lamented that contemporary Africans had lost the ability to govern themselves. It seems fairer to say that the postcolonial gamble denied them the opportunity to govern. In the absence of that opportunity, they and others in the postcolonial world have preferred to exercise their outside option against the state.

[140] Guha 1994.
[141] Scott 2009, xii.

8

Full Circle

A nation without a national government is, in my view, an awful spectacle.

Alexander Hamilton[1]

A society in captivity must produce an illegal literature because it must know the truth about itself, see an unfalsified picture of itself, hear its own genuine voice. The existence of illegal literature is a prerequisite for the fight against captivity of the spirit.

Adam Michnik[2]

In 1999, Vaclav Havel spoke to the Canadian Parliament about his support for the NATO bombing campaign in Yugoslavia. His own electorate in the Czech Republic did not support the intervention. Havel justified overriding the views of Czech citizens by invoking a claim—human rights—that exceeded that of the state: "There is every indication that the glory of the nation-state as the culmination of every national community's history, and its highest earthly value—the only one, in fact, in the name of which it is permissible to kill, or for which people have been expected to die—has already passed its peak."[3]

Havel exemplified a sense that with the Cold War over, the modern state had outlived its usefulness. New patterns of trade created a need for different organizational entities, like "region-states" and "virtual states" oriented around cities more integrated with the global economy than with their national economies.[4] Migration had expanded the claims of citizenship beyond the national community.[5] Human rights movements challenged states to bring about a transnational civil society, even a nascent transnational democracy.[6] "New wars" devoid

[1] Hamilton, Madison, and Jay 1996, 455 [*Federalist* 85].
[2] Michnik 1985, 207.
[3] Havel 1999.
[4] E.g., Ohmae 1993.
[5] Soysal 1995.
[6] Kaldor 1999a; Appadurai 2002.

of ideological content and focused purely on personal enrichment showed the inability of states to prevent warlordism and criminality.[7]

Yet two years after Havel linked the bombing of Yugoslavia to the coming obsolescence of the state, the United Nations released a document, *The Responsibility to Protect*, recommending building states to prevent humanitarian catastrophes from recurring, and NATO forces invaded Afghanistan to construct a modern state in that war-torn region. In this chapter, I will show how the modern state has come full circle, from an exchange between a central authority and population that developed to prosecute war without concern for human rights, to a central authority to be built by outside actors to prevent war and protect human rights. Human rights movements originated as a challenge to state power. As responses to the excesses of state formation, human rights revealed the self-undermining nature of the modern state, and as states faced a variety of challenges, these responses could have led to decentralized or polycentric orders. However, in the last decade, policymakers have proposed that the best way to protect human rights is to construct a centralized state that abjures war. Ironically, this makes state-building more difficult because the process of state formation documented in this book has precluded previous state-making strategies as human rights violations, such as war and dispossession, even as demands on the state to deliver a range of goods it never previously supplied have increased. The conditions under which the centralized state would be self-enforcing and the population would supply the state at a high level do not hold. These problems bedevil state-builders, even as they assert that states are "necessary to achieve the dignity, justice, worth and safety of their citizens."[8]

No "Gift of the Magistrate"

In 1964, Malcolm X urged his fellow African Americans to go before the United Nations because "we need to expand the civil-rights struggle to a higher level—to the level of human rights."[9] The "level" of human rights would allow African Americans to make common cause with yellow and brown brothers from across the world—"to take Uncle Sam before a world court"—while civil rights "kept African-Americans in Uncle Sam's pocket."[10] Human rights embodied a political claim prior to the exchange with the central authority to which one was subject—"human rights are something you were born with"—that would

---

[7] For a discussion of "new" wars, see Kalyvas 2001.

[8] United Nations 2004, 17.

[9] Quoted in Asad 2003, 141.

[10] Asad 2003, 142.

enable African Americans to define their own rights rather than receive rights codified by others, especially a state constituted by excluding them. Malcolm X's use of human rights had a predecessor: leading up to the American Revolution, Thomas Jefferson had described rights as bestowed by "the law of nature, and not as the gift of the chief magistrate."[11] The commonality between the two arguments is that human rights, or its precursor natural rights,[12] creates the possibility of claiming civil rights, defined by the US state, *or some other rights*, and by implication some other institutional structure within which those rights could be realized. Human rights function as an outside option with which to challenge the state and potentially found an alternative to it. In theory, human rights were about claiming one's own rights without having to found a state or be a member of one.

In the case of Eastern European dissidents, the tactical challenge of human rather than civil rights—asking their governments to respect the Helsinki Accords (1975) that they had themselves signed—eventually became an alternative that the population could prefer to the state.[13] In 1975, Havel had written that "there is no one in our country who is not, in a broad sense, existentially vulnerable" because the communist states only functioned by violating the human rights of the population.[14] If the population had rights, it was at the discretion of the state, the "gift of the magistrate." Denied any way to challenge or change this situation within an ever-more overbearing state, dissidents argued instead for what was loosely referred to as the "parallel polis." The anti-statism was conveyed in expressions like "social self-organization," "social self-defense," and "anti-politics."[15] The "parallel polis," however, was initially less an organized opposition than a practice of self-making and cultural regeneration.

Just living in an Eastern European state forced individuals to become a subject in a particular way, namely, one whose everyday behavior was expected to perpetuate the state.[16] Havel described the mundane example of a greengrocer who put a sign "workers of the world unite!" in his shop.[17] Neither the greengrocer nor his customer necessarily believed in the sign; the former may have put it up only to avoid censure from apparatchiks, and the latter just ignored it, even though she unreflectively put a similar sign up in her own workplace. Did either of them want to tear down the sign? Did either of them truly believe

---

[11] Quoted in Bailyn 1992, 188, 185–189.
[12] Hunt 2007, 22.
[13] Judt 2005, 566–568.
[14] Havel 1986, 6–7.
[15] Ash 1986; Konrad 1984.
[16] Havel 1986, 52.
[17] Havel 1986, 41–57.

in the sign? It did not matter—it was sufficient for the sign to exist—and that, Havel argued, was the problem. Insofar as the Czechoslovakian state functioned, it functioned entirely as a system of rituals and signs that not just had no connection with the political preferences of the population but was designed to disable the population from forming preferences, individual or collective, at all. These rituals and signs were not incidental: they were the mode through which the state persisted even as large sections of the population might have preferred to overthrow it. The Eastern European state was not self-enforcing as the central authority reneged on the exchange, like the "tyranny" described in Chapter 2, and relied on Soviet support for defense, and foreign loans for financing.[18] But there were no outside options that the population could prefer so the state sputtered on despite lacking popular support. As Havel put it, "Individuals need not believe all these mystifications, but they must behave as though they did."[19] The initial goal of dissidence was not to overthrow the state or even recover the true preferences of the population that their behavior obscured;[20] it was to enable the population to form preferences in the first place (what Havel called "living within the truth"). This required, before a political program, the "regeneration of our cultural and intellectual life."[21]

By focusing on "culture" and other seemingly apolitical causes like environmentalism, one could establish a space exterior to state power, variously referred to as "self-administration" or "destatification."[22] Sometimes, one could combine the two: in a short story, Ivan Klima commented on the smoke and sulfur in the Prague air.[23] (The reader will recall from Chapter 5 that the state is increasingly expected to reduce pollution and otherwise intervene in environmental issues.) At the same time, these apolitical causes offered a bridge to a transnational community beyond what Milan Kundera called the "small nations" of Central Europe that had not survived as independent states for any length of time.[24] This history compelled them to reach beyond their own borders—a cosmopolitanism of losers, so to speak.

> Central Europe as a family of small nations has its own vision of the world, a vision based on a deep distrust of history. History, that goddess of Hegel and Marx, that incarnation of reason that judges us and arbitrates our fate—that is the history of conquerors. The people of Central

[18] Kotkin 2009.
[19] Havel 1986, 45.
[20] Kuran 1991.
[21] Benda et al. 1988, 242.
[22] Respectively, Benda et al. 1988, 245; Konrad 1984.
[23] Quoted in Judt 2005, 571.
[24] Miszlevitz 1998, 31.

Europe are not conquerors. They cannot be separated from European history; they cannot exist outside it; but they represent the wrong side of this history; they are its victims and outsiders. It's this disabused view of history that is the source of their culture, of their wisdom, of the "nonserious" spirit that mocks grandeur and glory. "Never forget that only in opposing History as such can we resist the history of our own day." I would love to engrave this sentence by Witold Gombrowicz above the entry gate to Central Europe.[25]

Similar to the history of the stateless people discussed in Chapter 7, Eastern European history was less the story of states and more the story of (mostly unsuccessful) struggles against the state, "a cultural-political anti-hypothesis."[26] Eastern/Central Europe was a fuzzy space on the map, sometimes including Russia, identified from the eighteenth century onward as a borderland between Europe and Asia, a link, in Balzac's term "between civilization and barbarism."[27] This imaginative geography was characterized by instability and imagined as a space of conquest from Voltaire onward.[28] Galicia, for example, was invented as a province of the Austro-Hungarian empire at the partition of Poland in 1772, then disappeared from the map in 1918.[29] The "Mitteleuropa" defined in 1915 by the German politician Friedrich Naumann, was a backward space to be colonized by the Germans.[30] This was appropriated after the Great War in an aborted effort to create a Central European federation modeled after the Poland-Lithuania commonwealth of the sixteenth to eighteenth centuries, where the rights of minorities like the Jews would be respected.[31] In calling for a federation, its authors acknowledged the difficulty (noted by Kwame Nkrumah, as described in Chapter 6!) for individual states emerging from the Austro-Hungarian empire to become viable on their own, and without the participation of minorities and diaspora communities.[32]

But years of war and Soviet-imposed rule had eroded this cosmopolitan culture and eliminated minorities. Further, the mass of the population were "passive" in the sense that they were unwilling to incur costs in protesting state power.[33] The state had infiltrated society to the degree that a civil society independent of the state—whether underpinned by property rights or autonomous

---

[25] Kundera 1984.
[26] The term is George Konrad's; quoted in Ash 1986.
[27] Quoted in Wolff 1994, 357.
[28] Wolff 1994, 361–365.
[29] Davies 2012.
[30] Ash 1986.
[31] Michnik 1985, 214–222.
[32] Miszlevitz 1998, 53–54.
[33] Michnik 1985, 153.

associations like church groups—did not exist and had to be made.[34] As a Hungarian colleague put it to Ash, "For us the struggle for civil society is a great daily drama."[35] To make civil society, dissidents had to create a culture both independent from the state and attractive to those stifled by communist ortho-doxy, yet not make it so oppositional as to drive away the passive population. Tactically, this pointed to a variety of collective but apolitical activities—Havel's "anti-political politics"[36]—like lobbying against acid rain or the Danube Circle protests against a dam on that river.[37] Such local causes would motivate indi-viduals who would otherwise not oppose the regime.[38] The seeming diffidence of this agenda did not impress Western observers. Francois Furet, the French historian, and Jurgen Habermas separately commented that 1989 marked a rev-olution with no new ideas.[39]

The seeming lack of ideas was, however, unavoidable. If self-making was to be a genuine process, dissident leaders could not impose an agenda on their sup-porters.[40] They had to enable their supporters to figure out their own preferences by creating a space of autonomy from the all-powerful and suffocating state. Michnik conceded state functions to the party (deemed beyond reform), denied that Solidarity aimed for political power, and pushed instead for greater auton-omy in society.[41] By avoiding the state, the Hungarian writer George Konrad argued, society could develop its own standards: "The success of this inde-pendent ferment cannot be measured by the replacement of one government by another, but by the fact that under the same government society is growing stronger, independent people are multiplying, and the network of conversations uncontrollable from above is becoming denser" and "let the government stay on top, we will live our own lives underneath it."[42] After exposure to this network of conversations, the greengrocer might have chosen *not* to put up the sign in his shop. But he could have decided that he really wanted to put the sign up. The dis-sidents did not, indeed could not, rule this out, hence the criticism that they had no new ideas. The stakes of dissidence, and their articulation with human rights,

[34] Kotkin 2009, 9, 96.

[35] Ash 1986.

[36] Havel 1986, 157.

[37] Eastern European critics in the 1960s had turned to ideas of the peasant maintaining his or her life in a parallel economy that was exterior to the otherwise centralizing state; Rev 1998.

[38] One study estimated that 90 percent of Eastern European grassroots organizations were apo-litical; Weigle and Butterfield 1992, 23; Miszlevitz 1998, 67–68.

[39] Quoted in Kaldor 1999a, 475.

[40] Timothy Garton Ash observed that the dissident leadership "made it up as they went along" during the Velvet Revolution in Czechoslovakia. They were as surprised by the changes as anyone else and scrambled to formulate policies in response; Ash 1990.

[41] Michnik 1985, 89, 129, 135–148.

[42] Konrad 1984, 176, 198.

was to establish an outside option through which the population could make political claims, not a specification of what those claims would be.

The "diffidence of dissidence" marked a slippage between what motivated and enabled dissidents and what would follow the end of communism (where dissidents would, with exceptions like Havel, not be in positions of power).[43] Havel would suggest years later to the Canadian Parliament that the Eastern European revolutions indicated the basis of a community beyond the national state. His logic seemed to confirm the success of a movement that articulated diverse goals of environmentalism, disarmament, and human rights to under-mine existing states. The historian and anti-nuclear activist E. P. Thompson had called this aspiration in 1981 "a détente of people rather than states—a move-ment of peoples which sometimes dislodges states from their blocs and brings them into a new diplomacy of conciliation, which sometimes runs beneath state structures, and which sometimes defies the ideological and security structures of particular states."[44] But to say that Eastern Europeans supported the dissi-dents because they wanted to become European or world citizens was a post hoc description of the dissident movements that was at variance with the language of dissident intellectuals in the 1970s and 1980s (and presaged a future where com-mitment to universal or post-national values would be an elite preference, not a popular one). The contours of this disagreement could be sensed in the 1980s, when a Czech dissident writing under the pseudonym Vaclav Racek pointed out to Thompson that the Eastern European movements promoted human rights as the necessary condition for disarmament rather than Thompson's focus on "the increasing rate of armament (as) the cause for the suppression of human rights."[45] Similarly, Havel and Michnik would aver that "the cause of the danger of war is not weapons as such but political realities," namely, continued Soviet dominance and the suppression of human rights.[46]

As this disagreement suggests, dissident movements were about the condi-tions under which choice could be possible at all, not particular choices. Positing an outside option through which the writ of the state could be refused—human rights—was a parametric shift in that individuals or a population could appeal to a principle that neither relied on the protection of a state nor required the found-ing of a state. One did not need to aspire to founding a state or having the pro-tection of a state to be a political actor that could refuse state power. By contrast,

---

[43] The Czech dissident Jirina Siklova predicted that it would be the "gray zone" of people who were neither dissidents nor party loyalists—"on neither side of the barricades"—who would come to power in the new regime; Siklova 1990.

[44] Thompson 1982, 181–182.

[45] Thompson 1982, 83–84; Judt 2005, 574.

[46] Quoted in Ash 1986.

stateless peoples in the nineteenth century or the "local cretinism" of peasant revolts virtually invited subjugation from those who had states; these state-making practices were put in question by human rights movements. Dissident intellectuals, for example, stressed local, apolitical mobilization to create space for a future political program without specifying what that program would be.[47]

Now, one could argue that under communist states, dissidents could not reveal their true goals. So any public arguments were Trojan horses that moti-vated the population with coded promises of future liberal democracy and markets. When reading, for example, "it would appear that traditional parliamentary democracies can offer no fundamental opposition to the automatism of techno-logical civilization and the industrial-consumer society.... I see a renewed focus of politics on real people as something far more profound than merely returning to the everyday mechanism of Western (or if you like bourgeois) democracy,"[48] Havel's supporters understood him as saying that he would, in fact, choose a Western democratic model once communism was overthrown. This interpreta-tion is implausible: it bespeaks a high level of coordination around the meaning of statements in an environment specifically designed to foil coordination and to obscure meaning. More fundamentally, it would contradict the whole pro-gram of "living in truth": someone who was arguing against the duplicity of the communist system where no one could form, much less articulate, preferences would be the worst sort of hypocrite if he adopted this strategy.[49] It seems more reasonable to suggest that dissidents searched far and wide for outside options, reaching internally to modes of life that stood apart from state power, and exter-nally to diverse oppositional movements like the nuclear disarmament groups in Western Europe that could serve as allies. Establishing such an outside option would enable the population to think for themselves and communicate honestly with each other.

Habermas's criticism that the Eastern European revolutions offered no new ideas has parallels with Richard Wright's letter to Kwame Nkrumah discussed in Chapter 6. Wright had emphasized that even as Nkrumah looked to Bandung and pan-Africanism, his popular support was limited to anti-colonial sentiment and was backward-looking rather than oriented toward the future. Similarly, Habermas described the revolutions in Eastern Europe as backward-looking, turning to symbols that predated the communist era rather than articulating new

[47] In any case, only in Poland, with Solidarity, was there an organized opposition, and even Solidarity did not aim to replace the government but "to reinvent the public realm to break the state's monopolization"; Kotkin 2009, 6, 121.

[48] Havel 1986, 116–117.

[49] In fact, dissidents with a preference for liberal democracy were often open about it; e.g., Michnik 1985, 115.

ideas for the future.[50] (Unlike Wright, he did not encourage Eastern European leaders to overcome this backward-looking tendency by force.) That the revolutions had popular support for evicting the regime, but no real sense of what would follow, was borne out by a poll that same year of East Germans, of whom a majority (78 percent) said they had not anticipated the forthcoming events.[51] Of course, revolutions are often unanticipated because participants have to believe that others will join them to participate in the first place, and this belief arises suddenly rather than as the culmination of a process. But this very suddenness means participants may be motivated only by the act of participation (or fear of punishment if they free-ride), not any prior political affiliation or future political program, or awareness of why others participate. Insofar as dissidence—the establishment of a parallel polis to enable self-making—*was* the alternative to the communist state, its lack of political program meant, implicitly, that not only did participants in the 1989 revolutions not anticipate the events they participated in but that they could not have any coordinated view of what would follow. As a Czech intellectual, and signatory of Charter 77, a 1977 petition demanding human rights in Czechoslovakia, put it in 1991, "For years citizens in this part of Europe have yearned for the freedom to voice their opinions, and all of a sudden they find they have no opinions, not even political ones."[52] Into this void would be projected all manner of ideas for what would follow: the borderless world of management thinkers, the end of history, the return of atavistic affiliations, cosmopolitan democracy, even the "coming anarchy." But the real lesson, if the argument of this book is persuasive, was that the state either was not, or never had been, self-enforcing in most of the world. I now turn to what this might have meant.

Alexander Hamilton in Puntland

Eastern European dissidents were one manifestation of a perceived redundancy or crisis of the state toward the end of the twentieth century, as the Soviet Bloc crumbled and insurgencies accumulated. Human rights movements and insurgents contesting state power indicated that the population was increasingly unwilling to supply the state. Instead, in the absence of costly war, the population could prefer alternatives that enabled them to contest state power when it was unduly repressive or extractive. Consequently, in the context of civil wars and collapsing states after the Cold War, establishing centralized states that would monopolize violence need not have been the logical response.

[50] Habermas 1990.
[51] Rev 1998, 75; Kuran 1991, 7–13.
[52] Siklova 1991, 766; Miszlevitz 1991, 797–798.

A thought experiment will illustrate this claim. Prosaically, the American Revolution originated as a revolt against the demands of the British Crown. At an intellectual level, it drew on a deep distrust of state power developing in seventeenth-century English thought, and, as seen above, the sense that rights were independent of and prior to state power, not granted by the state.[53] But the authors of what became the *Federalist Papers*, especially Alexander Hamilton,[54] were advocating a centralized state where one did not exist, against a really existing alternative.[55] This alternative was the American Confederacy, a pluralist association of states they compared to "feudal baronies," "Grecian republics," and medieval Germany.[56] These entities were engaged in a patchwork of treaties and alliances with diverse Indian tribes.[57] As the reader will recall from Chapter 3, Hegel had more or less contemporaneously made similar arguments of Germany, namely, that confederacies were vulnerable to domestic divisions and external threats. On the one hand, the state governments could not be disbanded, for they were the source of what Madison called the "general authority (which came) . . . entirely from the subordinate authorities" to the extent that the Constitution, he averred, was "of a mixed nature" composed "of many coequal sovereignties."[58] The state governments and their militias also represented a defense against standing armies, which their revolutionary predecessors saw as reducing previously free nations like Denmark to vassalage and despotism.[59] To this end, the delegate Tench Coxe inveighed that the new army would not be a standing army because its budget would last only two years and had to be approved by the House, and Hamilton noted that building a "janissary" army would, because it required these appropriations, take a long time and prove easy to counter.[60]

On the other hand, the multiple sovereignties of a confederacy created insoluble collective action problems that Hamilton, in particular, castigated. These problems could only be overcome by a centralized state that would deny the states any outside option like exit.[61] The newly independent states faced rivals

[53] Pocock 1975, 411–412.

[54] Madison was most concerned with limiting the power of the state as it was being founded, so focused on checks and balances; Wolin 1989, 114–119. Similarly, Thomas Jefferson wanted to provide for the revision of the Constitution at "stated periods" so each generation could govern according to their specific needs; Arendt 1963, 235–238. Hamilton's views were different; Pocock 1975, 528–533.

[55] Wood 1972, 532–534.

[56] Hamilton, Madison, and Jay 1996, 74–97 [*Federalist* Nos. 16–20].

[57] Williams 1997, 40–123.

[58] Respectively, quoted in Arendt 1963, 164, 164–170; quoted in Wood 1972, 529–530.

[59] Bailyn 1992, 61–65, 338–340.

[60] Bailyn 1992, 355–357.

[61] Hamilton, Madison, and Jay 1996, 120–124 [*Federalist* 25]; Pocock 1975, 531; Wolin 1989, 111–114.

against whom an army needed to be raised and financed: "savage tribes" in the West, the British, the Spanish, and alliances between these rivals.[62] Left to themselves, individual states would choose to free-ride on the efforts of those immediately threatened; over time, those states paying the cost of war would not support others, and each would become vulnerable to much stronger rivals.

Therefore, the authors demanded that some functions be placed under central authority and proscribed any outside option like exit (though the states retained militias, these were to be placed under central command in the event of war). In his claim that only a centralized state could govern an area as large as the New World,[63] Hamilton argued that "a firm Union will be of the utmost interest to the peace and liberty of the States, as a barrier against domestic faction and insurrection."[64] Madison, more cautious of the central government, would acknowledge that "faction" was an inevitable byproduct of individual differences, and the role of the Union was not to eliminate its causes but to manage its effects, especially the risk that "an interested and overbearing majority" would rule over the rest.[65] For Madison, the center was not the "gorgon" threatening the states but the institution that would "extend the sphere" of rule such that factions would balance each other out.[66] Eventually, Hamilton and Madison would separate over the formation of a central bank, but, as Pocock puts it, Hamilton's key insight was that in a world of expanding specialization and commerce, "there would be war, and there must be strong government; and on the other side of the ledger, he suspected that Madison's theory of balancing interests made too little of the dangers of sectional conflict within a union of states."[67]

Could the lessons of the *Federalist* be applied to the weak and failed states of the 1990s? There, the threat of foreign conquest had diminished significantly, for reasons, as we saw in Chapters 4 and 6, that were endogenous to the process of state formation. Further, it was not a lack of centralization that was the problem in many cases, as the insurgents of Chapter 7 and the dissidents of the last section seemed to suggest, but too much of it.[68] Further, the equivalents of

---

[62] Hamilton, Madison, and Jay 1996, 118 [*Federalist* No. 24].

[63] This was in contrast to Anti-Federalist arguments, drawing on Montesquieu, that such a large territory could only be controlled by military force; Wood 1972, 499–500.

[64] Hamilton, Madison, and Jay 1996, 36 [*Federalist* No. 9].

[65] Hamilton, Madison, and Jay 1996, 44 [*Federalist* No. 10]; Wood 1972, 502.

[66] Bailyn 1992, 366–367.

[67] Pocock 1975, 531.

[68] It is hard to assess the claim that states are the greater threat to their population than rebels waging intrastate wars or rival states waging interstate wars. Certainly, the numbers of those killed by organized state campaigns and famines between 1945 and 1999—China's Great Leap Forward, for example, which killed 45 million—far exceed the battle deaths of all interstate and intrastate wars combined (approximately 20 million). But war deaths, especially in civil wars, may be ten to fifteen

Hamilton's "savage tribes" could no longer be treated as they had been in the nineteenth century. The problems that the authors of the *Federalist* counted on to drive popular support for their centralizing agenda over alternative arrangements were far less salient. If Alexander Hamilton went to Puntland, a de facto state within the territory of the de jure state of Somalia, what solution could he have advocated for Somalia's ills?

This is not a facetious question, because in a 1992 document called the *Agenda for Peace*, the United Nations charged itself to take "action to identify and support structures which will tend to strengthen and solidify peace in order to prevent relapse into conflict."[69] The *Agenda for Peace* reveals the parametric shifts conditioning state-making that a modern-day Hamilton had to operate under. The authors of the *Federalist* had favored a centralized, self-enforcing state as better suited to wage war over a confederal structure with multiple sources of order. War was then understood to be more or less inevitable; the only question was how it could be prosecuted better. By contrast, the UN's desired "structures" were intended to *prevent* conflict, not prosecute it better, as the post-1945 state was no longer a primarily war-making entity. Further, Puntland's equivalent of "savage tribes" had become "minorities"—possessing human rights irrespective of their membership in a state—toward whom the modern Hamilton was compelled to show "special sensitivity" in the UN's language.[70] To give a sense of this shift, Figure 8.1 shows the frequency of three terms—"savages," "minorities," "human rights"—in English language books indexed in Google Books.

The terms "minorities" and "human rights" were virtually unused in the nineteenth century, but the term "savages" was used frequently, as frequently, in fact, as the term "minorities" in the 1990s. While "savages" has declined to an eighth of its usage in 1900, the frequency of the other two terms has increased by many multiples since 1900: twenty-three times in the case of "minorities" and twenty-nine times in the case of "human rights."

In sum, a would-be Hamilton in Puntland would be facing a confederacy whose members had fewer incentives to give up their outside options and centralize the means of organized violence than the American confederacy of 1787. Also, centralization was likely to be costlier given that one could not ride roughshod over "minorities" who now had "human rights." Centralization in

---

times the number of battle deaths as most of the casualties are civilians who often die not from direct violence but from disease and other externalities of the conflict. At a causal level, it may be that a state provoked rebels or a rival state into fighting and hence the war deaths were a consequence of the behavior of the state; Rummel 1994; Fearon and Laitin 2003; Lacina and Gleditsch 2005; Dikotter 2010.

[69] Secretary General of the United Nations 1992, para. 21.
[70] Secretary General of the United Nations 1992, para. 18.

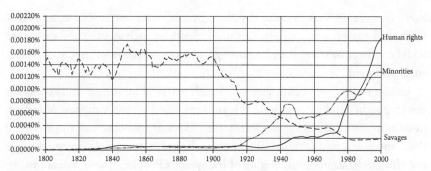

Figure 8.1 Frequency of terms "savages," "minorities," "human rights," 1800–2000

such a context was not the obvious solution to the travails of such a confederacy. Rather, in the absence of war, local motivations to engage in violence and protect territory would take priority, often to the detriment of forming a united front.[71] (This is, again, why civil wars should not usually be expected to build states.) The benefits of centralization had to be weighed against its costs, namely, the high odds of resistance and the higher costs, relative to the nineteenth century, of that resistance. The performance of centralized states, whether in terms of economic development or democracy or human rights, had been less than stellar. Consequently, armed groups, or "factions," had come into conflict with the state and/or other factions. The modern Hamilton's challenge was to get these factions to first, stop fighting, and second, to cooperate with each other to build "structures" that would prevent future conflict.

Given this transformed context, a modern Hamilton could not assume agreement between factions on the desirability of disarming—a condition for establishing a self-enforcing exchange with a central authority. Instead, he could expect that factions would be preoccupied with local concerns and see centralizing actors as either a threat, or at best, a possible ally against a local, rather than a foreign, rival. Such an alliance would have limits, however. The faction would be unwilling to disarm entirely, preserving an outside or exit option in case the centralizing actor reneged on an agreement.[72] A century earlier, as we saw in Chapter 3, such factions could have been dismissed as "lower races" cowed by superior firepower (Callwell), or "barbarians" to be conquered by science (Churchill) and massive force unleashed on them. This course of action had

[71] Most civil wars, for example, see combatant groups break into smaller factions; Christia 2012, 9.

[72] In Mozambique, for example, the rebel group Renamo did not disarm or relinquish its power in rural areas after the peace agreement of 1992. Thus confident it could defend itself in case its rival Frelimo reneged on power-sharing agreements, Renamo contested elections in 1994, and, when its rival Frelimo reneged, Renamo continued to control the provinces it won electorally in a form of "double administration" without a recurrence of the war; Walter 1999.

become more difficult because the "lower races" were better able to aggregate their local struggles through modernized identities such as tribe and caste into wider conflicts, or claim their human rights in international forums, and contest such treatment.

Unlike in the nineteenth century, statelessness is no longer a criterion for denying rights and recognition. This is exemplified by the struggles of indigenous activists confronting modern states, like Canada, that had dispossessed their ancestors, and forming alliances to shape international agreements like the UN Declaration on the Rights of Indigenous Peoples. These claims can, on the one hand, be settled in the courts and by the laws of the states within which the indigenous groups live. On the other, the claim to the land prior to the formation of the state introduces the possibility of other modes of relating to the land beyond property rights and alternative modes of governance altogether than that of the centralized state.[73] Statelessness is here an outside option with which to challenge the state and claim rights from the state. This is novel, because statelessness has historically been a means to escape state power, not to claim rights from the state, and nineteenth-century state formation involved intense efforts to eliminate statelessness and incorporate the stateless.[74] Analyzing the horrors of totalitarianism, Hannah Arendt had argued there was no abstract subject of human rights: one had to be a member of a state, that is, have the rights of a citizen, to have human rights.[75] The Jews, neither having a state of their own nor receiving the protection of existing states, had found that when they had only their human rights, they had no rights at all and could be exterminated.[76]

Arendt criticized a concept of human rights that took for its object individuals abstracted from the social context in which they lived, given its inadequacy in protecting the Jews. This abstract concept was, in fact, preferred by postwar proponents of international law like Quincy Wright, who criticized anti-colonial movements for articulating collective rights to self-determination. Anti-colonial movements were not, in the view of international lawyers, human rights movements, and on that basis self-determination should not have been included in UN resolutions on human rights.[77] These legalistic arguments did have a point: nineteenth-century campaigns that put collective mobilization as the condition for individual rights had frequently led to exclusionary behavior, especially behavior targeted against minority groups.[78] Mazzini, for example,

---

[73] Tully 1995, 54.
[74] Scott 2009; Osterhammel 2014, 322–330.
[75] Arendt 1968, 291–292; Asad 2003, 143–144.
[76] Arendt 1968, 279.
[77] Moyn 2010, 198–199.
[78] Hunt 2007, 181–186.

had asked, "What is a country . . . but the place in which our individual rights are most secure?" But, as we saw in Chapter 3, he answered that to build the country required war and conquest.[79] The activism of indigenous groups suggested neither the abstract individualism favored by international lawyers nor the determination to form a state. That is, these groups belied the binary that rights could be realized only through the institutions of the state that had dispossessed them or the establishment of their own state. By mobilizing as a community that was not a state, through, for example, exercising the (new) human right to engage in previously suppressed cultural practices, indigenous groups sought to claim collective rights against the states that had dispossessed them.[80] In one sense, Arendt was correct to say that abstract individuals had no rights; the individual had to belong to a community. But indigenous activism implied that the community need not have been organized as a state in the past, nor did it need to aspire to establish a state. This was a parametric shift in how rights were conceptualized in relation to the state, because statelessness, the condition to deny these groups rights in the past as we saw in Chapter 3, is no longer a valid basis to deny rights.

These claims have faced opposition. In the *Delgamuukw* case, two indigenous groups claimed rights to a large chunk of territory in British Columbia on the basis that they had used the land prior to colonization. The chief justice of the Court of Appeals in British Columbia dismissed the evidence, presented as oral history, that the groups had possessed the land. He dismissed the claim because "the plaintiff's ancestors had no written language, no horses or wheeled vehicles, slavery and starvation was not uncommon, wars with neighboring people were common, and there is no doubt, to quote Hobbes, that aboriginal life in the territory was, at best, 'nasty, brutish, and short.' "[81] Note that the judge dismissed not just the claim but also the basis for making the claim: that the groups had history, if orally transmitted; and that these traditions made the groups communities that could bargain with the Crown.[82] This statement was made in 1991 and recalls colonial arguments.[83] The echo of colonial arguments indicates the high stakes of such challenges to states. These claims threaten a future in which indigenous groups could reduce the supply of the Canadian state without having

---

[79] Quoted in Hunt 2007, 177.

[80] Lightfoot 2009, 64–66.

[81] Quoted in Tully 1995, 132. For similar language in the decision in *Calder*, a prior case, see Asch 2014, 13.

[82] Similarly, in 1979, future US chief justice, then an associate justice, William Rehnquist had written that Indian tribal courts, though improved on their nineteenth-century predecessors, were still characterized by "a want of fixed laws [and] of competent tribunals of justice" in *Oliphant vs. Suquamish Tribe*; quoted in Williams 1997, 19.

[83] Bell and Asch 1997, 64–71.

to form new states. The meaning (and threat) of indigenous mobilization is not that these societies were states—the lack of which was cause for their dispossession in the nineteenth century—or that they aspire to establish independent states,[84] but that stateless societies could not be subjugated as they had been.

To bastardize Norbert Elias, this has turned the civilizing process on itself. Elias argued that the rise of centralized states was the necessary condition for individuals to exercise self-control because they were no longer insecure and reliant on survival instincts that caused them to lash out at every perceived threat.[85] But history is not linear; indigenous groups challenged the acts through which they had been "civilized," and with it the state that had formed through those acts. Not only can indigenous groups, and marginalized groups more generally, now demand more services and obstruct previously accepted state-building policies like land displacements, imposing costs on the state, but these demands can shrink the supply of the state through another mechanism. I have argued that a combination of equality of sacrifice in costly war *and* dispossession of natives had driven the self-enforcing exchange in Europe and North America. In the first half of the twentieth century, the supply of the state increased significantly because of progressive taxation that equalized sacrifice. In the absence of costly war, the equality of sacrifice imperative has waned, and as marginalized groups demand services, the willingness to supply the state on the part of wealthier groups can shrink further.

Bargaining without War

All these changes suggest that building a centralized state in an environment where two or more factions retain the capacity for organized violence is only a possibility *as long as the factions accept it*, as Americans did in 1787.[86] If they oppose centralization, then alternatives to the state are not just desirable but necessary. These alternatives do not preclude building a state in the long term, but they mean beginning with decentralized, confederal, or "polycentric" governance structures.[87] To some degree, these structures exist in practice in conflict zones, where rebel groups, international organizations, and humanitarian organizations uneasily coexist with the nominal state authority.[88] These decentralized structures are inefficient, increasing transaction costs—such as tolls on roads

---

[84] On this point, see Asch 2014, 59–68.
[85] Elias 1982, 237–241; Mazlish 2001, 293–294.
[86] Wood 1972, 471–475.
[87] Ostrom 2010.
[88] Fearon and Laitin 2004, 7.

controlled by rebels or even security forces forced to collect their own wages[89]—and the redundancy involved in maintaining separate armed forces and service providers. Yet, precisely because these transaction costs are a source of rents to powerful local actors, doing away with them is likely to provoke a backlash.[90]

Once they have assurances against the breaking of agreements, factions can begin the process of rebuilding, possibly with some third-party mediation to ensure against reneging on agreements. Several institutional outcomes become possible. One is a centralized state, but this raises the risk of one faction capturing the state and repressing others, as occurred in Rwanda, the most centralized African state.[91] Or, in the expectation of such repression, the other factions might rebel. Centralization is either an exchange that emerges under very restrictive conditions, as theorized in Chapter 2, or a top-down gamble with significant downside, as theorized in Chapters 6 and 7. To mitigate the risks, an alternative institutional form might have been a federation in which each partner exercises power over a particular territory with pooling of common functions such as trade, or heteronomous power-sharing between a central and several local authorities, basically, to institutionalize politics as practiced, even if it did not approximate a centralized state.[92] This was not dissimilar to various federated structures envisioned at decolonization in West Africa, the Caribbean, and South Asia.

The logic underlying such polycentric alternatives to a centralized state is that repeated interactions over time allow factions to build trust and develop patterns of cooperation. But factions also require the ability to bring pressure, by staying armed, or by exit (i.e., some outside option). To use the example of the prisoner's dilemma game from Chapter 1, a long shadow of the future facilitates cooperation in the present, but fear of being exploited in the short term leads factions to arm in self-protection or reserve the right to exit.[93] For a faction to be willing to cooperate, it first needs the confidence that it can survive even if the other side reneges, for which an outside option—remaining armed or being able to exit—or a credible third-party guarantee is necessary. Conversely, to remove a faction's outside option risks immediate rebellion or exit. Instead, the logical starting point for peace-building would be to facilitate early cooperation—manifested in treaties or alliances that stopped the fighting—between factions retaining the capacity for self-defense, and defer centralization.

[89] Mbembe 2001, 77–89.

[90] Kalyvas 2006, 391.

[91] Mamdani 2001a.

[92] E.g., Roger Myerson, "Rethinking the Fundamentals of State-Building." Available at http://home.uchicago.edu/rmyerson/research/prism10.pdf.

[93] Axelrod 1986; Ostrom 2010.

Logically and historically, a centralized state exercising a monopoly on violence was one way, but not the only one, to "build peace." Historically, such states are rare, and they developed under very restrictive conditions, which are unlikely to obtain in the present. When factions have little incentive to prefer the state to alternatives—by combining forces in the face of external threat, as in the formation of the American Union in 1787—but are willing to stop fighting each other, what makes sense is a heteronomous, or polycentric, system, possibly with third-party enforcement from international actors, until the factions trust each other enough to allow a monopoly of violence and a centralized state. History, where state formation was contingent and always partial, should have urged openness to a range of institutional arrangements. A diversity of institutional arrangements would have acknowledged that in the absence of costly war, the population would prefer alternatives to the state so that they could refuse to supply the state at a high level and/or demand services.

A more provocative way of putting this is to say that if Alexander Hamilton went to Puntland, he may not have recommended a union at all. Rather, he may have been forced to adopt the treaty-making diplomacy that Europeans had practiced with the "savage Indians" prior to the nineteenth century. In the seventeenth and eighteenth centuries, when Europeans were unable to overpower Indian tribes, they often signed treaties, like the Iroquois Covenant Chain of 1677. This treaty recognized each side's right to remain armed and committed to collective self-defense, and respected the autonomy of each side's customs.[94] Transported to the 1990s, the modern-day Hamilton was unable to rely on popular willingness to prefer the state over alternatives and faced high costs of centralization, as factions were more organized and harder to repress—both as an outcome of 200 years of state formation. Consequently, he had to forge power-sharing agreements that would likely fall short of a self-enforcing exchange, and may indeed have precluded it as a condition for securing cooperation. A modern-day Hamilton might have advocated an outcome—a confederacy lacking a monopoly on violence, containing several wielders of violence and authority, brought together by treaties they could renegotiate or exit rather than an overarching constitution to which they were subject—that the authors of the Federalist excoriated and tried to eradicate in 1787, and the opposite of what his successors in the US government would advocate in the twenty-first century. This Hamilton, recognizing the parametric shifts conditioning the exchange between any would-be central authority and population, might have recommended an institutional arrangement Jay described as "destitute of an effectual government."[95]

---

[94] Williams 1997, 116–123; Tully 1995, 127–129.
[95] Hamilton, Jay, and Madison 1996, 16 [Federalist No. 4].

A range of problems faced interveners dealing with insurgencies and state collapse after the Cold War. Factions might not stop fighting, much less cooperate, for diverse reasons, in which case external intervention was likely to be problematic, as the UN's 2000 Brahimi Report acknowledged.[96] One faction might have thought it could win a decisive victory, in which case external actors were interlopers. Alternatively, the entry of external actors with significant resources might increase the value of capturing the state (or increase the cost of being squeezed out of the state). Finally, external actors might have neither the resources nor the knowledge to manage a variety of local conflicts.[97] Yet even as evidence accumulated of the failure of "peace enforcement" in places where factions had not signed a peace agreement,[98] and the failure of every US state-building effort except postwar Germany and Japan,[99] scholars and policymakers came to argue that, to paraphrase the title of one such book, to build peace, build states.[100]

Restaging (or Déjà Vu All Over Again)

I began this chapter with Vaclav Havel telling the Canadian Parliament that as a consequence of human rights movements, it was no longer permissible to kill for the glory of the state, nor could individuals be expected to die for it any longer. The population was no longer willing to bear such sacrifices anymore. Given that the state had developed through demanding such sacrifices, could states be constructed anymore?

In 2001, the International Commission on Intervention and State Sovereignty, constituted by the United Nations and the Canadian government, answered in the affirmative. Acknowledging that states were constrained in ways they had not been in the past, the Commission still averred that

> the conditions under which sovereignty is exercised—and intervention is practiced—have changed dramatically since 1945. Many new states have emerged and are still in the process of consolidating their identity. Evolving international law has set many *constraints* on what states can do, and not only in the realm of human rights. The emerging concept of human security has created additional *demands and expectations* in relation to the way states treat their own people. And many new actors

[96] Fearon and Laitin 2004, 14–19.
[97] Kalyvas 2006.
[98] Doyle and Sambanis 2006.
[99] Dobbins et al. 2003.
[100] Call and Wyeth 2008.

are playing international roles previously more or less the exclusive pre-serve of states. All that said, sovereignty does still matter. It is strongly arguable that effective and legitimate states remain the best way to ensure that the benefits of the internationalization of trade, investment, technology and communication will be equitably shared.[101]

The reader will observe an acknowledgment that the conditions within which state-building occurs had changed. Kwame Nkrumah, the reader will recall, had made this point more starkly, writing that leaders like him were expected to "work miracles" in 1958. I argued in the last section that such parametric shifts might have led to the establishment of alternatives to the state, at least until the population chose to give up their outside options. Yet, as this statement indi-cates, representatives of the international community asserted the opposite. They asserted that centralized states remained the optimal organizational form for world politics and should be built by outside actors.

As in the *Agenda for Peace* a decade prior, the state envisioned here is not the same entity that the authors of the *Federalist* had advocated to fight foreign enemies and "savage tribes." Rather, the commission argued that individual states were primarily responsible for world order, but when they failed to pro-tect the human rights of their "savage tribes," now "minorities" or "citizens," or threatened other states, the international community had the responsibility to intervene, and then rebuild states that would protect human rights.[102] State sovereignty—in the narrow, post-1945 sense of the right of non-interference from foreign powers—was made conditional on the state's ability and/or will-ingness to protect the human rights of its population (which, in turn, had come to be seen as predictive of external aggression).[103] States unwilling to protect the rights of their populations under international law were defined as "rogue" states, and states unable to do so as "failed" states.[104] In such "rogues" and "failures" that threatened human rights in different ways, it was for other states to step into the breach and construct a state that would respect human rights. Human rights, previously used to contest state power, were now to be delivered by the state. If Havel had argued that the state was no longer the highest value worth sacrificing for and killing for, the commission agreed, *and sought to construct states around that principle.*

Yet movements invoking human rights, much like insurgent movements and indigenous activists, signaled a refusal to supply the state by preferring

---

[101] ICISS 2001, 7, emphasis mine; Ignatieff 2001, 35; United Nations 2004, 17.
[102] This was reaffirmed in United Nations 2004, 17.
[103] Finnemore 2003, 135.
[104] Chowdhury 2011, 38–43.

alternatives, not a plea to build states. Michnik illustrated this when he wrote that an "illegal literature is a prerequisite for the fight against captivity of the spirit." It was by engaging in an act prohibited by the state, by transgressing its writ—in this case, by creating and disseminating *illegal* literature—that the dissidents constituted their movement. Movements claiming human rights can seek to define their own rights within institutions different from the modern state. Indigenous movements, for example, under the term "self-determination" assert a prior right to form a community that can then consent to, or reject, membership or policies of the state in which they reside.[105] The refusal of the writ of the state, rendering it not self-enforcing, is a fundamental, arguably constitutive, part of these movements: they are founded through such transgressions, and this makes it more difficult to compel sacrifice for the state.[106] For the state to internalize human rights—a principle prior to state power that enables the refusal of state power—is arguably to internalize the possibility of rebellion and transgression.

But advocates of state-building confine the solution to human rights violations to building a centralized state, and explicitly reject alternatives to the state. A UN study concluded,

> The best solution (to incapacitated and criminalized states) is to strengthen and legitimize states rather than overthrow the system of states .... [A] world of capable, efficient and legitimate states will help to achieve the goals of order, stability and predictability and promote national and human security.[107]

This statement, and others like it,[108] reveals that a particular type of state is the condition for the realization of human rights. By implication, human rights cannot be realized in other types of states—as in the Eastern Bloc where the central authority reneged on the exchange and the regime survived until the population could coordinate a revolution (the "tyranny" described in Table 2.1)—or in the absence of a state.

In these arguments, the population were expected to prefer the state to alternatives. If they did not, they could not be allowed to support such alternatives if

---

[105] For example, Article 5 of the Declaration on the Rights of Indigenous Peoples reads: "Indigenous peoples have the right to maintain and strengthen their distinct political, legal, economic, social, and cultural institutions, while retaining their right to participate fully, *if they so choose*, in the political, economic, social and cultural life of the State"; quoted in Lightfoot 2009, 333, emphasis mine.

[106] Chowdhury and Duvall 2014, 200.

[107] Chesterman, Ignatieff, and Thakur 2005, 359; United Nations 2004, 18.

[108] E.g., Ghani and Lockhart 2009, 27.

that would compromise human rights, such as restricting the rights of minorities, for example. Michael Ignatieff, an early proponent of state-building in Iraq, argued that these alternatives, whether or not they had popular support, could not threaten human rights, understood as primarily negative rights of protection of life, property, and speech.[109] In effect, state institutions had to be established *before* any exchange or bargaining between the central authority and population (this was closer to the postcolonial gamble than state-builders acknowledged).[110] The priority of the monopoly on violence is evident in the "sequencing" of tasks for state-builders in various policy prescriptions: the first task is always to provide security and disarm combatants.[111] The US military prefers to avoid the terms "nation-building" or "state-building," yet its counterinsurgency field manual states "the cornerstone of any [counterinsurgency] effort is establishing security for the civilian populace .... [W]ithout a security environment, no permanent reforms can be implemented and disorder spreads."[112]

Implicitly and explicitly, state-builders reserve the right to proscribe political contestation because "if democracy means risking civil war and the disintegration of the state, then the risk, in human rights terms, may not be worth running."[113] Ignatieff's position was echoed by a later high-level UN panel that made a telling juxtaposition: "Any event or process that leads to large-scale death or lessening of life chances and undermines States as the basic unit of the international system is a threat to international security."[114] If the argument in this book is correct, of course, the process that led to large-scale death and undermined states is state formation itself!

At this point, the reader may feel déjà vu on hearing of *another* service—human rights—that had to be delivered to recalcitrant subjects unable or unwilling to supply it for themselves. In Chapter 6, I described Jomo Kenyatta telling his compatriots on Independence Day that they should not expect the police and prisons to disappear. Kenyatta, like other anti-colonial leaders, suspected that the support of many Kenyans was restricted to the removal of coercive institutions. Insofar as he anticipated retaining these institutions to deliver development, he expected opposition. Others, like Nehru, misrecognized support for the anti-colonial movements for support for the interventions of the postcolonial state, and castigated civil disobedience like strikes as tactics whose time had gone. Consequently, anti-colonial alliances between rulers and the population

---

[109] Ignatieff 2001, 171–173.
[110] Paris 2004, 186–211, 235.
[111] E.g., Rotberg 2004, 32; Orr 2004, 23; Dobbins et al. 2007, xiii.
[112] Department of Army 2007, 42.
[113] Ignatieff 2001, 172. For a more recent statement, see Fukuyama 2014, 29–30.
[114] United Nations 2004, 2, 23.

dissolved over time (to the extent that we may now reinterpret these alliances as tactical, not indicative of popular commitment to sacrifice for the postcolonial state), leading in some cases to existential threats to the postcolonial state like insurgencies, or more mundane but persistent challenges to its writ, such as mobilizations that retained the capacity for transgression and violence. These outside options could not be eliminated in the absence of costly war, and the population could prefer them to challenge the gamble they had not consented to in the first place.

Viewing the breakdown of African states in 1987, Chinua Achebe's character Ikem reflected that "it can't be the massive corruption, though its scale and pervasiveness are truly intolerable; it isn't the subservience to foreign manipulation, degrading as it is; it isn't even this second-class, hand-me-down capitalism, ludicrous and doomed." The real problem was "the failure of our rulers to re-establish inner links with the poor and dispossessed of this country."[115] This book suggests that the problem is even more fundamental: over history, the population, especially the poor and dispossessed, have rarely ever preferred, much less demanded, the construction of a modern centralized state, and they have been unwilling to make the necessary sacrifices for it outside the rare, and now unlikely, exigency of costly war.

The indifference the population showed toward the wars of sovereigns prior to the French Revolution has, 200 years later, been replaced by heightened expectations placed on the institutions responsible for order. I have suggested that expectations of order derive, to some degree, from proposed alternatives to the modern state, because these alternatives highlight perceived failures of the state. Consequently, expectations of order develop in opposition to the state. Insofar as the state is restaged to satisfy these expectations, *the state is expected to do more than it has already failed to do*, hence the persistent gap between the demand for services and the supply of the state. Evidence of these heightened expectations abounds in what state-builders understand their tasks to be: it is not a modest mission they have set themselves. For example, theUS Department of Defense, in a 2005 directive, reissued in 2009, defined "stability operations"—"to establish or maintain order when civilians cannot do so"— as a "core mission" on par with combat operations. To this end, the Defense Department would disarm former combatants, play a role in "strengthening governance and the rule of law," and "fostering economic stability and development."[116] Another plan to "fix failed states" describes "ten functions of the

---

[115] Quoted in Davidson 1992, 290–291.

[116] DoDI 3000.05, September 16, 2009, 3. Available at http://www.dtic.mil/whs/directives/corres/pdf/300005p.pdf.

state": "rule of law," "monopoly on the legitimate means of violence," "administrative control," "sound management of public finances," "investments in human capital," "creation of citizenship rights through social policies," "provision of infrastructure services," "formation of a market," "management of public assets," and "effective public borrowing."[117] To measure "state weakness in the developing world," a Brookings Institution study looks at the indicators such as access to water, primary school completion, and GDP growth, indicating just how much the state has become responsible for.[118] In contrast with neoliberal arguments, the state is seen as necessary for markets to function: "a capable and accountable state creates opportunities for poor people, provides better services, and improves development outcomes."[119]

Such prescriptions are not just the wish list of armchair strategists: in addition to the US Defense Department, the authors of the above analyses include a prime minister of Afghanistan (Ashraf Ghani), a US National Security Advisor (Susan Rice), and the World Bank. These prescriptions embody the belief that state weakness is not, ultimately, a problem of material capacity. Rather, state weakness is another way of saying that the *demand for services* exceeds the willingness of the population in most parts of the world to *supply the state*.

Full Circle

We have now come full circle. State formation through costly war and conquest, as the costs of war increased, made costly war less likely. In the absence of costly war, the population could not be compelled to give up alternatives to the state. They have consequently preferred these alternatives, as outside options, to challenge the state and demand more services. Thus, the supply of the state has fallen short of the demand for services. Contemporary state weakness is the latest manifestation of this gap, because the state is expected to abjure precisely those processes—costly war and conquest—that forced the population to prefer the state to alternatives and supply it at a high level. The prevalence of state weakness is the consequence of state formation.

In this chapter I have highlighted human rights as motivation for the contemporary project of state-building. Ironically, human rights movements originated

---

[117] Ghani and Lockhart 2009, 124–163. Other "guides" to state-building have a similarly expansive list of prescriptions—for example, Rotberg 2004; Eizenstat, Porter, and Weinstein 2005; Dobbins et al. 2007.

[118] Rice and Patrick 2008, 9.

[119] World Bank 2012, 7; Fukuyama 2004, 22.

as challenges to the state, identifying the costs of previous state-making behavior as excessive, and gestured to alternatives to the state. This is not to say that states cannot observe human rights; but it is to say that establishing a state today is difficult, because human rights violations can be challenged while previously states were constructed with little regard for human rights. State weakness in the contemporary era—when repressive states that monopolize violence are seen as weak because they violate human rights and can unravel quickly and violently (like Libya pre-2011), and states without the repressive capacity to protect the human rights of their citizens are also seen as weak (like Libya post-2011)—is the manifestation of this difficulty.

At the same time, surely expectations of order could be achieved in different ways. Because European state formation was a violent process does not mean centralized states can only form through costly war and conquest. Even if we grant this argument, state-builders ignored two lessons from this history that compromised their enterprise. For the modern state to be a self-enforcing exchange rather than one imposed or propped up by outside actors, the population had to be willing to supply the state, by giving up the means of self-defense to a central authority and paying taxes, not just making demands on the state. By definition, in weak or failed states the population had not done so, and state-builders had to supply the state instead.

Second, state collapse and state weakness were not new. The crises of the state brought on in different ways by insurgencies and human rights movements should have suggested, at the very least, openness to alternative institutional arrangements that would have mitigated violence in the short run. The worst situation state-builders could find themselves in would be to promote an institution that sections of the population, capable of organized violence, deemed threatening. In such contexts, distrust of external powers or fear that internal rivals might capture state power would drive groups within the society to prefer their outside option and arm and/or use violence in self-defense. The insistence that states were the only possible outcome if human rights were to be protected ironically increased the odds of violence and human rights violations.

A paradox from Iraq will illustrate this unhappy outcome. In 2007, four years after the invasion, a poll indicated that a majority of Iraqis surveyed (51 percent) supported attacks on US forces, yet a majority (65 percent) also did not want the United States to leave. An ex-advisor to the US mission complained that "if supporting violence against the same soldiers you wish would stay is not confusion, then nothing is."[120] What might this group (between 16 percent and 51 percent of respondents) have been thinking? By desiring US forces to

---

[120] Noah Feldman, "The Undeparted," *New York Times Magazine*, April 8, 2007.

remain while attacking them, the Iraqis would achieve a rough balance of power in which no group was strong enough to control the state and disarm everyone else. By exercising their outside option of violence, they could force the United States to bargain with them. The outcome was a civil war, no monopoly on violence, and a weak, if not failed, state. State-building had produced the very outcome it aimed to avert.

9

A World of Weak States

Three stories from present and past: one, in March of 2015, prisoners awaiting trial in an Indian prison went to court to demand their fundamental right to watch the ongoing cricket World Cup. The judge granted their claim and directed the prison officials to install a cable connection within the week.[1] Two, in December of 2014, three health workers engaged in a polio eradication campaign in Pakistan were killed by militants. More than sixty health workers or police officers protecting them had been killed in that country between 2012 and 2014.[2] Three, in July 1874 during a devastating famine that ravaged much of South Asia, the *Economist* criticized the famine relief programs of the lieutenant-governor. The error of these programs, the writer inveighed, was that they would lead the natives to expect, for the first time in history, that "it is the duty of the Government to keep them alive."[3]

These vignettes concretize the argument of this book. Over the last 200 years, the process of state formation—initially through war and empire—has transformed expectations of what the state should do. These "expectations of order" have been double-edged. On the one hand, they have led to a reduction in conquest and interstate war and an increase in life expectancy of populations: a transformation of the state from a war-making entity to a developmental one. This transformation reflects increasing demands for services, even in weak states, from the questionable right to watch cable TV to more serious legislations such as the right to food. The standards for statehood have gone up. On the other, rising standards of statehood have been accompanied by frequent refusals of the writ of the state, such as long-running insurgencies. This opposition is *also* a product of the state's expanded role; as it has moved into more and more aspects of everyday life under capacious categories like "security" and "development," the population has moved from general indifference and occasional

---

[1] BBC News, "Indian Prisoners Win Right to Watch Cricket World Cup," March 5, 2015.
[2] BBC News, "Pakistan Gunmen Kill Four Polio Workers in Quetta," November 26, 2014.
[3] *Economist*, "The Indian Famine and the Indian Revenue," July 4, 1874, 802.

disaggregated struggle to more consistent and enduring opposition to the state. The paradox this book has addressed is that the state is incapable of fulfilling its fundamental tasks yet remains the central unit of world politics.

I have argued that the modern state should be understood as a self-undermining institution. State formation through costly war has, as the costs of war have risen, made costly war less likely. In the absence of costly war, the population is not compelled to support the state at high sacrifice over alternatives. Rather, they can support these alternatives as outside options to demand more services or sacrifice less for the state. The odd prospect of criminals demanding and getting cable TV as a matter of right and militants shooting health workers dispensing polio vaccine is a metaphor for the gap between the demand for services and the willingness to supply the state.

The modern state has come to be represented as the driver of the civilizing process wherein everyday life becomes less violent.[4] As such, it is said to be the necessary condition for peace and development in the international system.[5] State weakness, the inability of most states to monopolize violence and provide public goods, is bemoaned as a barrier to security and development. But to understand state weakness and its solution (rebuilding states) as primarily a material problem that can be solved through intervention and foreign aid is misleading. State weakness is no aberration but the consequence of how the modern state has developed over time. From its nineteenth-century origins, the modern state has rarely been self-enforcing, and popular willingness to supply the state has not been sufficient to satisfy expectations of order. Therefore, the category of state weakness as something anomalous and fixable is misleading, which begs three questions: first, what are the prospects for foreign policy in a world of weak states; second, what is the future of the state; third, what are the prospects for alternatives to the state?

Agreement before Institutions

I have argued that the war-making/state-making relationship is self-undermining because it raises the costs of war to a point where the population is no longer willing to supply the war-making state. As the parameters within which the costs of war are calculated are also the parameters conditioning the exchange between central authority and population, the shift toward the idea that interstate war and conquest is both too costly and avoidable means that the war-making/state-making relationship cannot be replicated in the contemporary moment.

[4] Elias 1982.
[5] ICISS 2001.

In the absence of costly but winnable war, the exchange between central authority and population is partial at best, operating weakly in some areas where large sections of the population are not recognized by the central authority. Even in "strong states," rights are now being limited and made a private rather than public responsibility, and the costs of services like education are increasingly externalized onto the population, suggesting that the exchange is subject to revision, not fixed for all time. There is a gap between the population's demand for services and its willingness to supply the state; and the population in many places is able to articulate historically disconnected local struggles to contest state power for long periods. This has three implications for foreign policy: the construction of centralized institutions, or state-building, is a misguided strategy; foreign aid that can be captured by the central authority is similarly problematic; and, given the ability of insurgent groups to prolong conflicts, it is imperative to bring a conflict situation to a negotiated settlement rather than seek a military victory.

State-building is a bad idea. The effort to "build institutions" does not occur in a historical vacuum but in a context in which prior efforts at centralization have failed and been resisted. "Building state capacity" in such a context is a Sisyphean task. Arguably, it is worse, because state-building is a choice, and Sisyphus had no choice but to push his rock. The rock that state-builders are pushing is popular unwillingness to supply the state. This means that insofar as state-builders get support from local actors, it will be limited to tactical alliances to secure local interests. These alliances do not necessarily mean broad support for centralization and the emergence of a monopoly on violence. Such centralization will be a threat to the diverse armed actors that operate in weak states, and they should be expected to balance against any actor that threatens to monopolize violence. At the same time, the routing of resources like aid through a presumptive central authority creates moral hazard: the availability of rents at the level of the state reduces the need to establish an exchange with the population and demand taxes from them. It also makes the state a prize to be captured and preserved from the population, rather than an institution constructed through bargaining with the population.

The moral hazard that routing resources through a central authority presents applies as well to foreign aid. The problems of the postcolonial state have mainly stemmed from its inability to get the population to disarm and to tax its population adequately; also, the resources provided by foreign powers have reduced the need or desire for leaders to establish an exchange with the population. As I argued in Chapter 6, rather than extract internally to wage war externally, postcolonial leaders could extract externally to either neglect or actively oppress their citizens. This relationship has proven doubly problematic: not only have postcolonial regimes been unpopular with their population, so have their foreign funders for supporting rulers who implement policies on behalf of foreign powers rather than their own people. Foreign aid and state-building do not occur in a historical vacuum but in relation to a population that is often ambivalent about foreign powers. The resources devoted to foreign aid might be better spent within donor states to lower the costs of products in poorer parts of the world *if capacity to make those products does not exist* and/or do research in those areas where the private sector does not. An example might be to pay drug companies to lower the cost of their medicines in Africa or Asia. Another might be funding environmental research that is then made accessible to groups in weak states. That said, one must be careful not to subsidize goods where poorer economies have a comparative advantage, like agriculture, for fear of undercutting producers in those economies (agricultural subsidies in Europe and North America provide a cautionary tale). Alternatively, why not disburse aid money directly to the poor in weak states and let them decide what services and providers are worth supporting?[6] Put another way, rather than supply the state from the outside, why not support the population and let them choose whether they want to support the state or some alternative institution?

If state-building and foreign aid are bad ideas, is there anything to be done? Contra the orthodoxy behind "building institutions" I offer a different formulation: "agreement before institutions." In weak states in general and conflict situations in particular, one cannot assume the population prefers the state to alternatives and is willing to sacrifice for it; indeed, it is more reasonable to assume the absence of such support and expect from the population a refusal to pay taxes and disarm. Rather than risk violence by imposing centralization (or aiding the central authority), it is productive to aim for the reverse—forming agreements that guarantee local autonomy in exchange for a cessation of violence. These agreements do create a role for foreign powers and international organizations, as enforcers of a peace deal, for example. Agreements to stop fighting can be extended to limited forms of cooperation designed to build trust but leaving each side with the outside option of retaking up arms. There is justifiable concern that hasty elections will foment violence.[7] However, democratic processes like elections and referendums, even if accompanied with a certain level of violence, are necessary

[6] Studies of cash transfers to poor people suggest that the poor generally make good decisions with money, contrary to paternalistic assumptions that they would squander it; Christopher Blattman, "Let Them Eat Cash," *New York Times*, June 29, 2014. Transfers are becoming easier to disburse with the spread of mobile banking and may not require a massive bureaucracy to administer. In Kenya, M-Pesa, a mobile-phone based money transfer system, had 17 million subscribers in 2014, in a population of 44 million. In 2012 M-Pesa processed transactions worth a third of Kenya's GDP; Murithi Mutiga, "Kenya's Banking Revolution Lights a Fire," *New York Times*, January 20, 2014.

[7] E.g., Ignatieff 2001, 172–173; Paris 2004.

to assess preferences and gain a popular mandate. The secondary motivation for enabling local actors to preserve their outside option, detailed below, is to compel them to bargain with the population in their areas of territorial control or broader community and extract some level of taxes. If I am correct that most states cannot compel their populations to make sacrifices equivalent to what they demand in services, then it is necessary to find other actors that can bargain with the population. To this end, it is not just pragmatic to not aspire for a monopoly on violence; it is potentially productive of future sources of revenue and the emergence of capable local actors. Foreign powers and international organizations should limit their role to "peacekeeping" and leave the "peacebuilding" to local actors.

Put another way, if our received wisdom about European state formation is that centralization preceded bargaining—that is, the need to fight external enemies compelled the population to disarm and pay taxes before making demands for representation and public goods—in the contemporary era, bargaining must precede centralization, and centralization may in fact never happen. For the short and medium term, bargaining between local actors designed to bring peace is likely to prevent the rise of a monopoly on violence. The role for a central authority, or foreign third parties, is then to enforce agreements between these actors, and to provide goods that cannot be provided locally. The reader will hear echoes of various proposals for federations as the colonial empires were ending, or versions of eighteenth-century treaty diplomacy between the colonists and native tribes of North America.[8] These, rather than the neo-imperial models mooted after 2001, are worth revisiting for their focus on reaching agreement. To get beyond the unsatisfying binary between the transcendence of the state in the face of markets and globalization and the reaffirmation of the state to provide security and institutions since 2001, it is necessary to revisit the relationship between the state and alternatives to it.

The Future of the State

Predictions of the state's impending obsolescence or demise have been frequent, and generally proven wrong. But resilience does not mean vitality. The process of state formation has undermined the prospect that the state can command the level of sacrifice necessary for it to deliver ever-expanding expectations of order. At the same time, the weakness of the state is not just because of the lack of costly but winnable war. Neoliberalism has altered the political economy of the modern state.

[8] E.g., Camus 2014; Tully 1995; Young 2000.

Recall that even as the nineteenth-century state expanded, it was still barely involved in many areas of life we now take for granted to be the state's responsibility. As the revenues of the state swelled because of war, it could provide a greater array of services. The effect of neoliberalism is not to return us to an era where the state has no responsibility for areas like health. Rather, neoliberalism's promotion of markets, privatization, and capital flows across borders has created alternatives to state provision of services. This has reduced the willingness of wealthy elites to fund public goods because they calculate, reasonably enough, that they don't wish to be taxed twice, once to provide for their own medical care or children's education and then to provide those services for others. This effect of neoliberalism is exacerbated by the rise of inequality in North America and Europe, as the wealthy mobilize to push for lower tax rates.[9] But the effect is particularly pronounced in the developing world, where wealth is lower and concentrated among a small elite.[10] Even if the state does not go away, the effect of this process is that the services it is expected to provide will either not be provided, as in the nineteenth century, or provided by other entities, of which more below.[11] But unlike the nineteenth century, the absence of these services will be blamed on the state, and unrest in the face of mass hunger or environmental degradation will be targeted at the state rather than local authorities, as in the nineteenth century.

Neoliberalism has placed constraints on the ability to extract, of which the more consequential may well be the promotion of private provision that reduces the willingness of elites to pay the extortionary rates of marginal tax they paid in the face of war. The diminishment of external threat and the inability of many states to fulfill basic functions suggest that even if the state remains the central unit, there is a role for other organizations better suited to provide certain goods. Protectorates, for example, may be the optimal way to provide security, given diminished threats.[12] Are we likely to see a return to arrangements of pooled sovereignty, like the Hanseatic League? I now turn to this question.

What, Then, of Alternatives?

State formation is the source of rising expectations of order. In contrast with arguments identifying exogenous constraints on the state-building enterprise, I have

[9] Piketty 2014.

[10] This is particularly pernicious when such elites purchase services overseas, because not only does their willingness to pay taxes diminish but the revenue and capacity of local institutions is also reduced. Kapur and Mehta estimate, for example, that in 2005–2006, Indian students studying abroad spent $3.5 billion in their host countries while the Indian government spent $4.3 billion on higher education at home; Kapur and Mehta 2008.

[11] Appadurai 2002; Slaughter 2004.

[12] Lake 2009.

suggested that the problem is endogenous: the costly wars necessary for the formation of centralized states have made state-building more difficult over time. These expectations have transformed the role of the modern, centralized state from war-fighting and conquest, the purpose for which it emerged in Europe. Not only is it more difficult, if not impossible, to replicate the European process of state formation; it is also difficult to see a situation under which the high level of sacrifice that made possible the expansion of social programs in Europe and America can be induced by existing states. In some ways, this is a good thing because state-building in the past was a violent process, and the world sees lower levels of war and conquest. But the exigencies of war and conquest also generated a greater willingness of the population to supply the state, and this is now lacking. Yet the population's expectations of order—of reduced conflict and better standards of living—have not diminished, and these expectations have developed in the process of struggle against the state. These expectations cannot be wished away; the question is how to achieve them if the state cannot. The preceding pages imply that alternatives to the state, almost by default, have to be part of the solution, but they also suggest a glaring lacuna in these alternatives.

Alternatives to the state identified the self-undermining nature of the modern state. But such alternative visions rarely addressed the problem of how to get the population to make the sacrifices necessary to satisfy increased expectations of rights, services, and representation. If anything, they have expanded expectations by *not* demanding sacrifices of the public, and/or internalizing costs previously externalized onto the population. Kwame Nkrumah identified this problem five decades ago at the success of the independence movement in Ghana: "The leaders are now expected, simply as a result of having acquired independence, to work miracles . . . . [T]he people look for new schools, new towns, new factories . . . . [T]hey *expect* political equality to bring economic equality . . . . [T]hey do not realize what it may cost."[13] Nkrumah himself would duck the problem by appealing for foreign aid. Rising expectations of order are a consistent theme, visible in the arguments in Chapter 5 that markets would improve the provision of goods like education, in the condemnations of the colonial and postcolonial state in Chapters 6 and 7, and are reflected in the prescriptions of state-builders in Chapter 8. But there is very little discussion of how to pay the costs, especially in the long term.

To this end, alternatives to the state can play two roles, one complementing the state and the other potentially opposing it. Alternatives can work to increase popular willingness to sacrifice on a variety of causes where the state is unable to induce sacrifice: they can make up some of the gap between the demand for services and the willingness to supply the state. At the same time, they can keep

---

[13] Nkrumah 1958, 51, emphasis mine.

alive the possibility of refusing the writ of the state, what I have called the outside option. We can expect the population in most of the world to be unwilling to pay taxes to the state. Indeed, as we saw in Chapter 5, the only condition under which the governed have been willing to pay an extortionate level of direct tax to the state is under the threat of costly war, and this was for a relatively brief period. It is unlikely that most states can compel that level of direct taxation now or in future.[14] Yet market mechanisms will probably undersupply goods like education, especially to the poorest. Therefore, it is necessary to look to other organizations that can levy taxes on production and transactions (or to mobilize the population's willingness to be taxed toward a more local cause, like public buses). The idea here is to construct "tax units" at various, and likely overlapping, scales that can then engage in bargaining with other "tax units" after having established some level of local support. At the local level, given the cost of tax collection at point of sale, the primary taxes can be taxes on goods, collected at production, with the costs passed on to consumers. Taxes can also be levied on the sale of assets like land. "Tax units" would obviously include existing states. But most states, even in Europe, are not very good at collecting direct taxes from their citizens. Rather than rely on the state, tax collection needs to be pluralized.[15] Various "tax units" can then reach agreements with others and pool revenue to provide goods that cross jurisdictions. This would be extremely inefficient, as transaction costs would be involved at different levels, and the net tax take would be lower than if an effective centralized state was taxing.

If this sounds like a repetition of the state-making process in North America, where goods like schooling were initially provided at a local level, there is an important difference. One cannot expect a return to large-scale interstate war and conquest. The process of state formation has increased the destructiveness of interstate wars and, through the generation of exclusive categories, made intrastate wars longer in duration: contemporary wars are unlikely to make states as wars did in the past. In lieu of this, more modest extraction has to be justified locally by promising goods like education, which can be monitored at a local level. Given that most tax units are likely to be restricted in terms of numbers of taxpayers and dependent on commerce for inputs, they will find it hard to fund and enforce protectionist policies, and also find it hard to run up foreign debts that eventually lead to painful adjustment or default. This is on aggregate a good thing because if it encourages the pursuit of comparative advantage and

---

[14] Direct taxes in non-OECD states account for proportionately less revenue (20 percent of revenue) than in OECD states (30 percent); Ross 2004. If we account for the difference in tax ratios, direct taxes account for about 4 percent of GDP outside the OECD and 10 percent within it.

[15] This does not require territorial control, for charities and religious groups can be tax units as well if they share a portion of their proceeds with other tax units.

relatively unencumbered trade, aggregate economic growth will be higher (in this sense neoliberal arguments have some validity and cannot be rejected in favor of a state-centric development model).

By contrast, many postcolonial states were so large that it was difficult to effectively tax remote regions or disarm their populations, yet large enough to enforce protectionist policies that over time and with the "help" of foreign aid, distorted their economies. Charles Tilly's great insight was that taxation and military service enabled the population to make demands on the state. Conversely, debt and foreign aid reduce the pressure on the state to recognize the demands of the population. As military service is unlikely to be as salient a mechanism in the contemporary era, it is essential to look at alternatives to the state that can increase the population's willingness to pay taxes (and reduce debt and foreign aid). In the absence of war and conquest, these tax units may not concede as many powers to the center as occurred in the late nineteenth century and on through the world wars (indeed, one of the implications of insurgencies is an unwillingness to cede the monopoly of violence to the state and to make it impossible to establish a self-enforcing exchange). The outcome may be polycentric forms of order that separate governance from government, then divide governance along several scales, leaving some to be provided locally within the tax unit (e.g., policing, primary education, health care), some through coordination between tax units (e.g., infrastructure, higher education), and others delegated to states (e.g., currencies and subsidies for research and development), or regional and international organizations serving particular functions (e.g., setting environmental standards). States would continue to exist; indeed, they would remain the most powerful actors in the system. But in the many places where existing states cannot induce their populations to pay taxes, other organizations serving as tax units can supplement or substitute for the state and enter into bargaining relationships with it and other entities. These "tax units" if recognized in more or less formal fashion could make up some of the gap between the demand for services—what I have called "expectations of order"—and the willingness to supply the state.

The other role alternatives to the modern state can play is to keep alive the possibility of refusing the writ of the state, as human rights movements emerged to do. There is a strategic element to this; namely, that an "outside option" in the form of an alternative to the state confers some bargaining power to populations otherwise at the mercy of the state but unable to establish a viable state of their own. More important, it remains clear that ordinary people expect something different from what their experience has given them; in this sense, they are modern.[16] If the history of state formation teaches us one thing, it is that

---

[16] Koselleck 2004.

making it the responsibility of the state to fulfill these expectations—to trust in what James Scott called "high modernism"—is a costly and only occasionally successful gamble.[17] High modernism has a monumental quality, from Baron Haussmann's boulevards in Paris to the carving out of the Amazonian rainforest to build Oscar Niemeyer's Brasilia. But this grandeur, which often came at the expense of the population, is now harder to replicate. Let us recall that the boulevards were built to enable a clear field of fire for Louis Napoleon's troops and the junta that built Brasilia was deposed because of such excesses.[18] In the 1960s the top-down nature of architectural modernism came under attack in theory and practice. Critics identified the irony that the cities of the future were being designed without much concern for those who would live in them. Most famously, Robert Moses's effort to build an expressway through Central Park in New York incited protests led by the urbanist Jane Jacobs. For the first time, Moses had to back down. Currently, the only places where such vaulting visions can be realized are in autocracies, where there are often concerns about the stability of the state. Hence the Burmese military junta has built a new capital in the jungle, just as Brazil did fifty years ago, and the Qatar monarchy has erected an entirely new sporting infrastructure with an imported and rightless workforce that outnumbers its own citizens.

The association of "high modernism" with violence hearkens back: Tsar Peter compelled every stonemason in the Russian Empire to build his new capital in St. Petersburg and prohibited building in stone anywhere else in his domain.[19] Stalin used 200,000 gulag prisoners to build the White Sea Canal. Both Peter and Stalin wished to establish their states on new foundations, to exceed their European rivals and "develop" their own people. But the convulsions of state-building in Russia exemplify the self-undermining tendency I have described in these pages. At the same time, these monuments exist, in fact and more importantly in the imagination. They have transformed expectations—epistemological and political—that is, expectations of what is possible and what one is due. Because one is unwilling to be evicted and pay taxes for wide boulevards does not mean one will not protest narrow, crowded streets.

If "high modernism" is too costly, maybe we can hope for a "low modernism." Low modernism begins with the realization that high modernism cannot be replicated. It is not a return to "traditional" modes of life—whether centralized polities like a caliphate or decentralized indigenous communities—because these emerge in relation to the modern state and its categories of governance. But it does involve engaging with the idiom of these modes of life—from veiled female

---

[17] Scott 1998, 4–5.
[18] Berman 1988, 150–152; Scott 1998, 60–62.
[19] Berman 1988, 176–178.

activists challenging interpretations of the Koran to indigenous people reviving previously banned practices like the potlatch—to establish a place from which to challenge the state or make demands on it. To paraphrase Giorgio Agamben, these groups are not always already in the place of politics; they must come into it. The formation of the modern state, we have seen, was predicated on the claim that some groups lacked a state, were outside of history, and thus could not be political beings. In response, they have become political beings by asserting their membership in collectivities that oppose the state or refuse its writ. Their history comes from their struggle against the state. But unlike a century ago, that history can no longer be disregarded. Alternatives to the state bring people into politics and give them a history, where the state will not. For this reason, alternatives to the state have, do, and will continue to be around us.

BIBLIOGRAPHY

Acemoglu, Daron, and James Robinson. 2006. *Economic Origins of Dictatorship and Democracy.* New York: Cambridge University Press.

Acemoglu, Daron, and James Robinson. 2012. *Why Nations Fail: The Origins of Power, Prosperity and Poverty.* New York: Crown.

Achebe, Chinua. 1958. *When Things Fall Apart.* New York: Vintage.

Achebe, Chinua. 2012. *There Was a Country: A Personal History of Biafra.* New York: Penguin.

Acheson, Dean. 1947. "The Requirements of Reconstruction." *Record of the Week,* May 18, 1947.

Amin, Shahid. 1995. *Event, Metaphor, Memory: Chauri Chaura, 1922–1992.* Berkeley: University of California Press.

Anderson, Benedict. 1991. *Imagined Communities: Reflections on the Origin and Spread of Nationalism.* London: Verso.

Ansell, Ben, and David Samuels. 2014. *Inequality and Democratization: An Elite-Competition Approach.* New York: Cambridge University Press.

Appadurai, Arjun. 1996. *Modernity at Large: Cultural Dimensions of Globalization.* Minneapolis: University of Minnesota Press.

Appadurai, Arjun. 2002. "Deep Democracy: Urban Governmentality and the Horizon of Politics." *Public Culture* 14(1): 21–47.

Arendt, Hannah. 1951. *Origins of Totalitarianism.* New York: Harvest.

Arendt, Hannah. 1963. *On Revolution.* New York: Viking.

Aron, Raymond. 1965. *The Great Debate: Theories of Nuclear Strategy.* (Trans. Ernst Pawel) New York: Garden City.

Aron, Raymond. 1966. *Peace and War: A Theory of International Relations.* New York: Doubleday.

Asad, Talal. 2003. *Formations of the Secular: Christianity, Islam, and Modernity.* Stanford, CA: Stanford University Press.

Asch, Michael. 2014. *On Being Here to Stay: Treaties and Aboriginal Rights in Canada.* Toronto: University of Toronto Press.

Ash, Timothy Garton. 1986. "Does Central Europe Exist?" *New York Review of Books* 33(15).

Ash, Timothy Garton. 1990. "Revolution of the Magic Lantern." *New York Review of Books* 36(21).

Atomic Scientists of Chicago. 1945. "Pearl Harbor Anniversary and the Moscow Conference." *Bulletin of Atomic Scientists* 1(1): 1–1.

Austin, J. L. 1975. *How to Do Things with Words.* Cambridge, MA: Harvard University Press.

Axelrod, Robert. 1986. *The Evolution of Cooperation.* New York: Basic.

Azikiwe, Nnamdi. 1937. *Renascent Africa.* London: Frank Cass.

Azikiwe, Nnamdi. 1961. *Zik: A Selection from the Speeches of Nnamdi Azikiwe.* Cambridge: Cambridge University Press.

Bagehot, Walter. 1873. *Physics and Politics.* London: Henry S. King.

Bailyn, Bernard. 1992. *The Ideological Origins of the American Revolution*. Cambridge, MA: Harvard University Press.

Balcells, Laia, and Stathis Kalyvas. 2014. "Does Warfare Matter? Severity, Duration and Outcomes of Civil Wars." *Journal of Conflict Resolution* 58(8): 1390–1418.

Ball, Desmond. 1982. "U.S. Strategic Forces: How Would They Be Used?" *International Security* 7(3): 31–60.

Barkawi, Tarak. 2006. *Globalization and War*. New York: Roman and Littlefield.

Barro, Robert. 1987. "Government Spending, Interest Rates, Prices and Budget Deficits in the United Kingdom, 1701–1918." *Journal of Monetary Economics* 20(2): 221–247.

Bartelson, Jens. 1995. *A Genealogy of Sovereignty*. New York: Cambridge University Press.

Bates, Robert. 2008. *When Things Fell Apart: State Failure in Late-Century Africa*. New York: Cambridge University Press.

Baum, Bruce. 2006. *The Rise and Fall of the Caucasian Race: A Political History of Racial Identity*. New York: New York University Press.

Baviskar, Amita. 1995. *In the Belly of the River: Tribal Conflicts over Development in the Narmada Valley*. New Delhi: Oxford University Press.

Bayly, C.A. 2004. *The Birth of the Modern World, 1780–1914*. Oxford: Blackwell.

Becker, Gary. 1962. "Investment in Human Capital: A Theoretical Analysis." *Journal of Political Economy* 70(5): 9–49.

Becker, Gary. 1981. "Altruism in the Family and Selfishness in the Marketplace." *Economica* 48:1–15.

Becker, Gary, and Nigel Tomes. 1986. "Human Capital and the Rise and Fall of Families." *Journal of Labor Economics* 4(3): S1–S39.

Bell, Duncan. 2007. *The Idea of Greater Britain: Empire and the Future of World Order, 1860–1900*. Princeton, NJ: Princeton University Press.

Bell, Catherine, and Michael Asch. 1997. "Challenging Assumptions: The Impact of Precedent in Aboriginal Rights Litigation." In Michael Asch (ed.), *Aboriginal and Treaty Rights in Canada*, 38–74. Vancouver: University of British Columbia Press.

Benda, Vaclav, et al. 1988. "Parallel Polis, or An Independent Society in Central and Eastern Europe: An Inquiry." *Social Research* 55(1/2): 211–246.

Ben-Porath, Sigal, and Rogers Smith (eds.). 2013. *Varieties of Sovereignty and Citizenship*. Philadelphia: Pennsylvania University Press.

Bergstrom, Theodore. 1989. "A Fresh Look at the Rotten Kid Theorem—and Other Household Mysteries." *Journal of Political Economy* 97(5): 1138–1159.

Berman, Marshall. 1988. *All That Is Solid Melts into Air: The Experience of Modernity*. New York: Penguin.

Beteille, Andre. 1998. "The Idea of Indigenous People." *Current Anthropology* 39(2): 187–191.

Beveridge, William. 1942. *Social Insurance and Allied Services*. London: His Majesty's Stationery Office.

Bhabha, Homi. 1994. *The Location of Culture*. New York: Routledge.

Bhukya, Bhagya. 2008. "The Mapping of the Adivasi Social: Colonial Anthropology and Adivasis." *Economic and Political Weekly* 43(39): 103–109.

Biddle, Tami Davis. 2002. *Rhetoric and Reality in Air Warfare: The Evolution of British and American Ideas about Strategic Bombing, 1914–1945*. Princeton, NJ: Princeton University Press.

Bose, Sugata. 1990. "Starvation amidst Plenty: The Making of Famine in Bengal, Honan, and Tonkin, 1942–1945." *Modern Asian Studies* 24(4): 699–727.

Bourguignon, Francois, and Christian Morrison. 2002. "Inequality among World Citizens: 1820–1992." *American Economic Review* 92(4): 727–744.

Boyer, John. 1995. "Drafting Salvation." *University of Chicago Magazine* 88(2).

Brands, Hal. 2006. "Rethinking Nonproliferation: L.B.J., the Gilpatric Committee, and U.S. National Security Policy." *Journal of Cold War Studies* 8(2): 83–113.

Braumoeller, Bear. 2012. *The Great Powers and the International System: Systemic Theory in Empirical Perspective*. New York: Cambridge University Press.

Brodie, Bernard (ed.). 1946. *The Absolute Weapon*. New York: Harcourt.

Brodie, Bernard. 1949. "Strategy as a Science." *World Politics* 1(4): 467–488.

Brodie, Bernard. 1959. *Strategy in the Missile Age*. Princeton, NJ: Princeton University Press.

Brodie, Bernard. 1973. *War and Politics*. New York: Macmillan.

Buckler, F.W. 1922. "The Political Theory of the Indian Mutiny." *Transaction of the Royal Historical Society* 5: 71–100.

Bundy, McGeorge. 1988. *Danger and Survival: Choices about the Bomb in the First Fifty Years*. New York: Random House.

Burbank, Jane, and Frederick Cooper. 2010. *Empires in World History: Power and the Politics of Difference*. Princeton, NJ: Princeton University Press.

Burke, Edmund. 1973. "Reflections on the Revolution in France." In Edmund Burke and Thomas Paine, *Two Classics of the French Revolution*, 15–266. New York: Anchor.

Burgess, John. 1890. *Political Science and Comparative Constitutional Law*, Volume 1. New York: Baker and Taylor.

Cabral, Amilcar. 1979. *Unity and Struggle*. (Trans. Michael Wolfers) New York: Monthly Review Press.

Call, Charles, and Vanessa Wyeth (eds.). 2008. *Building States to Build Peace*. Boulder, CO: Lynne Rienner.

Camus, Albert. 2014. *Algerian Chronicles*. (Trans. Arthur Goldhammer) Cambridge, MA: Harvard University Press.

Carr, E. H. 2001. *The Twenty Years' Crisis*. New York: Harper Perennial.

Casement, Roger. 1915. *The Crime against Europe: A Possible Outcome of the War of 1914*. Philadelphia: Celtic Press.

Carter Commission. 1966. *Report of the Royal Commission on Taxation*. Ottawa: Government of Canada.

Centeno, Miguel. 2002. *Blood and Debt: War and the Nation-State in Latin America*. University Park: Pennsylvania State University Press.

Chakrabarty, Dipesh. 2007. "'In the Name of Politics': Democracy and the Power of the Multitude in India." *Public Culture* 19(1): 35–57.

Chaloupka, William. 1992. *Knowing Nukes: The Politics and Culture of the Atom*. Minneapolis: University of Minnesota Press.

Chang, Gordon. 1988. "J.F.K., China, and the Bomb." *Journal of American History* 74(4): 1287–1310.

Chatterjee, Partha. 1993. *The Nation and Its Fragments: Colonial and Postcolonial Histories*. New Delhi: Oxford University Press.

Chesterman, Simon, Michael Ignatieff, and Ramesh Thakur (eds.). 2005. *Making States Work: State Failure and the Crisis of Governance*. New York: United Nations Press.

Chowdhury, Arjun. 2011. "The Giver or the Recipient? The Peculiar Ownership of Human Rights." *International Political Sociology* 5(1): 35–51.

Chowdhury, Arjun. 2012. "Shocked by War: The Non-Politics of Orientalism." In Tarak Barkawi and Keith Stanski (eds.), *Orientalism and War*, 19–37. New York: Columbia University Press.

Chowdhury, Arjun, and Raymond Duvall. 2014. "Sovereignty and Sovereign Power." *International Theory* 6(2): 191–223.

Christia, Fotini. 2012. *Alliance Formation in Civil Wars*. Cambridge: Cambridge University Press.

Clapham, Christopher. 1996. *Africa and the International System: The Politics of State Survival*. Cambridge: Cambridge University Press.

Clastres, Pierre. 1989. *Society against the State*. (Trans. Robert Hurley) New York: Zone.

Clark, Tom, and Andrew Dilnot. 2002. *Long Term Trends in British Taxation and Spending*. Institute for Fiscal Studies Briefing Note 25.

von Clausewitz, Carl. 1976. *On War*. (Trans. Michael Howard and Peter Paret) Princeton, NJ: Princeton University Press.

Coase, Ronald. 1976. "Adam Smith's View of Man." *Journal of Law and Economics* 19(3): 529–546.

Coggan, Philip. 2012. *Paper Promises: Debt, Money, and the New World Order*. New York: Public Affairs.

Colley, Linda. 1992. *Britons: Forging the Nation, 1707–1837*. New Haven, CT: Yale University Press.

Collier, Paul. 2007. *The Bottom Billion: Why the Poorest Countries Are Failing and What Can Be Done about It*. New York: Oxford University Press.

Collier, Paul, and Anke Hoeffler. 1998. "Greed and Grievance in Civil War." *Oxford Economic Papers* 56(4): 563–595.

Comaroff, Jean, and John Comaroff. 1991. *Of Revelation and Revolution*, Volume 1: *Christianity, Colonialism, and Consciousness in South Africa*. Chicago: University of Chicago Press.

Comaroff, Jean, and John Comaroff. 2009. *Ethnicity, Inc.* Chicago: University of Chicago Press.

Cooper, Frederick. 2005. *Colonialism in Question: Theory, Knowledge, History*. Berkeley: University of California Press.

Council of Economic Advisers. 1950. *The Economics of National Defense: Fifth Annual Report to the President by the Council of Economic Advisors*. Washington, DC: White House.

Cullather, Nick. 2010. *The Hungry World: America's Cold War Battle against Poverty in Asia*. Cambridge, MA: Harvard University Press.

Dahl, Robert. 1953. "Atomic Energy and the Democratic Process." *Annals of the American Academy of Political and Social Science* 290: 1–6.

Damodaran, Vinita. 2006. "The Politics of Marginality and the Construction of Indigeneity in Chotanagpur." *Postcolonial Studies* 9(2): 179–196.

Daunton, M. J. 1996. "How to Pay for the War: State, Society, and Taxation in Britain, 1917–1924." *English Historical Review* 111: 882–919.

Davidson, Basil. 1969. *The Liberation of Guinea: Aspects of an African Revolution*. New York: Penguin.

Davidson, Basil. 1992. *The Black Man's Burden: Africa and the Curse of the Nation-State*. New York: Times Books.

Davis, Mike. 2001. *Late Victorian Holocausts: El Nino Famines and the Making of the Third World*. New York: Verso.

Davis, Mike. 2006. *Planet of Slums*. New York: Verso.

Davies, Norman. 2012. *Vanished Kingdoms: The Rise and Fall of States and Nations*. New York: Viking.

Deaton, Angus. 2013. *The Great Escape: Health, Wealth, and the Origins of Inequality*. Princeton, NJ: Princeton University Press.

Demos, T. J. 2003. "Circulations: In and Around Zurich Dada." *October* 105: 147–158.

Department of Army. 2007. *US Army/Marine Corps Counterinsurgency Field Manual*. Chicago: University of Chicago Press.

de Tocqueville, Alexis. 2001. *Writings on Empire and Slavery*. (Trans. Jennifer Pitts) Baltimore: Johns Hopkins University Press.

Devi, Mahshweta. 1995. *Imaginary Maps: Three Stories by Mahashweta Devi*. (Trans. Gayatri Chakravorty Spivak) New York: Routledge.

Dhanagare, D. N. 1974. "Social Origins of the Peasant Insurrection in Telangana (1946–1951)." *Contributions to Indian Sociology* 8(1): 109–134.

Dikotter, Frank. 2010. *Mao's Great Famine: The History of China's Most Devastating Catastrophe, 1958–1962*. New York: Walker.

Diop, Cheikh Anta. 1978. *Black Africa: The Economic and Cultural Basis for a Federated State*. (Trans. Harold Salemson) Westport, CT: Lawrence Hill.

Dirks, Nicholas. 2001. *Castes of Mind: Colonialism and the Making of Modern India*. Princeton, NJ: Princeton University Press.

Dirks, Nicholas. 2006. *The Scandal of Empire: India and the Creation of Imperial Britain*. Cambridge, MA: Belknap Press.

Dobbins, James, et al. 2003. *America's Role in Nation Building from Germany to Iraq*. Santa Monica: RAND.

Dobbins, James, et al. 2007. *The Beginner's Guide to Nation-Building*. Santa Monica: RAND.

Doyle, Michael, and Nicholas Sambanis. 2006. *Making War and Building Peace: United Nations Peace Operations*. Princeton, NJ: Princeton University Press.

Drelichman, Mauricio, and Hans Joachim Voth. 2008. "Debt Sustainability in Historical Perspective: The Role of Fiscal Repression." *Journal of the European Economic Association* 6(2/3): 657–667.

Duara, Prasenjit. 2001. "The Discourse of Civilization and Pan-Asianism." *Journal of World History* 12(1): 99–130.

Du Bois, W. E. B. 1917. "Of the Culture of White Folk." *Journal of Race Development* 7(4): 434–447.

Dubois, Laurent. 2011. *Haiti: The Aftershocks of History*. New York: Metropolitan Books.

Eizenstat, Stuart, John Porter, and Jeremy Weinstein. 2005. "Rebuilding Weak States." *Foreign Affairs* 84(1): 134–145.

Eksteins, Modris. 1989. *Rites of Spring: The Great War and the Birth of the Modern Age*. Boston: Houghton Mifflin.

Elias, Norbert. 1982. *Power and Civility, The Civilizing Process*, Volume II. (Trans. Edmund Jephcott) New York: Pantheon Books.

Elwin, Verrier. 1963. *A New Deal for Tribal India*. New Delhi: Ministry of Home Affairs.

Engerman, Stanley, and Kenneth Sokoloff. 2012. *Economic Development in the Americas since 1500: Endowments and Institutions*. New York: Cambridge University Press.

Escobar, Arturo. 1995. *Encountering Development: The Making and Unmaking of the Third World*. Princeton, NJ: Princeton University Press.

Esdaile, Charles. 1988. "War and Politics in Spain, 1808–1814." *Historical Journal* 31(2): 295–317.

Esenbel, Selcuk. 2004. "Japan's Global Claim to Asia and the World of Islam: Transnational Nationalism and World Power, 1900–1945." *American Historical Review* 109(4): 1140–1170.

Eucken, Walter. 1948. "On the Theory of the Centrally Administered Economy: An Analysis of the German Experiment, Part II." (Trans. T. W. Hutchison) *Economica* 15(59): 173–193.

Eucken, Walter, and Fritz Meyer. 1948. "The Economic Situation in Germany." *Annals of the American Academy of Political and Social Science* 260: 53–62.

Fabian, Johannes. 1982. *Time and the Other: How Anthropology Makes Its Object*. (Trans. Matti Bunzl) New York: Columbia University Press.

Fanon, Frantz. 1963. *The Wretched of the Earth*. New York: Grove Press.

Fanon, Frantz. 1967. *Black Skin, White Masks*. (Trans. Charles Markmann) New York: Grove Press.

Faust, Drew Gilpin. 2009. *This Republic of Suffering: Death and the American Civil War*. New York: Random House.

Fazal, Tanisha. 2007. *State Death: The Politics and Geography of Conquest, Occupation, and Annexation*. Princeton, NJ: Princeton University Press.

Fearon, James. 1995. "Rationalist Explanations for War." *International Organization* 49(3): 379–414.

Fearon, James. 2004. "Why Do Some Civil Wars Last So Much Longer than Others?" *Journal of Peace Research* 41(3): 275-301.

Fearon, James. 2011. "Self-Enforcing Democracy." *Quarterly Journal of Economics* 126(4): 1661–1708.

Fearon, James, and David Laitin. 2003. "Ethnicity, Insurgency, and Civil War." *American Political Science Review* 97(1): 75–90.

Fearon, James, and David Laitin. 2004. "Neotrusteeship and the Problem of Weak States." *International Security* 28(4): 5–47.

Ferguson, James. 1994. *The Anti-Politics Machine: "Development," Depoliticization, and Bureaucratic Power in Lesotho*. Minneapolis: University of Minnesota Press.

Ferguson, Niall. 1994. "Public Finance and National Security: The Domestic Origins of the First World War Revisited." *Past & Present* 142: 141–168.

Finnemore, Martha. 2003. *The Purpose of Intervention: Changing Beliefs and the Use of Force*. Ithaca, NY: Cornell University Press.

Fischer, Sibylle. 2004. *Modernity Disavowed: Haiti and the Cultures of Slavery in the Age of Revolution*. Durham, NC: Duke University Press.

Foucault, Michel. 2003. *Society Must Be Defended: Lectures at the College de France, 1975–1976.* (Trans. David Macey) New York: Picador.

Foucault, Michel. 2008. *The Birth of Biopolitics: Lectures at the College De France, 1978–1979.* (Trans. Graham Burchell) Basingstoke: Palgrave Macmillan.

Freedgood, Elaine. 1995. "Banishing Panic: Harriet Martineau and the Popularization of Political Economy." *Victorian Studies* 39(1): 33–53.

Freedman, Lawrence. 1989. *The Evolution of Nuclear Strategy.* London: Macmillan.

Frieden, Jeffry. 2006. *Global Capitalism: Its Fall and Rise in the Twentieth Century.* New York: Norton.

Friedman, Milton. 1943. "The Spending Tax as a Wartime Fiscal Measure." *American Economic Review* 33(1): 50–62.

Friedman, Milton. 1973. "The Voucher Idea." *New York Times Magazine* 23: 22–23, 65–72.

Friedman, Milton. 1982. *Capitalism and Freedom.* Chicago: University of Chicago Press.

Friedman, Milton, and Rose D. Friedman. 1998. *Two Lucky People: Memoirs.* Chicago: University of Chicago Press.

Friedrich, Carl. 1955. "The Political Thought of Neo-liberalism." *American Political Science Review* 49(2): 509–525.

Fukuyama, Francis. 2004. *State-Building: Governance and World Order in the 21st Century.* Ithaca, NY: Cornell University Press.

Fukuyama, Francis. 2011. *The Origins of Political Order: From Prehuman Times to the French Revolution.* New York: Farrar, Straus and Giroux.

Fukuyama, Francis. 2014. *Political Order and Political Decay: From the Industrial Revolution to the Globalization of Democracy.* New York: Farrar, Straus and Giroux.

Furedi, Frank. 1998. *The Silent War: Imperialism and the Changing Perception of Race.* London: Pluto Press.

Fussell, Paul. 2009. *The Great War and Modern Memory.* New York: Sterling.

Galbraith, John Kenneth. 1969. *The Affluent Society.* Boston: Houghton Mifflin.

Gallagher, Catherine. 1986. "The Body Versus the Social Body in the Works of Thomas Malthus and Henry Mayhew." *Representations* 14: 83–106.

Ganapathy. N. D. "LIC Is the Cruelest Counter-Revolutionary War of the Imperialists," Manuscript.

Gandhi, M. K. 1938. *Hind Swaraj.* Ahmedabad: Navajivan Trust.

Gandhi, M. K. 1942. *My Appeal to the British.* New York: John Day.

Gandhi, M. K. 1962. *Village Swaraj.* Ahmedabad: Navajivan Trust.

Gandhi, M. K. 1965. *My Picture of Free India.* Bombay: Bharatiya Vidya Bhavan.

Garvey, Marcus. 1989. "A Solution for World Peace—1922." In *Philosophy and Opinions of Marcus Garvey: Or Africa for the Africans,* 31–32. New York: Routledge.

Gavin, Francis. 2012. *Nuclear Statecraft: History and Strategy in America's Atomic Age.* Ithaca, NY: Cornell University Press.

Gavin, Francis. 2015. "Strategies of Inhibition: U.S. Grand Strategy, the Nuclear Revolution, and Nonproliferation." *International Security* 40(1): 9–46.

Gay, Peter. 1994. *The Cultivation of Hatred: The Bourgeois Experience, Victoria to Freud,* Volume 3. New York: Norton.

Ghani, Ashraf, and Clare Lockhart. 2009. *Fixing Failed States: A Framework for Rebuilding a Fractured World.* Oxford: Oxford University Press.

Ghobarah, Hazem Adam, Paul Huth, and Bruce Russett. 2003. "Civil Wars Kill and Maim People—Long after the Shooting Stops." *American Political Science Review* 97(2): 189–202.

Gidwani, Vinay. 2008. *Capital, Interrupted: Agrarian Development and the Politics of Work in India.* Minneapolis: University of Minnesota Press.

Gilder, George. 2012. *Wealth and Poverty: A New Edition for the Twenty-First Century.* Washington: Regnery.

Gilroy, Paul. 1992. *The Black Atlantic: Modernity and Double Consciousness.* Cambridge, MA: Harvard University Press.

Glaser, Charles. 2010. *Rational Theory of International Politics: The Logic of Competition and Cooperation.* Princeton, NJ: Princeton University Press.

Goldstein, Joshua. 2011. *Winning the War on War: The Decline of Armed Conflict Worldwide.* New York: Plume.

Goodin, Robert. 1988. *Reasons for Welfare: The Political Theory of the Welfare State.* Princeton, NJ: Princeton University Press.

Gopal, Sarvepalli. 1976. *Jawaharlal Nehru: A Biography,* Volume 1: *1889–1947.* Cambridge, MA: Harvard University Press.

Gopal, Sarvepalli. 1980. *Jawaharlal Nehru: A Biography,* Volume 2: *1947–1956.* Cambridge, MA: Harvard University Press.

Gombrich, E. H. 2006. *The Story of Art.* New York: Phaidon.

Gramsci, Antonio. 1957. *The Modern Prince and Other Writings.* New York: International Publishers.

Greif, Avner, and David Laitin. 2004. "A Theory of Endogenous Institutional Change." *American Political Science Review* 98(4): 633–652.

Grovogui, Siba. 1996. *Sovereigns, Semi-Sovereigns and Africans: Race and Self-Determination in International Law.* Minneapolis: University of Minnesota Press.

Grynaviski, Eric. 2014. *Constructive Illusions: Misperceiving the Origins of International Cooperation.* Ithaca, NY: Cornell University Press.

Guha, Ramachandra. 1996. "Savaging the Civilized: Verrier Elwin and the Tribal Question in Late Colonial India." *Economic and Political Weekly* 31(35/37): 2375–2389.

Guha, Ramachandra. 2000. *The Unquiet Woods: Ecological Change and Peasant Resistance in the Himalaya.* Berkeley: University of California Press.

Guha, Ramachandra. 2007a. *India after Gandhi: The History of the World's Largest Democracy.* New York: Ecco.

Guha, Ramachandra. 2007b. "Adivasis, Naxalites, and Indian Democracy." *Economic and Political Weekly* 42(32): 3305–3312.

Guha, Ranajit. 1994. "The Prose of Counter-Insurgency." In Nicholas B. Dirks, Geoff Eley, and Sherry B. Ortner (eds.), *Culture/Power/History: A Reader in Contemporary Social Theory,* 336–371. Princeton, NJ: Princeton University Press.

Guha, Ranajit. 1997. *Dominance without Hegemony: History and Power in Colonial India.* Cambridge, MA: Harvard University Press.

Guha, Ranajit. 1999. *Elementary Aspects of Peasant Insurgency in Colonial India.* Durham, NC: Duke University Press.

Guha, Ranajit. 2002. *History at the Limit of World-History.* New York: Columbia University Press.

Guha, Sumit. 1999. *Environment and Ethnicity in India, 1200–1991.* Cambridge: Cambridge University Press.

Gupta, Akhil. 2012. *Red Tape: Bureaucracy, Structural Violence, and Poverty in India.* Durham, NC: Duke University Press.

Haas, Ernst. 1964. *Beyond the Nation-State: Functionalism and International Organization.* Stanford, CA: Stanford University Press.

Haas, Ernst. 1967. "The Uniting of Europe and the Uniting of Latin America." *Journal of Common Market Studies* 5(4): 315–343.

Habermas, Jurgen. 1975. *Legitimation Crisis.* (Trans. Thomas McCarthy) Boston: Beacon Press.

Habermas, Jurgen. 1986. "The New Obscurity: The Crisis of the Welfare State and the Exhaustion of Utopian Energies." (Trans. Phillip Jacobs) *Philosophy and Social Criticism* 11(2): 1–18.

Habermas, Jurgen. 1990. "What Does Socialism Mean Today? The Rectifying Revolution and the Need for New Thinking on the Left." *New Left Review* 183: 3–21.

Hall, Stuart. 1980. "Thatcherism: A New Stage?" *Marxism Today* 24(2): 26–28.

Hamilton, Alexander, James Madison, and John Jay. 1996. *The Federalist.* London: Everyman.

Hardiman, David. 1981. *Peasant Nationalists of Gujarat: Kheda District, 1917–1934.* New Delhi: Oxford University Press.

Hardiman, David. 1987. *The Coming of the Devi: Adivasi Assertion in Western India.* New Delhi: Oxford University Press.

Hardt, Michael, and Antonio Negri. 2004. *Multitude: War and Democracy in the Age of Empire.* New York: Penguin.

Hart, Basil Liddell. 1946. *Revolution in Warfare*. New Haven, CT: Yale University Press.

Havel, Vaclav. 1986. *Living in Truth*. (Trans. Various) London: Faber and Faber.

Havel, Vaclav. 1999. "Kosovo and the End of the Nation-State." (Trans. Paul Wilson) *New York Review of Books* 46(10): 4–6.

Hayek, F. A. 1940. "Review of "How to Pay for the War" by J. M. Keynes." *Economic Journal* 50: 321–326.

Hayek, F. A. 1944. "Scientism and the Study of Society, Part III." *Economica* 11(41): 27–39.

Hegel, G. W. F. 1967. *Philosophy of Right*. (Trans. T. M. Knox) London: Oxford University Press.

Hegel, G. W. F. 1988. *Introduction to the Philosophy of History*. (Trans. Leo Rauch) Indianapolis: Hackett.

Hegel, G. W. F. 1999. *Political Writings*. Cambridge: Cambridge University Press.

Herbst, Jeffrey. 2000. *States and Power in Africa: Comparative Lessons in Authority and Control*. Princeton, NJ: Princeton University Press.

Herz, John. 1959. *International Politics in the Atomic Age*. New York: Columbia University Press.

Himmelfarb, Gertrude. 1984. *The Idea of Poverty: England in the Early Industrial Age*. New York: Knopf.

Hironaka, Ann. 2005. *Never Ending Wars: The International Community, Weak States and the Perpetuation of Civil War*. Cambridge, MA: Harvard University Press.

Hobsbawm, Eric. 1987. *The Age of Empire, 1875–1914*. New York: Pantheon Books.

Hochschild, Adam. 1999. *King Leopold's Ghost: A Story of Greed, Terror and Heroism in Colonial Africa*. Boston: Mariner.

Hoffman, Paul. 1949. "Statement on European Economy." Economic Cooperation Administration File, P. G. Hoffman Papers, October 31, 1949. Harry S. Truman Library: Independence, MO.

Hoffman, Paul. 1953. "Interview with Paul Hoffman." Oral History Interview File, Price Papers, January 28, 1953. Harry S. Truman Library: Independence, MO.

Hoffman, Stanley. 1966. "Obstinate or Obsolete? The Fate of the Nation-State and the Case of Western Europe." *Daedalus* 95(3): 862–915.

Holsti, Kalevi. 1996. *The State, War, and the State of War*. Cambridge: Cambridge University Press.

Hull, Isabel V. 2005. *Absolute Destruction: Military Culture and the Practices of War in Imperial Germany*. Ithaca, NY: Cornell University Press.

Hunt, Lynn. 2007. *Inventing Human Rights: A History*. New York: Norton.

Husserl, Edmund. 1970. *The Crisis of European Sciences and Transcendental Phenomenology*. (Trans. David Carr) Evanston, IL: Northwestern University Press.

ICISS (International Commission on Intervention and State Sovereignty). 2001. *The Responsibility to Protect*. Ottawa: International Development Research Center.

Ignatieff, Michael. 2001. *Human Rights as Politics and Idolatry*. Princeton, NJ: Princeton University Press.

Ikenberry, John G. 2001. *After Victory: Institutions, Strategic Restraint, and the Rebuilding of Order after Major Wars*. Princeton, NJ: Princeton University Press.

Iriye, Akira. 2004. *Global Community: The Role of International Organizations in the Making of the Contemporary World*. Berkeley: University of California Press.

Isaacman, Allen. 1976. *The Tradition of Resistance in Mozambique: The Zambezi Valley, 1850–1921*. London: Heinemann.

Jackson, Patrick. 2006. *Civilizing the Enemy: German Reconstruction and the Invention of the West*. Ann Arbor: University of Michigan Press.

Jagan, Chhedi. 1966. *The West on Trial: My Fight for Guyana's Freedom*. London: Joseph.

Jakobson, Roman. 1987. *Language in Literature*. Cambridge, MA: Harvard University Press.

Jalal, Ayesha. 1990. *The State of Martial Rule: The Origins of Pakistan's Political Economy of Defense*. Cambridge: Cambridge University Press.

James, C. L. R. 1989. *The Black Jacobins*. New York: Vintage.

Jervis, Robert. 1989. *The Meaning of the Nuclear Revolution: Statecraft and the Prospect of Armageddon*. Ithaca, NY: Cornell University Press.

Judt, Tony. 2005. *Postwar: A History of Europe since 1945*. New York: Penguin.

Kaes, Anton. 2009. *Shell-Shock Cinema: Weimar Culture and the Wounds of War*. Princeton, NJ: Princeton University Press.

Kahn, Herman. 1960. *On Thermonuclear War*. Princeton, NJ: Princeton University Press.

Kahn, Herman. 1962. "The Arms Race and World Order." In Morton Kaplan (ed.), *The Revolution in World Politics*, 332–351. Princeton, NJ: Princeton University Press.

Herman Kahn. 1965. *On Escalation: Metaphors and Scenarios*. New York: Praeger.

Kaldor, Mary. 1999. "The Ideas of 1989: The Origins of the Concept of Global Civil Society." *Transnational and Contemporary Problems* 9: 475–488.

Kaldor, Nicholas. 1963. "Will Underdeveloped Countries Learn to Tax?" *Foreign Affairs* 41(2): 410–419.

Kalyvas, Stathis. 2001. "'New' and 'Old' Civil Wars: A Valid Distinction?" *World Politics* 54(1): 99–118.

Kalyvas, Stathis. 2006. *The Logic of Violence in Civil War*. New York: Cambridge University Press.

Kalyvas, Stathis, and Laia Balcells. 2010. "International System and Technologies of Rebellion: How the End of the Cold War Shaped Internal Conflict." *American Political Science Review* 104(3): 415-429.

Kant, Immanuel. 1983. *Perpetual Peace and Other Essays*. (Trans. Ted Humphrey) Indianapolis: Hackett.

Kaplan, Fred. 1983. *The Wizards of Armageddon*. New York: Simon and Schuster.

Kapur, Devesh, and Pratap Bhanu Mehta. 2008. "Mortgaging the Future? Indian Higher Education." *Brookings-NCAER India Policy Forum* 4: 101–157.

Karlsson, Bengt. 2003. "Anthropology and the 'Indigenous Slot': Claims to and Debates about Indigenous Peoples' Status in India." *Cultural Anthropology* 23(4): 403–423.

Kaviraj, Sudipta. 2010. *The Imaginary Institution of India: Politics and Ideas*. New York: Columbia University Press.

Kay, David. 1967. "The Politics of Decolonization: The New Nations and the United Nations Political Process." *International Organization* 21(4): 786–811.

Kenyatta, Jomo. 1968. *Suffering without Bitterness: The Founding of the Kenya Nation*. Nairobi: East African Publishing House.

Keohane, Robert. 2001. "Governance in a Partially Globalized World." *American Political Science Review* 95(1): 1–13.

Keynes, John Maynard. 1914. "War and the Financial System." *Economic Journal* 24(95): 460–486.

Keynes, John Maynard. 1920. *The Economic Consequences of the Peace*. London: Macmillan.

Keynes, John Maynard. 1939. "A Problem of Social Justice." *Times*, November 14, 1939.

Keynes, John Maynard. 1940. *How to Pay for the War: A Radical Plan for the Chancellor of the Exchequer*. London: Macmillan.

Keyserling, Leon. 1972. "Discussion." *American Economic Review* 62(2): 134–142.

Khama, Seretse. 1980. *From the Frontline*. London: Rex Collings.

Killingray, David. 2010. *Fighting for Britain: African Soldiers in the Second World War*. Woodbridge: James Currey.

Kindleberger, Charles. 1947. "Charles Kindleberger to John C. de Wilde." State Department File, Kindleberger Papers, March 24, 1947. Harry S. Truman Library: Independence, MO.

Kissinger, Henry. 1957. *Nuclear Weapons and Foreign Policy*. New York: Harper.

Kissinger, Henry. 1994. *Diplomacy*. New York: Simon and Schuster.

Konrad, George. 1984. *Antipolitics: An Essay*. New York: Harcourt.

Korpi, Walter. 2003. "Welfare-State Regress in Western Europe: Politics, Institutions, Globalization and Europeanization." *Annual Review of Sociology* 29: 589–609.

Koselleck, Reinhart. 2004. *Futures Past: On the Semantics of Historical Time*. (Trans. Keith Tribe) New York: Columbia University Press.

Kotkin, Stephen. 2009. *Uncivil Society: 1989 and the Implosion of the Communist Establishment*. New York: Modern Library.

Krebs, Christopher. 2011. *A Most Dangerous Book: Tacitus's Germania from the Roman Empire to the Third Reich*. New York: Norton.

Krebs, Ronald. 2006. *Fighting for Rights: Military Service and the Politics of Citizenship*. Ithaca, NY: Cornell University Press.

Kull, Steven. 1988. *Minds at War: Nuclear Reality and the Inner Conflicts of Defense Policymakers*. New York: Basic Books.

Kundera, Milan. 1984. "The Tragedy of Central Europe." (Trans. Edmund White) *New York Review of Books* 31(7): 33–38.

Kupchan, Charles. 2010. *How Enemies Become Friends: The Sources of Stable Peace*. Princeton, NJ: Princeton University Press.

Kuran, Timur. 1991. "Now Out of Never: The Element of Surprise in the East European Revolution of 1989." *World Politics* 44(1): 7–48.

Lacina, Bethany, and Nils Peter Gleditsch. 2005. "Monitoring Trends in Global Combat: A New Dataset of Battle Deaths." *European Journal of Population* 21(2–3): 145–166.

Lake, David. 2009. *Hierarchy in International Relations*. Ithaca, NY: Cornell University Press.

Lake, Marilyn, and Henry Reynolds. 2008. *Drawing the Global Colour Line: White Men's Countries and the International Challenge of Racial Equality*. New York: Cambridge.

Lasswell, Harold. 1949. "'Inevitable' War: A Problem in the Control of Long-Range Expectations." *World Politics* 2(1): 1–39.

Lawrence, Adria. 2013. *Imperial Rule and the Politics of Nationalism: Anti-Colonial Protest in the French Empire*. New York: Cambridge University Press.

Leach, Edmund. 1964. *Political Systems of Highland Burma: A Study of Kachin Social Structure*. London: Athlone Press.

Legro, Jeffrey. 2005. *Rethinking the World: Great Power Strategies and International Order*. Ithaca: Cornell University Press.

Lewis, Mary Dewhurst. 2013. *Divided Rule: Sovereignty and Empire in French Tunisia, 1881–1938*. Berkeley: University of California Press.

Lewis, W. Arthur. 1966. *Development Planning: The Essentials of Economic Policy*. London: Allen and Unwin.

Lightfoot, Sheryl. 2009. *Indigenous Global Politics*. PhD Dissertation, University of Minnesota.

Lindert, Peter H. 2004. *Growing Public: Social Spending and Economic Growth since the Eighteenth Century*. New York: Cambridge University Press.

Luilevicius, Vejas Gabriel. 2000. *War Land on the Eastern From: Culture, National Identity and German Occupation in World War I*. New York: Cambridge University Press.

Lyall, Jason, and Isaiah Wilson. 2009. "Rage against the Machines: Explaining Outcomes in Counterinsurgency Wars." *International Organization* 63(1): 67–106.

MacDonald, James. 2003. *A Free Nation Deep in Debt: The Financial Roots of Democracy*. New York: Farrar, Straus and Giroux.

MacDonald, Paul. 2013. "Retribution Must Succeed Rebellion: The Colonial Origins of Counterinsurgency Failure." *International Organization* 67(2): 253–286.

Mahan, Alfred Thayer. 1970. *The Problem of Asia*. Port Washington, NY: Kennikat Press.

Mahoney, James, and Kathleen Thelen (eds.). 2010. *Explaining Institutional Change: Ambiguity, Agency, and Power*. New York: Cambridge University Press.

Mamdani, Mahmood. 1996. *Citizen and Subject: Contemporary Africa and the Legacy of Late Colonialism*. Princeton, NJ: Princeton University Press.

Mamdani, Mahmood. 2001a. *When Victims Become Killers: Colonialism, Nativism, and the Genocide in Rwanda*. Princeton, NJ: Princeton University Press.

Mamdani, Mahmood. 2001b. "Beyond Settler and Native as Political Identities: Overcoming the Political Legacy of Colonialism." *Comparative Studies in Society and History* 43(4): 651–664.

Mamdani, Mahmood. 2012. *Define and Rule: Native as Political Identity*. Cambridge, MA: Harvard University Press.

Manley, Michael. 1970. "Overcoming Insularity in Jamaica." *Foreign Affairs* 49(1): 100–110.

Manley, Michael. 1982. *Jamaica: Struggle in the Periphery*. London: Third World Media.

Manley, Norman. 1971. *Manley and the New Jamaica: Selected Speeches and Writings, 1938–68*. (Ed. Rex Nettleford) New York: Africana.

Mann, Michael. 1993. *The Sources of Social Power*, Volume II: *The Rise of Classes and Nation-States, 1760–1914*. New York: Cambridge University Press.

Marshall, T. H. 1965. "The Right to Welfare." *Sociological Review* 13(3): 261–272.

Marx, Karl. 1973. *Grundrisse: Foundations of the Critique of Political Economy*. New York: Penguin.

Mayaram, Shail. 2003. *Against History, against State: Counterperspectives from the Margins*. New York: Columbia University Press.

Mazlish, Bruce. 2001. "Civilization in a Historical and Global Perspective." *International Sociology* 16(3): 293–300.

Mazower, Mark. 2012. *Governing the World: The History of an Idea*. New York: Penguin Press.

Mazzini, Guiseppe. 2009. *A Cosmopolitanism of Nations*. (Trans. Stefano Recchia) Princeton, NJ: Princeton University Press.

Mbembe, Achille. 2001. *On the Postcolony*. Berkeley: University of California Press.

McClintock, Anne. 1995. *Imperial Leather: Race, Gender, and Sexuality in the Colonial Contest*. New York: Routledge.

Mearsheimer, John. 2001. *The Tragedy of Great Power Politics*. New York: Norton.

Memmi, Albert. 1967. *The Colonizer and the Colonized*. (Trans. Howard Greenfeld) Boston: Beacon.

Metcalf, Thomas. 1990. *The Aftermath of Revolt: India, 1857–1870*. New Delhi: Manohar.

Michnik, Adam. 1985. *Letters from Prison and Other Essays*. Berkeley: University of California Press.

Mikesell, Raymond. 1994. "The Bretton Woods Debates: A Memoir." *Essays in International Finance* 192: 1–64.

Mill, John Stuart. 1975. *On Liberty*. New York: Norton.

Mill, John Stuart. 1994. *Principles of Political Economy*. Oxford: Oxford University Press.

Miller, Benjamin. 2007. *States, Nations, and the Great Powers: The Sources of Regional War and Peace*. Cambridge: Cambridge University Press.

Mishra, Pankaj. 2012. *From the Ruins of Empire: The Intellectuals Who Remade Asia*. New York: Farrar, Straus and Giroux.

Miszlevitz, Ferenc. 1991. "The Unfinished Revolutions of 1989: The Decline of the Nation State." *Social Research* 58(4): 781–804.

Miszlevitz, Ferenc. 1998. *Illusion and Realities: The Metamorphosis of Civil Society in a New European Space*. Szombathely, Hungary: Savaria University Press.

Mitchell, Timothy. 1988. *Colonising Egypt*. Berkeley: University of California Press.

Mitchell, Timothy. 2002. *Rule of Experts: Egypt, Techno-Politics, Modernity*. Berkeley: University of California Press.

Mitranyi, David. 1948. "The Functional Approach to World Organization." *International Affairs* 24(3): 350–363.

Morgenthau, Hans. 1962. "A Political Theory of Foreign Aid." *American Political Science Review* 56(2): 301–309.

Morgenthau, Hans. 1964. "The Four Paradoxes of Nuclear Strategy." *American Political Science Review* 58(1): 23–35.

Moyn, Samuel. 2010. *The Last Utopia: Human Rights in History*. Cambridge, MA: Harvard University Press.

Mudimbe, Y. V. 1988. *The Invention of Africa: Gnosis, Philosophy, and the Order of Knowledge*. Bloomington: Indiana University Press.

Murray, Charles. 1984. *Losing Ground: American Social Policy, 1950–1980*. New York: Basic Books.

Murray, Charles. 1994. "Does Welfare Bring More Babies?" *Public Interest* 115: 17–30.

Naipaul, V. S. 1967. *The Mimic Men*. London: Andre Deutsch.

Nasser, Gamal Abdel. 1955. "The Egyptian Revolution." *Foreign Affairs* 33(2): 199–211.

National Security Council. 1950. "United States Objectives and Programs for National Security." Washington, DC: White House.

Nehru, Jawaharlal. 1938. "The Unity of India." *Foreign Affairs* 16(2): 231–243.

Nehru, Jawaharlal. 2004. *The Discovery of India*. New Delhi: Penguin.

Neuberger, Benyamin. 1976. "The African Concept of Balkanisation." *Journal of Modern African Studies* 14(3): 523–529.

Niebuhr, Reinhold. 1949. "The Illusion of World Government." *Foreign Affairs* 27(3): 379–388.

Nkrumah, Kwame. 1958. "African Prospect." *Foreign Affairs* 37(1): 45–53.

Nkrumah, Kwame. 1961. *I Speak of Freedom: A Statement of African Ideology*. New York: Praeger.

Nkrumah, Kwame. 1962. *Towards Colonial Freedom: Africa in the Struggle against World Imperialism*. London: Heinemann.

Nkrumah, Kwame. 1963. *Africa Must Unite*. New York: Praeger.

North, Douglass, and Barry Weingast. 1989. "Constitutions and Commitment: The Evolution of Institutions Governing Public Choice in Seventeenth Century England." *Journal of Economic History* 49(4): 803–832.

North, Douglass, John Joseph Wallis, and Barry Weingast. 2009. *Violence and Social Orders: A Conceptual Framework for Interpreting Recorded Human History*. New York: Cambridge University Press.

Nyerere, Julius. 1968. *Freedom and Socialism*. Dar es Salaam: Oxford University Press.

Nyerere, Julius. 1974. *Man and Development*. New York: Oxford University Press.

Oberoi, Harjot. 1994. *The Construction of Religious Boundaries: Culture, Identity, and Diversity in the Sikh Tradition*. Chicago: University of Chicago Press.

Ohmae, Kenichi. 1993. "The Rise of the Region State." *Foreign Affairs* 72(2): 78–87.

Olson, Mancur. 1993. "Dictatorship, Democracy, and Development." *American Political Science Review* 87(3): 567–576.

Omissi, David. 1990. *Air Power and Colonial Control: The Royal Air Force, 1919–1939*. Manchester: Manchester University Press.

Oren, Ido. 2003. *Our Enemies and US: America's Rivalries and the Making of Political Science*. Ithaca, NY: Cornell University Press.

Orr, Robert (ed.). 2004. *Winning the Peace: An American Strategy of Post-Conflict Reconstruction*. Washington: CSIS.

Orwell, George. 2009. *Shooting an Elephant and Other Essays*. New York: Penguin.

Osterhammel, Jurgen. 2014. *The Transformation of the World: A Global History of the Nineteenth Century*. Princeton, NJ: Princeton University Press.

Ostrom, Elinor. 2010. "Beyond Markets and States: Polycentric Governance of Complex Economic Systems." *American Economic Review* 100: 1–33.

Paine, Thomas. 1973. "Rights of Man." In Edmund Burke and Thomas Paine, *Two Classics of the French Revolution*, 267–515. New York: Anchor.

Pandey, Gyanendra. 1990. *The Construction of Communalism in Colonial North India*. New Delhi: Oxford University Press.

Pandita, Rahul. 2011. *Hello Bastar: The Untold Story of India's Maoist Movement*. Chennai: Tranquebar.

Paris, Roland. 2004. *At War's End: Building Peace after Civil Conflict*. Cambridge: Cambridge University Press.

Parker, Christopher. 2009. *Fighting for Democracy: Black Veterans and the Struggle against White Supremacy in the Postwar South*. Princeton, NJ: Princeton University Press.

Pedersen, Susan. 1993. *Family, Dependence, and the Origins of the Welfare State: Britain and France, 1914–1945*. New York: Cambridge University Press.

Petersen, Stephen. 2004. "Explosive Propositions: Artists React to the Atomic Age." *Science in Context* 17(4): 579–609.

Philipsen, Dirk. 2015. *The Little Big Number: How G.D.P. Came to Rule the World and What We Can Do about It*. Princeton, NJ: Princeton University Press.

Philpott, Daniel. 2001. *Revolutions in Sovereignty: How Ideas Shaped Modern International Relations*. Princeton, NJ: Princeton University Press.

Pierson, Paul. 2000. "Increasing Returns, Path Dependence, and the Study of Politics." *American Political Science Review* 94(2): 251–267.

Pigou, Arthur. 1918. "A Special Levy to Discharge War Debt." *Economic Journal* 28(110): 135–156.

Pigou, Arthur. 1919. "The Burden of War and Future Generations." *Quarterly Journal of Economics* 33(2): 242–255.

Pigou, Arthur. 1936. "Mr. J. M. Keynes' General Theory of Employment, Interest and Money." *Economica* 3(10): 115–132.

Piketty, Thomas. 2014. *Capital in the Twenty-first Century*. Cambridge, MA: Harvard University Press.

Piketty, Thomas, and Emmanuel Saez. 2007. "How Progressive Is the U.S. Federal Tax System? A Historical and International Perspective." *Journal of Economic Perspectives* 21(1): 3–24.

Pinker, Steven. 2011. *The Better Angels of Our Nature: Why Violence Has Declined*. New York: Penguin.

Pocock, J. G. A. 1975. *The Machiavellian Moment: Florentine Political Thought and the Atlantic Republican Tradition*. Princeton, NJ: Princeton University Press.

Pocock, J. G. A. 2000. "Waitangi as Mystery of State: Consequences of the Ascription of Federative Capacity to the Maori." In Duncan Ivision, Paul Patton, and Will Sanders (eds.), *Political Theory and the Rights of Indigenous Peoples*, 25–35. New York: Cambridge University Press.

Polanyi, Karl. 1944. *The Great Transformation*. Boston: Beacon.

Pollack, Sheldon. 2009. *War, Revenue, and State Building: Financing the Development of the American State*. Ithaca, NY: Cornell University Press.

Poovey, Mary. 1998. *A History of the Modern Fact: Problems of Knowledge in the Sciences of Wealth and Society*. Chicago: University of Chicago Press.

Porter, Bruce. 1994. *War and the Rise of the State: The Military Foundations of Modern Politics*. New York: Free Press.

Powell, Robert. 2006. "War as a Commitment Problem." *International Organization* 60(1): 169–203.

Ralston, David. 1996. *Importing the European Army: The Introduction of European Military Techniques and Institutions in the Extra-European World, 1600–1914*. Chicago: University of Chicago Press.

Record of the Proceedings of the First Universal Races Congress. 1911. London: P. S. King and Son.

Remarque, Erich Maria. 1982. *All Quiet on the Western Front*. New York: Fawcett Crest.

Reus-Smith, Christian. 2013. *Individual Rights and the Making of the International System*. New York: Cambridge University Press.

Rev, Istvan. 1998. "Retrotopia: Critical Reason Turns Primitive." *Current Sociology* 46(2): 51–80.

Ricardo, David. 1821. *On the Principles of Political Economy and Taxation*. London: John Murray.

Rice, Susan, and Stewart Patrick. 2008. *Index of State Weakness in the Developing World*. Washington, DC: Brookings Institution.

Root, Hilton. 1994. *The Fountain of Privilege: Political Foundations of Markets in Old Regime France and England*. Berkeley: University of California Press.

Rosenberg, David Alan. 1983. "The Origins of Overkill: Nuclear Weapons and American Strategy, 1945–1960. *International Security* 7(4): 3–71.

Ross, Michael. 2004. "Does Taxation Lead to Representation?" *British Journal of Political Science* 34(2): 229–249.

Ropke, Wilhelm. 1947. *The Solution of the German Problem*. New York: G. P. Putnam's Sons.

Rotberg, Robert (ed.). 2004. *When States Fail: Causes and Consequences*. Princeton, NJ: Princeton University Press.

Ruggie, John. 1993. "Territoriality and Beyond: Problematizing Modernity in International Relations." *International Organization* 47(1): 139–174.

Rummel, R. J. 1994. *Death by Government*. New Brunswick: Transaction.

Russell, Bertrand. 2009. *Common Sense and Nuclear Warfare*. New York: Routledge.

Said, Edward. 1978. *Orientalism*. New York: Vintage.

Said, Edward. 1993. *Culture and Imperialism*. New York: Vintage.

Sainath, P. 1996. *Everybody Loves a Good Drought: Stories from India's Poorest Districts*. New York: Penguin.

Sarkar, Sumit, and Tanika Sarkar. 2009. "Notes on a Dying People." *Economic and Political Weekly* 44(26/27): 10–14.

Sassen, Saskia. 2006. *Territory, Authority, Rights: From Medieval to Global Assemblages*. Princeton, NJ: Princeton University Press.

Schelling, Thomas. 1960. *The Strategy of Conflict*. Oxford: Oxford University Press.

Schelling, Thomas. 1966. *Arms and Influence*. New Haven, CT: Yale University Press.

Schelling, Thomas. 2008. *Arms and Influence: With a New Preface and Afterword*. New Haven, CT: Yale University Press.

Scheuerman, William. 2010. "The (Classic) Realist Vision of Global Reform." *International Theory* 2(2): 246–282.

Scheve, Kenneth, and David Stasavage. 2010. "The Conscription of Wealth: Mass Warfare and the Demand for Progressive Taxation." *International Organization* 64(4): 529–561.

Scheve, Kenneth, and David Stasavage. 2012. "Democracy, War and Wealth: Lessons from Two Centuries of Inheritance Taxation." *American Political Science Review* 106(1): 81–102.

Schmitt, Carl. 2003. *Nomos of the Earth in the International Law of the Jus Publicum Europaeum*. (Trans. G. L. Ulmen) New York: Telos.

Schmitt, Carl. 2004. *The Theory of the Partisan: A Commentary/Remark on the Concept of the Political*. (Trans. A. C. Goodson) East Lansing: Michigan State University Press.

Schuler, Kurt, and Andrew Rosenberg (eds.). 2013. *The Bretton Woods Transcripts*. New York: Center for Financial Stability.

Schwendemann, Heinrich. 2003. "'Drastic Measures to Defend the Reich at the Oder and the Rhine . . .' A Forgotten Memorandum of Albert Speer of 18 March 1945." *Journal of Contemporary History* 38(4): 597–614.

Scott, James. 1977. "Protest and Profanation: Agrarian Revolt and the Little Tradition, Part II." *Theory and Society* 4(2): 211–246.

Scott, James. 1998. *Seeing like a State: How Certain Schemes to Improve the Human Condition Have Failed*. New Haven, CT: Yale University Press.

Scott, James. 2009. *The Art of Not Being Governed: An Anarchist History of Upland Southeast Asia*. New Haven, CT: Yale University Press.

Sebald, W. G. 2005. *Campo Santo*. New York: Modern Library Paperbacks.

Secretary General of the United Nations. 1992. *An Agenda for Peace: Preventative Diplomacy, Peacemaking and Peace-Keeping*. United Nations, A/47/277-S/24111.

Seligman, Edwin. 1918. "Loans versus Taxes in War Finance." *Annals of the American Academy of Political and Social Science* 75: 52–82.

Seligman, Edwin, and Robert Haig. 1917. "How to Finance the War." In *War Finance Primer*, 19–48. New York: National Bank of Commerce.

Senghor, Leopold. 1964. *On African Socialism*. (Trans. Mercer Cook) London: Pall Mall.

Seth, Vanita. 2010. *Europe's Indians: Producing Racial Difference, 1500–1900*. Durham, NC: Duke University Press.

Shah, Alpa. 2011. "Alcoholics Anonymous: The Maoist Movement in Jharkhand, India." *Modern Asian Studies* 45(5): 1095–1117.

Shepperson, George. 1960. "Notes on Negro American Influences on the Emergence of African Nationalism." *Journal of African History* 1(2): 299–312.

Shilliam, Robbie. 2006. "What about Marcus Garvey? Race and the Transformation of Sovereignty Debate." *Review of International Studies* 32(3): 379–400.

Siklova, Jirina. 1990. "The 'Grey Zone' and the Future of Dissent in Czechoslovakia." *Social Research* 57(2): 347–363.

Siklova, Jirina. 1991. "The Solidarity of the Culpable." *Social Research* 58(4): 765–773.

Simpson, Gerry. 2004. *Great Powers and Outlaw States: Unequal Sovereigns in the International Legal Order*. Cambridge: Cambridge University Press.

Skaria, Ajay. 1999. *Hybrid Histories: Forests, Frontiers and Wildness in Western India*. New Delhi: Oxford University Press.

Slaughter, Anne-Marie. 2004. *A New World Order*. Princeton, NJ: Princeton University Press.

Smith, Adam. 2000. *The Wealth of Nations.* New York: Modern Library Paperbacks.

Snyder, Timothy. 2010. *Bloodlands: Europe between Hitler and Stalin.* New York: Basic Books.

Soysal, Yasemin Nuhoglu. 1995. *Limits of Citizenship: Migrants and Postnational Membership in Europe.* Chicago: University of Chicago Press.

Spencer, Herbert. 1892. *The Man versus the State.* London: D. Appleton.

Spiers, Edward. 1992. *The Late Victorian Army, 1868–1902.* Manchester: Manchester University Press.

Sprague, O. H. W. 1918. "Loans and Taxes in War Finance." *American Economic Review* 7(1): 199–213.

Spruyt, Hendrik. 1996. *The Sovereign State and Its Competitors: An Analysis of Systems Change.* Princeton, NJ: Princeton University Press.

Spruyt, Hendrik. 2005. *Ending Empire: Contested Sovereignty and Territorial Partition.* Ithaca, NY: Cornell University Press.

Steil, Benn. 2013. *The Battle of Bretton Woods: John Maynard Keynes, Harry Dexter White, and the Making of a New World Order.* Princeton, NJ: Princeton University Press.

Steiner, Zara. 2007. *The Lights That Failed: European International History 1919–1933.* Oxford: Oxford University Press.

Steinmo, Sven. 1993. *Taxation and Democracy: Swedish, British and American Approaches to Financing the Modern State.* New Haven, CT: Yale University Press.

Steinmo, Sven. 2010. *The Evolution of Modern States: Sweden, Japan, and the United States.* New York: Cambridge University Press.

Stigler, George. 1981. *Economics or Ethics? The Tanner Lectures on Human Values.* Salt Lake City: University of Utah.

Stoler, Ann Laura. 2002. *Carnal Knowledge and Imperial Power: Race and the Intimate in Colonial Rule.* Berkeley: University of California Press.

Stolper, Wolfgang. 1963. "Economic Development in Nigeria." *Journal of Economic History* 23(4): 391–413.

Sundar, Nandini. 2007. *Subalterns and Sovereigns: An Anthropological History of Bastar, 1854–2006.* New Delhi: Oxford University Press.

Tarrow, Sidney. 2013. "War, Rights, and Contention: Lasswell vs. Tilly." In Sigal Ben Porath and Rogers Smith (eds.), *Varieties of Sovereignty and Citizenship,* 35–57. Philadelphia: University of Pennsylvania Press.

Taussig, Michael. 1987. *Shamanism, Colonialism, and the Wild Man: A Study in Terror and Healing.* Chicago: Chicago University Press.

Teera, Joweria, and John Hudson. 2004. "Tax Performance: A Comparative Study." *Journal of International Development* 16(6): 785–802.

Thelen, Kathleen. 2004. *How Institutions Evolve: The Political Economy of Skills in Germany, Britain, the United States, and Japan.* New York: Cambridge University Press.

Theweleit, Klaus. 1989. *Male Fantasies,* Volume 2: *Psychoanalyzing the White Terror.* Minneapolis: University of Minnesota Press.

Thompson, E. P. 1982. *Beyond the Cold War: A New Approach to the Arms Race and Nuclear Annihilation.* New York: Pantheon Books.

Tilly, Charles (ed.). 1975. *The Formation of National States in Western Europe.* Princeton, NJ: Princeton University Press.

Tilly, Charles. 1985. "War-Making and State-Making as Organized Crime." In Peter Evans, Dietrich Rueschmeyer, and Theda Skocpol (eds.), *Bringing the State Back In,* 169–191. New York: Cambridge University Press.

Tilly, Charles. 1986. "European Violence and Collective Action since 1700." *Social Research* 53(1): 159–184.

Tilly, Charles. 1992. *Coercion, Capital, and European States, AD 990–1992.* Cambridge: Blackwell.

Tolstoy, Leo. 2010. *War and Peace.* (Trans. Aylmer Maude and Louise Maude) London: Oxford University Press.

Tomz, Michael. 2007. *Reputation and International Cooperation: Sovereign Debt across Three Countries.* Princeton, NJ: Princeton University Press.

Trachtenberg, Marc. 1988. "A 'Wasting Asset': American Strategy and the Shifting Nuclear Balance, 1949–1954." *International Security* 13(3): 5–49.

Trachtenberg, Marc. 1989. "Strategic Thought in America, 1952–1966." *Political Science Quarterly* 104(2): 301–334.

Trachtenberg, Marc. 1999. *A Constructed Peace: The Making of the European Settlement, 1945–1963.* Princeton, NJ: Princeton University Press.

Treff, Karin, and David Perry. 2003. *Finance of the Nation: A Review of Expenditures and Revenues of the Federal, Provincial and Local Government of Canada.* Toronto: Canadian Tax Foundation.

Tribe, Keith. 1995. *Strategies of Economic Order: German Economic Discourse, 1750–1950.* New York: Cambridge University Press.

Tully, James. 1995. *Strange Multiplicity: Constitutionalism in an Age of Diversity.* Cambridge: Cambridge University Press.

United Nations. 2004. *A More Secure World: Our Shared Responsibility.* New York: United Nations Foundation.

Voeten, Erik. 2011. "The Practice of Political Manipulation." In Emanuel Adler and Vincent Pouliot (eds.), *International Practices,* 255–279. New York: Cambridge University Press.

Vitalis, Robert. 2010. "The Nobel American Science of Imperial Relations and Its Laws of Race and Development." *Comparative Studies in Society and History* 52(4): 909–938.

Wagner, R. Harrison. 2007. *War and the State: The Theory of International Politics.* Ann Arbor: University of Michigan Press.

Wahrman, Dror. 2004. *The Making of the Modern Self: Identity and Culture in Eighteenth Century England.* New Haven, CT: Yale University Press.

Wallis, John Joseph. 2000. "American Government Finance in the Long Run: 1790 to 1900." *Journal of Economic Perspectives* 14(1): 61–82.

van Walraven, Klaas. 2009. "Decolonization by Referendum: The Anomaly of Niger and the Fall of Sawabia, 1958–1959." *Journal of African History* 50(2): 269–292.

Walter, Barbara. 1999. "Designing Transitions from Civil War: Demobilization, Democratization, and Commitments to Peace." *International Security* 24(1): 127–155.

Waltz, Kenneth. 1979. *Theory of International Politics.* Boston: Addison Wesley.

Weber, Eugen. 1976. *Peasants into Frenchmen: The Modernization of Rural France, 1870–1914.* Palo Alto, CA: Stanford University Press.

Weigle, Marcia, and Jim Butterfield. 1992. "Civil Society in Reforming Communist Regimes: The Logic of Emergence." *Comparative Politics* 25(1): 1–23.

Wells, H. G. 1906. *Socialism and the Family.* London: Fifield.

Wendt, Alexander. 1999. *Social Theory of International Politics.* New York: Cambridge University Press.

Weinstein, Jeremy, et al. 2004. "On the Brink: Weak States and US National Security." Washington, DC: Center for Global Development.

Williams, Eric. 1993. *Eric E. Williams Speaks: Essays on Colonialism and Independence.* Amherst: University of Massachusetts Press.

Williams, Robert. 1997. *Linking Arms Together: American Indian Treaty Visions of Law and Peace, 1600–1800.* New York: Oxford University Press.

Wilkins, David Eugene, and Tsianina Lomawaima. 2001. *Uneven Ground: American Indian Sovereignty and Federal Law.* Norman: University of Oklahoma Press.

Wimmer, Andreas. 2013. *Waves of War: Nationalism, State Formation, and Ethnic Exclusion in the Modern World.* New York: Cambridge University Press.

Wimmer, Andreas, and Brian Min. 2009. "The Location and Purpose of Wars around the World: A New Global Dataset, 1816–2001." *International Interactions* 35(4): 390–417.

Wohlstetter, Albert. 1958. "The Delicate Balance of Terror." RAND P-1472. Santa Monica: RAND.

Wolff, Larry. 1994. *Inventing Eastern Europe: The Map of Civilization on the Mind of the Enlightenment.* Stanford, CA: Stanford University Press.

Wolin, Sheldon. 1989. *The Presence of the Past: Essays on the State and the Constitution.* Baltimore, MD: Johns Hopkins University Press.

Wood, Gordon. 1972. *The Creation of the American Republic, 1776–1787*. New York: Norton.

World Bank. 2012. "Strengthening Governance, Tackling Corruption: The World Bank's Updated Strategy and Implementation Plan." Washington, DC: World Bank Group.

Wright, Richard. 2008. *Black Power: Three Books from Exile: Black Power; the Colour Curtain; and White Man, Listen!* New York: Harper Perennial.

Xaxa, Virginius. 1999. "Tribes as Indigenous People of India." *Economic and Political Weekly* 34(51): 3589–3595.

Yergin, Daniel. 1977. *Shattered Peace: The Origins of the Cold War and the National Security State*. New York: Houghton Mifflin.

Young, Crawford. 1994. *The African Colonial State in Comparative Perspective*. New Haven, CT: Yale University Press.

Young, Iris Marion. 2000. "Hybrid Democracy: Iroquois Federalism and the Postcolonial Project." In Duncan Ivision, Paul Patton, and Will Sanders (eds.), *Political Theory and the Rights of Indigenous Peoples*, 237–258. New York: Cambridge University Press.

Young, Robert J. C. 1995. *Colonial Desire: Hybridity in Theory, Culture and Race*. London: Routledge.

Young, Robert J. C. 2001. *Postcolonialism: An Historical Introduction*. Oxford: Blackwell.

Zacher, Mark. 2001. "The Territorial Integrity Norm: International Boundaries and the Use of Force." *International Organization* 55(2): 215–250.

Zelizer, Julian. 1998. *Taxing America: Wilbur D. Mills, Congress and the State, 1945–1975*. New York: Cambridge University Press.

Ziblatt, Daniel. 2006. *Structuring the State: The Formation of Italy and Germany and the Puzzle of Federalism*. Princeton, NJ: Princeton University Press.

INDEX

Note: Figures and tables are indicated by italic "*f*" and "*t*" following the page number. Endnote material is indicated by italic "*n*" and note number.

Absolute war (Clausewitz), 20, 71–74, 76–77.
See also Europe, during age of empire
Achebe, Chinua, 166, 174–175, 190, 213
Acheson, Dean, 86–87
Adenauer, Konrad, 87, 89
Adivasi, in India, 179–188
Aerial bombing, 55, 56, 58
Afghanistan, 4
Africa. See also individual countries and leaders
anti-colonial movements in, 25
concentration camps in during Boer War, 55, 58
Herero in southwest, 57
Pan-African movements, 148–151
African Party of Independence of Guinea and Cape Verde (PAIGC), 149
Agamben, Giorgio, 227
Algeria, 47, 151
Alternatives to the state. See also Regional federations, as alternative to the state
development as, 28, 29, 30–31
militias as, 1, 22t, 28
restaged states and, 66–71
self-undermining states and, 27–33
summary conclusion, 222–227
Altruism, 128–129
American Revolution, 38, 200
Angolan People's Movement for the Liberation of Angola (MPLA), 149
Anti-colonial movements, 25, 133, 204. See also Postcolonial state-building
internalization of costs, 30–31
leaders of, 135t
Anti-political politics (Havel), 194, 196
Arendt, Hannah, 42, 93, 204, 205
Aron, Raymond, 73, 75
Ash, Timothy Garton, 196

Atomic age. See Restaged state
Authority-elite bargains, 34
Azikiwe, Nnamdi, 135t, 142, 153, 172

Bagehot, Walter, 45
Baker, Phillip Noel, 134
Ball, Hugo, 64
Balzac, Honoré de, 195
Bargaining model of war (Fearon), 26–27
Barrow, John, 58
Baruch Plan, 70
Becker, Gary, 128–129
Belgium, 58–59
Bellicist model (Tilly), 18, 19, 22, 26–27
Beveridge, William, 100–101, 113
Black Star Line, 148
Boer War, 55, 58
Booth, Charles, 99
Boxing, 24
Braumoeller, Bear, 14n17
Bretton Woods agreements, 84–85
Brexit, 29n50
Brodie, Bernard, 79, 81–82, 83, 92
Brookings Institution, on measures of state weakness, 214
Burgess, John, 61, 86
Burke, Edmund, 45–48, 54
Burnham, Forbes, 150

Cabral, Amilcar, 135t, 142–143, 149
Callwell, C. E., 56, 203
Camus, Albert, 151
Canada
    Delgamuukw case, 205–206

Canada (*cont.*)
  income taxes, 37, 109, 115–116
  indigenous activism, 204, 205–206
Cannibalism, 54
Caribbean Federation, 29, 145, 146–147
Carr, E. H., 61–62, 63, 68, 74, 76
Casement, Roger, 58–59, 60, 61
Cash transfers, 220, 220*n*6
Centeno, Miguel, 76
Centralized states. *See* Strong modern states
Cesaire, Aime, 149
Chamberlain, Austen, 60–61
Christophe, Henry, 134
Churchill, Winston, 50, 55, 69, 81–82, 203
Civil society, 191–192, 195–196
Classical liberalism, 97, 122–131
Clastres, Pierre, 189
Clausewitz, Carl von, 20, 42, 56, 57, 71–74,
  76–77, 187
Clemenceau, Georges, 62
Colby, Eldridge, 56
Collective punishment, 56, 57–59
Confederacies (Hegel), 49, 200
Congo. *See* Democratic Republic of Congo
Conrad, Joseph, 58
Contemporary state weakness, 191–216
  overview, 191–192
  bargaining without war, 206–209
  as consequence of state formation, 214–216
  Hamilton and the centralized state, 199–206
  human rights claims as outside option, 192–199
  restaging and, 209–214
Corsica, 97
Counterinsurgency theory, during nineteenth
  century, 55–56
Coxe, Tench, 200
Crisis of the family (Reagan), 130–131
Crowther, Samuel Ajayi, 54
Cust, Edward, 139
Custom and development, as outside option, 9,
  161–190
  overview, 161–163
  colonial vs. postcolonial insurgency,
    175–178, 177*t*
  exchange/non-exchange vs. postcolonial
    gamble, 170–171, 171*t*
  giving vs. claiming of rights and custom,
    163–174
  neglect of intended beneficiaries, 179, 181, 182
  summary conclusion, 188–190
  weaponization of custom and rejection of,
    174–188
Customary identities
  collective action and, 20, 172–175, 189
  as exclusive categories, 163, 178–181
  postcolonial state inheritance of, 9, 188–189
Czechoslovakia, former, 193–194, 196*n*40

Dahl, Robert, 73
d'Azegelio, Massimo, 49–50
Debt defaults, 105
Declaration on the Granting of Independence to
  Colonial Countries (1960), 147
Decolonization. *See* Custom and development, as
  outside option; Postcolonial state-building
de Gaulle, Charles, 49, 74
Delgamuukw case (Canada), 205
Demand for services vs. willingness to supply the
  state, overview, 4–9, 13–14, 18–20, 218–220,
  223, 225
Democratic Republic of Congo, 2, 58–59
Denationalization of military power
  (Einstein), 69–70
Desastres de le Guerra (etchings), 40–41
Desmoisilles d'Avignon (Picasso), 60
Dessalines, Jean-Jacques, 133–134, 137
Détente of people rather than states
  (Thompson), 197
de Tocqueville, Alexis, 45, 47, 55, 58
Development, as alternative to the state, 28,
  29, 30–31
Devi, Mahasweta, 171, 174
Diop, Cheikh Anta, 149–150
Disarmament, 69–70, 74, 81–82, 197
Dominance without hegemony (Guha), 136
Dominican Republic, 133–134
Dostoevsky, Fyodor, 53
Drug trafficking, 1–2
Du Bois, W.E.B., 62, 143, 148
Dulles, Allen, 86, 88
Dulles, John Foster, 70, 87

Eastern Europe, dissidence movements, 191–199
East India Company, 39, 48, 54
Education, financing of, 123–125
Egypt, 148, 149, 153–154, 155–156
Einstein, Albert, 62–63, 68, 69–70
Eisenhower, Dwight D., 73, 75
Elias, Norbert, 206
Elwin, Verrier, 181
Emulation of the West, 134*n*6, 140–141, 143–144
Enemy partners (Aron), 75
Engels, Friedrich, 97
Environmentalism, 118, 118*f*, 194
Erhard, Ludwig, 88
Estonia, 67
Eucken, Walter, 88, 89–90
Europe. *See also individual countries*
  dissidence movements in Eastern, 191–199
  EU inability to compel popular sacrifice, 29*n*50
  during interwar era, 67
  pattern of warfare, 21, 25
Europe, during age of empire, 8–9, 20, 23, 37–64.
  See also individual colonies

overview, 37–39
  interstate conflicts (1816–2000), 45f
  lessons of Great War, 37, 60–64
  limiting of conflict costs, 50–60
  management of popular participation, 44–50
  new wars and popular participation, 39–44, 42n24
European Coal and Steel Community, 85, 87
European Defense Community, 86
Expectations of order
  alternatives to costly war and, 5–6
  expansion of, 3, 5–6
  history of state formation and, 217–227
  neoliberalism and, 131
  Nkrumah and development, 187–188
  state weakness as function of, 189, 213
  tax units and, 225
Extraction, defined, 14

Factions, 203–204, 206–209
Failed state, defined, 210
Failed States Index (Fund for Peace), 3–4, 3t
Family wage, 128
Famines, 30–31, 55, 183–184, 201n68, 217
Fanon, Frantz, 136, 137–138, 140, 165, 172
Fearon, James, 22n36, 26
Federalist Papers, 200–202, 210
Federations. See Regional federations, as
  alternative to the state
Foreign aid, 6n8, 20, 135, 158, 160, 218–221,
  223, 225
Foucault, Michel, 88–89, 90, 95–96, 123
Fragile States Index (Foreign Policy), 1
France. See also individual colonies
  burial practices, 97
  as centralized state (13th–14th c.), 33
  debt defaults, 105
  financing of wars with debt, 102–103
  during nineteenth century empire, 47,
  47n52
  social transfers as percentage of GDP
  (1880–1980), 98f
French Revolution, 37, 38, 41
Freud, Sigmund, 63
Friedman, Milton, 108–109, 112, 114,
  124–126, 128
Friendly Societies, 99–100
Fulbright, William, 68
Fund for Peace, Failed States Index, 3–4, 3t
Funk, Walter, 84
Furet, Francois, 196

Galbraith, John Kenneth, 114, 158
Gallup poll, on international military power, 67
Ganapathy, 182, 183

Gandhi, Mohandas K.
  as anti-colonial leader, 135t
  on avoidance of emulation of the West,
  140–141, 143
  critique of India, 152, 156, 162, 163
  on Japanese defeat of Russia (1906), 134
  on protest demonstrations, 183
  stance on Indian independence, 139, 145,
  147–148, 154
  on state as violence, 144
Garvey, Marcus, 148
GDP (Gross Domestic Product)
  origin of measure, 120–121
  social transfers as percentage of GDP
  (1880–1980), 98f, 102
  tax to GDP ratios, 159, 159n156
George, Lloyd, 62
Germany
  during Great War, 62, 63
  Marshall Plan, 85–86
  Nazi regime, 2–3, 39, 63–64, 87–88, 89, 143
  during nineteenth century, 49, 57
  Ordoliberalism, 88–90
  social transfers as percentage of GDP
  (1880–1980), 98f
  Thirty Years' War, 40, 41
Ghana, 153, 154–155, 223
Ghana Airways, 160
Ghandy, Kobad, 183, 184
Ghani, Ashraf, 214
Gilder, George, 130
Gold reserves, 103
Gorbachev, Mikhail, 74
Gorchakov, Aleksandr, 52–53
Goya, Francisco de, 40–41, 41
Gramsci, Antonio, 164
Great Britain, during empire. See also United
  Kingdom (UK); individual colonies
  aspirations for United States of Britain, 51
  Beveridge Report, 100–101
  Commission on the Poor Laws in Britain, 99
  Friendly Societies, 99–100
  India Bill (1858), 48
  public health services, 97–98
  use of foreign armies, 44
Great War
  Freud on, 63
  German treatment of irregular fighters, 57
  lessons of, 37, 60–64
  war as too costly, 24–25, 60–64
Guha, Ranajit, 136, 152, 163–164, 178
Guinea-Bissau, 142–143, 149

Habermas, Jurgen, 95–96, 131, 196, 198–199
Haig, Robert, 104
Haiti, 4, 133–134, 137, 140

Hall, Stuart, 96, 126, 131
Hamilton, Alexander, 200–202, 208
Hastings, Warren, 46–47
Havel, Vaclav, 191–192, 193–194, 196, 197, 198, 209, 210
Hayek, Friedrich, 101–102, 109, 112, 127–128
Hegel, G.W.F., 49, 59, 200
Helsinki Accords (1975), 193
Herder, Johann Gottfried, 49
Herz, John, 76
High modernism (Scott), 225–226
Hiroshima (Klein), 65, 66
Hitler, Adolph, 63
Hobbes, Thomas, 53, 205
Hobhouse, Emily, 58, 60
Hoffman, Paul, 85–86
Hoffman, Stanley, 6, 67, 74, 80
Houphouet-Boigny, Félix, 150
Hudson Bay Company, 39
Human rights, use of term (1800–2000), 202, 203f
Human rights movements, 191–192. *See also* Contemporary state weakness
Hutchins, Robert, 68

Ignatieff, Michael, 212
Illegal literature (Michnik), 211
Imperialism. *See also* Europe, during age of empire
    Arendt on, 42–43
    Azikiwe on, 142
    history of, 2–3
    Nehru on, 143
    subcontracting of war to private actors under, 21, 44
    war and commitment problems, 27
    wars of conquest, 44, 45f
India. *See also* Gandhi, Mohandas K.; Nehru, Jawaharlal
    Adivasi peoples, 179–188
    Bengal famine (1941–1943), 30–31
    caste/religion/tribes, 167–170, 174
    Communist Party of India, 183
    Famine Commission (1880), 183–184
    Home Rule negotiations, 59, 147
    Indian Mutiny (1857), 47–48, 180
    Land Acquisition Act (1894), 179
    Naxalites-Maoist insurgency, 179–188
    postcolonial state-building, 140–141, 145–146, 147, 153, 156
    poverty rate, 184
    Tribal Affairs, Ministry of, 181
    as weak but stable, 1
Indigenous peoples. *See also* Racial categories
    recognition of by European explorers, 4, 47n50
    statelessness and, 204–206
    use of census to control, 168–169
    use of term, 25–26

Inequality, rise of, 113, 125, 180, 222
Insurgencies
    colonial vs. postcolonial, 175–181, 177t, 189
    threshold for, 163–164
International Commission on Intervention and State Sovereignty (2001), 209–210
International Monetary Fund (IMF), 84, 85
Interstate war, 17
    during 1945–1995, 142
    civilian casualties, 201n68
    conscription costs, 18
    decline of, 26, 37
    number of conflicts (1816-2000), 45f
    as war of peoples, 37
Iraq, US invasion/wars, 77, 215–216
Ireland, British proposal of Home Rule for, 59
Iroquois Covenant Chain treaty (1677), 208
Italy, 49–50, 59

Jacobs, Jane, 226
Jagan, Chhedi, 135t
Jakobson, Roman, 62–63
Jamaica, 29, 146–147
James, C.L.R., 136, 148, 149
Japan, 134, 134n6
Jay, John, 208
Jefferson, Thomas, 193, 200n54
Jinnah, Mohammed Ali, 150
Johnson, Lyndon B., 115
Jung, Carl, 60

Kahn, Herman, 83
Kaldor, Nicholas, 159n156
Kant, Immanuel, 26n44, 27n45
Kaviraj, Sudipta, 168
Kennan, George, 83, 86, 88
Kennedy, John F., 114–115
Kenya, 152, 212
Kenyatta, Jomo, 135t, 150, 152, 153, 212
Keynes, John Maynard
    deferred payment plan, 112
    on GDP measure, 120
    How to Pay for the War, 101–102
    on length and cost of war, 24, 61–62, 66, 103–104
    Pigovian theory and, 107–108
    on postwar sense of personal security, 91
    on survival of the fittest, 126
    on unrestrained economic competition, 84–85
Keyserling, Leon, 91, 114
Khama, Sereste, 135t
Kim (Kipling), 43
Kindleberger, Charles, 85
Kissinger, Henry, 80, 83
Klein, Yves, 65, 82, 92
Klima, Ivan, 194

Konrad, George, 196
Kundera, Milan, 194–195

Language of weakness/failure/fragility, 2–3,
  122–123
Laswell, Harold, 68
Latin America, during nineteenth century, 39–40
Leach, Edmund, 167
League of Nations, 148
Legitimization crisis (Habermas), 95
Lenin, Vladimir, 144
Lewis, George Cornewall, 44
Lewis, W. Arthur, 159
Libya
  aerial bombing of during First World War, 55
  militias and Islamist groups in, 2
  ranking in Fragile States Index, 1, 2n4
  unrest and rebellion (2011), 1
  as weak state at risk of failure, 2, 215
Liddell Hart, Basil, 74, 79
Liebniz, Gottfried W., 53
Limited wars, by superpowers, 77–79
Lippmann, Walter, 116
Local cretinism (Trotsky), 164, 197–198
Locke, John, 58
Lorimer, James, 52
L'Ouverture, Toussaint, 137
Low modernism, 226–227
Luxford, Ansel, 84

Macaulay, Thomas B., 137, 138, 157
Madison, James, 200–202, 200n54
Major war and stability. See also Absolute war
    (Clausewitz); Interstate war; individual wars
  high/low cost of war, 20–21, 21t
  lessons during European empire, 39–44,
    42n24, 60–64
  state weakness and bargaining without war,
    206–209
  war and state-making, post 1945, 71–79,
    75n54, 78t
  war as costly but winnable in self-undermining
    state, 17–27, 21–22t, 22n36, 26n44, 27n45
  war as too costly, 24–25, 60–64
Malcolm X, 192–193
Malthus, Thomas, 99
Manley, Michael, 146
Manley, Norman, 135t, 143, 145, 146
Market forces. See also Neoliberalism, and post-
    1945 self-undermining state
  elite preference for minimal services, 14, 222
  as means to providing services, 9
  Ordoliberals on, 88–90
  Polanyi on, 100
  Spencer on, 100

Marshall, George, 87
Marshall, T. H., 98
Marshall Plan, 85–87
Marx, Karl, 99, 100, 126
Mass taxation, 107–113
Maulding, Reginald, 115
Mazower, Mark, 67–68
Mazzini, Giuseppe, 25, 50, 134, 204–205
Mercantilism, 100, 127
Metternich, Klemens von, 50
Mexico, as weak but stable, 1–2
Michnik, Adam, 196, 197, 211
Militias
  as alternative to the state, 1, 22t, 28
  large-scale war and, 17
  in Libya, 2
  mobilization by Prussia (1813), 56–57
  in US confederacy, 200–201
Mill, James, 48, 135
Mill, John Stuart, 48, 123, 124–125, 128, 139, 162
Mimic Men, The (Naipaul), 138
Minorities, use of term (1800–2000), 202, 203f
Modern states. See Strong modern states
Montaigne, Michel de, 53
Morel, Edmund, 58, 59
Morgenthau, Hans, 75, 76, 158
Morgenthau, Henry, 85, 86
Morgenthau Plan, 86
Moser, Carl von, 49
Moses, Robert, 226
Moynihan Report, 130
Mudimbe, Y. V., 53
Murray, Charles, 129–130, 131
Myrdal, Gunnar, 95

Naipaul, V. S., 138
Napoleonic wars, 20, 21, 40–41, 49, 56
Nasser, G. A., 135t, 149, 153–154, 155–156, 157
National Bureau of Economic Research (NBER),
    111–112
Nationalism
  conflation of anti-colonialism with, 136
  Fanon on, 165
  Jakobson on zoological, 62–63
  Nehru on, 172–173
  Nkrumah on, 165, 172
  S. Hoffman on, 67
National security state, 91–93
Naumann, Friedrich, 195
Naxalites-Maoist insurgency, in India, 179–188
Nazism. See Germany
Nehru, Jawaharlal
  as anti-colonial leader, 135t
  critique of India, 153, 162
  on federations, 144, 150
  on imperialism and racialism, 143

Nehru, Jawaharlal (*cont.*)
　on limits of nationalism, 172–173
　on postcolonial state-building, 175, 212–213
　stance on Indian independence, 145–146, 156,
　　157, 184
Neocolonialism, use of term, 146, 150, 188
Neoliberalism, and post-1945 self-undermining
　　state, 23, 95–131
　overview, 31–32, 95–97, 221–222
　contingency of welfare, 95–101, 98*f*
　paying for new services, 101–113
　summary conclusion, 221–225
　sympathy for neoliberalism, 122–131
　tax burden as percentage of income,
　　in UK, 108*t*
　tax reform during 1980s and, 113–122
　World Values Survey, 117–119, 118–120*f*
Niebuhr, Reinhold, 71
Nigeria, 174–175
Nkrumah, Kwame
　on African state sovereignty, 150
　as anti-colonial leader, 135*t*
　on challenges of development, 187–188,
　　210, 223
　critique of nationalism, 165, 172
　on imperialism and racialism, 143
　Padmore and, 148–149
　retention of colonial bureaucrats, 157
　on state development through war as
　　self-undermining, 144–145, 151
　Wright and, 154–155, 164–166, 198–199
North, Douglass, 33–34
North Atlantic Treaty Organization (NATO),
　　87, 192
Nuclear deterrence, 9, 29, 66, 80–83, 90–91.
　　See also Restaged state
Nuclear disarmament, 69–70, 198
Nyerere, Julius, 135*t*, 146, 165–166, 174, 188

Oman, Charles, 51
Oppenheimer, Robert, 69–70, 74–75
Organisation for Economic Co-operation and
　　Development (OECD)
　The Crisis of the Welfare State, 95
　social transfers as percentage of GDP
　　(1880–1980), 98*f*, 102
Orr, Verne, 83
Orwell, George, 97

Padmore, George, 148–149
Paine, Thomas, 37, 64
Pakistan, 150
Pal, Bipin Chandra, 138, 139, 157
Pan-African movements, 148–151
Parallel polis, 193, 199

Peasant revolts, 163–164. *See also* Custom and
　　development, as outside option
Petty, William, 120, 121
Pigou, Arthur, 107–108, 109, 112
Piketty, Thomas, 119
Pocock, J.G.A., 201
Polanyi, Karl, 62, 100
Pollock, Jackson, 65
Pollution control. *See* Environmentalism
Popular participation. *See* Europe, during
　　age of empire
Postcolonial state-building, 9, 19, 133–160
　overview, 133–136
　anti-colonial leaders, 135*t*
　colonial non-exchange, 136–140
　discipline and extraction level, 152–159
　economic development and expanded state,
　　140–159
　one-sidedness as self-undermining, 159–160
Poverty, historical view of, 98–100, 183–184.
　　See also Neoliberalism, and post-1945
　　self-undermining state
Power, positive concept of, 164–165, 173, 178,
　　180–181, 183
Prisoner's dilemma game, 7–8, 207
Property rights, 14, 33–35, 97, 189, 195, 204
Prussia, 56–57, 186–187
Pufendorf, Samuel von, 53

Qaddafi, Muammar, 1

Racial categories. *See also* Indigenous peoples
　as destructive of colonizers, 142–143
　fluidity of in postcolonial places, 167–168
　mimicry vs. rights, 137–139
　during nineteenth century, 25, 43,
　　50, 57*n*120
　as nonbinding, 63
　skin color and, 168
　stateless vs. states and, 52–56, 59
　Teutonic race, use of term, 61
Rathbone, Eleanor, 99
Reagan, Ronald, 130
Regional federations, as alternative to the state,
　　9, 19, 22*t*, 28, 195, 207, 221. *See also*
　　Postcolonial state-building
Renan, Ernest, 53
Restaged state, 20–21, 23, 65–93
　overview, 65–66
　alternatives to the state, 66–71
　defined, 32
　economic intervention and conflict
　　prevention, 84–91
　prevention of war via capability for absolute
　　war, 79–84

security as self-enforcing or self
    undermining, 91–93
war and state-making, post 1945, 71–79,
    75n54, 78t
Rhodes, Cecil, 42–43, 188
Ricardo, David, 99, 123, 125–126, 127
Rice, Susan, 214
Rite of Spring (Stravinsky), 60
Rogue state, defined, 210
Romano, Giovanni, 53–54
Ropke, Wilhelm, 88, 89
Rotten kid theorem (Becker), 129
Russell, Bertrand, 69, 122
Russia, 52–53, 195, 226. *See also* Soviet Union,
    former Said, Edward W., 169

St. Petersburg Declaration (1868), 55
Salmond, John, 58
Sartre, Jean-Paul, 166
Savages, use of term, 25–26, 52, 202, 203f
Schelling, Thomas, 40, 68n11, 82
Schuman, Robert, 87
Schuman Plan, 85, 87
Scott, James, 225–226
Seal, Brajendranath, 134
Sebald, W. G., 97
Second of May, The (Goya), 40, 41
Self-determination, 147, 204–205, 211
Self-enforcing state, defined, 14
Self-undermining state, 11–35. *See also*
    Neoliberalism, and post-1945
    self-undermining state
    overview, 11–14
    alternatives to the state, 27–33
    bargains given variation in costs of fighting, 28t
    costly but winnable wars, 17–27, 21–22t,
        22n36, 26n44, 27n45
    informal theory of, 13–17, 16t
    other mechanisms for state formation, 33–35
Seligman, Edwin, 104
Senghor, Leopold, 135t, 148, 150
Shell shock, use of term, 60
Shilliam, Robbie, 137
Small Wars (Callwell), 56
Smith, Adam, 120, 124–129
Somalia, 2
Soviet Union, former, 77–79, 195–196.
    See also Russia
Spain, 40–41, 56, 105
Speer, Albert, 64
Spencer, Herbert, 100, 123, 126
Spruyt, Hendrik, 23, 33
Staley, Eugene, 84
Stalin, Joseph, 226
State incapability and centrality, overview, 1–10
    agreements and local autonomy, 218–221

alternatives to the state, 222–227
analytical approach, 7–8
Failed States Index (Fund for Peace), 3–4, 3t
future of the state, 221–222
modern weak states. *see* Contemporary state
    weakness
organization of book, 8
restaging. *see* Restaged state
self-undermining states. *see*
    Self-undermining state
State-phobia sentiment (Foucault), 95–96,
    122–123
State weakness, definitions, 213–214
Stein, Lorenz von, 51, 87
Stigler, George, 129
Stimson, Henry, 70
Stolper, Wolfgang, 158
Strong modern states. *See also* Contemporary state
    weakness; Self-undermining state
    ability to repress and extract, 17
    as anomaly during nineteenth century,
        39, 44, 50
    as the exception, 2–4, 11, 13
    extraction of GDP, 14
    taxation and, 6, 14
    tax to GDP ratios, 159, 159n156
Sukarno, 135t
Supplying the state. *See* Demand for services vs.
    willingness to supply the state, overview
Surrey, Stanley, 114
Sweden, 109, 117

Tagore, Rabindranath, 148
Tanzania, villagization in, 165–166
Tax to GDP ratios, 159, 159n156
Test Ban Treaty, 78
Teutonic race, use of term, 61
Thatcher, Margaret, 96, 126
Thirty Years' War, 40, 41
Thompson, E. P., 197
Tilly, Charles, 17, 18, 20, 26, 225
Tolstoy, Leo, 41–42, 56
Tönnies, Ferdinand, 134
Toure, Sekou, 150
Tribal customs, 166–167. *See also* Custom
    and development, as outside option
Tribal protest, conditions for (Devi), 174
Trotsky, Leon, 164
Truman, Harry, 71, 79

UN Atomic Energy Commission, 70
UN Declaration on the Rights of Indigenous
    Peoples, 204, 211n105
UN Multidimensional Poverty Index, 184
UN Universal Declaration of Human Rights, 147

UN Working Group on Indigenous Populations, 185
Underdeveloped states. *See also* Custom and development, as outside option; Postcolonial state-building; *individual countries*
 economic development of, 158
 tax to GDP ratios, 159, 159*n*156
United Kingdom (UK). *See also* Great Britain, during empire
 colonial relations with India, 147
 English cost of credit (17th c.), 33–34
 income taxes, 37, 102, 115
 public debt, 104–105
 social transfers as percentage of GDP (1880–1980), 98*f*, 102
 tax burden as percentage of income, 108*t*
 Trade Union Congress on taxation, 107–108
United Nations (UN). *See also individual agencies*
 Agenda for Peace (1992), 202, 210
 Brahimi Report (2000), 209
 Gallup poll on, 67
 popularity of world government and, 67–71
 on relevance of state sovereignty, 13, 211, 212
 The Responsibility to Protect, 192
 Systems of Accounts, 121
 under trusteeship system, 148
United Negro Improvement Association (UNIA), 148
United States (US)
 Council of Economic Advisers, 91, 109–110
 early confederate militias, 200–201
 The Economics of National Defense report (1950), 91
 Employment Act (1946), 91
 financing of wars with debt, 102
 income taxes, 37, 82–83, 108, 110*f*, 112, 114–115, 117
 invasion/wars with Iraq, 77, 215–216
 limited wars of, 77–79
 military expenditures, 83
 National Security Act (1947), 90
 NSC-68 document, 70–71, 82–83
 Single Integrated Operational Plan, 75
 social transfers as percentage of GDP (1880–1980), 98*f*
 Vandenberg Resolution (1948), 68–69

Universalism (Herz), 76
US Council of Economic Advisers, 109–110
 The Economics of National Defense report (1950), 91
US Defense Department, on stability operations, 213–214
US Economic Cooperation Administration, 85–86
US-Iraq war (1991), 77

Vauban, 121
Versailles Peace Treaty, 62, 86, 147
Vitoria, Francisco de, 53

Wallerstein, Immanuel, 151
War and state-making. *See* Major war and stability; Restaged state
Wars of conquest. *See* Imperialism
Weak but stable status, 1–2
 Failed States Index (Fund for Peace), 2*n*4, 3–4, 3*t*
Weak state at risk of failure status, 2
 Failed States Index (Fund for Peace), 2*n*4, 3–4, 3*t*
Wealth of Nations (Smith), 124
Weingast, Barry, 33–34
Welfare state, 31–32, 95–101, 98*f*.
 See also Neoliberalism, and post-1945 self-undermining state
Wells, H. G., 128, 130
White, Harry Dexter, 85
Williams, Eric, 135*t*
Wilson, Woodrow, 61, 86
Wimmer, Andreas, 175
Wohlstetter, Albert, 83
World Bank, 85, 165, 185, 214
World government, 67–69, 70–71, 74, 79
World Values Survey, 117–119, 118–120*f*
Wright, Quincy, 204
Wright, Richard, 154–155, 164–166, 198–199

Yergin, Daniel, 90